REFERENCE GUIDES IN LITERATURE

Jack Salzman, *Editor*

Harriet Beecher Stowe:
A Reference Guide

Jean W. Ashton

G. K. HALL & CO., 70 LINCOLN STREET, BOSTON, MASS.

Copyright © 1977 by Jean W. Ashton

Library of Congress Cataloging in Publication Data

Ashton, Jean.
    Harriet Beecher Stowe : a reference guide.

    (Reference guides in literature)
    Includes index.
    1. Stowe, Harriet Elizabeth Beecher, 1811-1896--
Bibliography.
Z8849.4.A84 [PS2957]   016.818'3'09   76-51433
ISBN 0-8161-7833-X

This publication is printed on permanent/durable acid-free paper
MANUFACTURED IN THE UNITED STATES OF AMERICA

Contents

Introduction

When Orestes Brownson diagnosed what he termed "Beecherism" in 1871, he suggested that the members of the Beecher family, including Harriet Beecher Stowe, had a peculiar talent for riding the crest of public interest and fortuitously aligning themselves with popular causes at precisely the moment that would enable them to "always appear as public leaders and gain the credit of having declared themselves, before success was known." However accurate Brownson's rather acerbic analysis of the family may be, Harriet, Henry, and to a lesser extent Catharine, Isabella, and Edward Beecher became and have since remained so strongly identified with the central social issues of mid-nineteenth-century America that examining the works of any one of them and the criticism they inspired is equivalent to undergoing a short course in the history of American culture.

From the 1840's onward, Beechers were the bellwethers of the liberal middle class in the United States. They made respectable causes that had been considered radical or extreme. Opposition to slavery, often suffused with a covert or unconscious but very conventional racial distrust, promulgation of the democratic religion of intuition, love, and social action in place of the rigorous spiritual elitism of New England Calvinism, a hesitant support of the less threatening demands of the feminist movement combined with worship of the home, and an ambivalent optimism that satisfied the business community by promising salvation as a reward for work and good feeling were preached from the pulpit at Plymouth Church by Beechers to increasingly large congregations and spoken by Beechers on platforms of crowded lecture halls across the midwest and northeast. Stories about and writings by the family filled the newspapers, both those that supported their liberal ideas and those that were aroused to fury by the mere mention of the Beecher name.

Harriet Beecher Stowe, because of the publication of <u>Uncle Tom's Cabin</u> in 1852, was for a decade the most famous woman of her day. Energetic, prudish, half-educated and impulsive, she was for Europeans and Americans alike the embodiment of national virtues and faults. Her works, like those of Poe, seemed to gain resonance abroad, and her defense of the oppressed in a period of social and political turmoil kindled admiration in such diverse authors as Tolstoi, Turgenev, Heine, and George Sand. Because she was a woman and because she was, as Kenneth Rexroth pointed out in 1969, the only major American author of the pre-war period to confront directly the problem of slavery in her work, her books evoked and still evoke in this country and abroad passionate and often confused responses where moral, aesthetic, and political judgments are closely intertwined. A survey of these responses, from 1850 until the present, thus seems less an act of literary criticism than an excursion into the broader ranges of American intellectual and cultural history.

*   *   *

Many articles, essays, and reviews have been written about Harriet Beecher Stowe and her work in the last 125 years. Although much of this material has been perfunctory or piously biographical, at least four major concerns can be traced throughout the serious work: the related issues of slavery and race; the definition and discussion of protest literature and its function; religion, i.e., the manifestation and fragmentation of nineteenth-century Calvinist thought; and, to a lesser degree, feminism. Other recurrent topics include examination of the relationship between Stowe's New England novels and the slightly later products of the local color movements, analysis of her use of dialect and folklore material, and discussion of the influence of her novels abroad. Of these, the major issues, primarily social or cultural rather than aesthetic, have inspired the most controversy and the most interesting writing.

Mrs. Stowe's descriptions of and opinions about Southern Negro slavery of course dominate almost all discussions of her work. Although she would have a secure, if minor, place in the history of regional writing without her first two novels, for most people she was and is the author of a single book. The fluctuations of American opinion about the issues of slavery and race have been reflected in the essays written about Uncle Tom's Cabin since it first appeared and in the kind of attention given to it in surveys and anthologies. Little of this criticism can be called strictly "literary": from the beginning, readers, even if they noted the author's powers of dramatization or character creation, responded primarily to the moral and political concerns of the novel. As one anonymous reviewer put it: "If this book does not make Americans ashamed of themselves, nothing done by man or woman can." Defenders of the Southern system lamented Mrs. Stowe's abilities because they gave her increased power to persuade and to convince the world of things that from their point of view were simply not true: her Negroes were idealized, her examples of cruelty unrepresentative, her attacks on the clergy illogical and unfair. They were convinced that the undercurrents of violence and eroticism in her work would arouse the passions of the ignorant here and stir up latent anti-Americanism abroad.

Introduction

Many early readers were concerned about the propriety of using
fiction to effect social change. Dickens had dealt with the abuses
of the workhouse system and Maria Edgeworth with absentee landlords,
but slavery was a more volatile issue than either of these and im-
pinged more directly upon the interests of the growing American middle
class, most of whom read novels. The author had learned much of her
craft from reading Scott, but that author's books were set safely in
the past; this one dealt with a subject that was already threatening
to split the country. Mrs. Stowe's audacity in using the manipulative
conventions of popular literature to preach political doctrine was
unprecedented and it forced reviewers--even those in England for whom
the problem of slavery was now relatively remote--to take a public
position on an issue not strictly literary. Fiction, of course, was
by definition not "true," but it was impossible to classify Uncle
Tom's Cabin as a romance; it was rather, as the English critic Nassau
Senior put it, "a political pamphlet in the guise of a novel" and
inherently dangerous.

It was clear that Mrs. Stowe herself regarded fiction not as an
end in itself but as the means to a very particular end--the abolition
of slavery and the transformation of society through the application
of brotherly, or more precisely, motherly love; and critics at first
spent most of their time discussing the probability and desirability
of this end. Reviews which began with consideration of fictional
techniques continually turned into essays on the history and causes
of American slavery, on the desirability of Liberian colonization, on
the past and future of the "African Race," and so forth. As the century progressed, the author's moral stand was less admired. She was
at first attacked for favoring Negroes, then later condemned for her
use of stereotypes and implicit racism. In both cases, readers and
critics tended to view Uncle Tom's Cabin and its companions, A Key to
Uncle Tom's Cabin and Dred: A Tale of the Great Dismal Swamp as illustrations of extra-literary convictions rather than as entities and
sometimes to ignore the novels altogether or distort grossly their
contents. Two influential modern attacks on the author, James Baldwin's "Everybody's Protest Novel" (1949.B1) and J. C. Furnas's Goodbye to Uncle Tom (1956.A1), for example, probe with great acuity
sensitive areas of American racial consciousness, or unconsciousness,
but tell us relatively little about the character the author actually
created.

Harriet Beecher Stowe was the daughter, sister, and wife of Con-
gregational ministers. She shared with them total commitment to a
variant of evangelical Christianity, and reforming or didactic im-
pulses so strong that even in the New England novels, where controversial political issues are generally avoided, action seems an
aspect of religious argument. For such critics as Alice Crozier and
Charles Foster, Harriet's long struggle with and final rejection of
the doctrines of her Calvinist father is the central theme of all her
fiction. From this point of view, the later novels, often ignored or
given condescending praise as regional miniatures by critics whose
main interest is in the more overtly political works, gain importance

as reflectors of a significant movement of religious thought in the nineteenth century, while Uncle Tom's Cabin and Dred appear as extended commentaries on religious texts or "providential" histories, straight out of the Puritan tradition. Edmund Wilson, who worked out his ideas about Mrs. Stowe in several New Yorker articles before expanding them into the first chapter of Patriotic Gore (1962.B5), saw the author as an important spokesman for the "holy war" sentiments that shaped responses to the rise and defeat of the Confederacy in much of the North and the South.

In these two novels, the transforming power of Christian love is juxtaposed with what Ellen Moers in another context called the "cash nexus" of American society that created and preserved the slave system. Mrs. Stowe is thus not so much a political propagandist as a sectarian moralist, working out a theory of salvation. Tom is less likely to be viewed as a black man, a slave, by these readers, than discussed as a black Christ or a black exemplar of Protestant virtue, and the author's villains in these novels and the later books--Legree, Byron, Burr--are identified as those who have been the victims of or the spokesmen for a distorted, perverted religion. Stowe's attacks on the corrupt or hypocritical clergymen who defend slavery and protect the consciences of slaveowners, her use of "evangels" or spiritual guides, and her vague anticipations of millenial catastrophe, although not always congruent with one another, become components of a vast dramatic sermon.

Humanitarian religion, embodying what James Smylie identifies in a 1973 article as "the sympathies of Christ," was not of course invented nor exclusively possessed by Harriet Beecher Stowe. In her shift away from the theology of predestination and eternal punishment that had dominated her childhood, she was anticipating, as Brownson noted her family always anticipated, a great popular trend. Through this Christ-centered religion, however, she gained metaphysical sanction for the qualities she praised throughout her works, fiction and non-fiction: emotion, intuition, impulsiveness. These qualities were, and are, widely regarded as "feminine," and critics who noted the place these held in her works or noted the irrationality and carelessness they felt went with the gender were often baffled by the unfeminine boldness of the author's subject matter and her direct approach to it. Those who approved of her political opinions praised her sensitivity and her awareness of slavery's inherent threat to the family; those who found her abolitionism abhorrent found her lack of modesty, her "indelicacy" equally repellent. They felt it necessary to apologize for their unchivalrous attacks on her by explaining that she had, in essence, "unsexed herself" by writing about slavery or Byron's purported incest, but then went on to note that her work was full of female evasions and wiles.

The problems involved in describing the personality of Mrs. Stowe and in defining her place in nineteenth-century culture are particularly evident here. She is hard to categorize because she often shifted her position or acted inconsistently. Her actions and her statements often point in different directions. She was called a radical feminist, for example, by some of her contemporaries, but the feminists themselves were less sure of her allegiance and were not quick to identify her as one of themselves. She wrote essays on interior decoration and the domestic duties of women--"she was a true home woman," says one of the pious tributes of her later years--and in 1865, the Nation, hardly a radical suffrage journal, took her to task for presenting housework as an end in itself and ignoring the intellectual training of the female young. At the same time, she spoke out--eventually--in favor of votes for women, argued questions of politics and theology with great vigor, and in general lived an independent and assertive life, speaking of the virtues of dependence but taking masculine advice only when she wished.

It was noted in several early reviews that the strong figures in all her books are female and that the home provides the primary moral sustenance of society, yet an undercurrent of protest against the female role was also identified within them. Elizabeth Cady Stanton and other writers for the women's journals of the 1860's and 70's saw her controversial Byron book as a protest against male license and applauded it, while in 1926, Constance Rourke argued convincingly that the motivating energy for Uncle Tom's Cabin had come from an underlying resentment of the burdens imposed by an impoverished and unworldly husband, an intellectually domineering father, too little money, and too many children. Other critics have noted since then that in terms of natural virtue, blacks and women are almost interchangeable in Stowe's hierarchy of value, and that both achieve moral triumphs in spite of or perhaps because of the oppressions of a predominantly masculine and commercial world.

Arguments over Harriet Beecher Stowe's position in the history of American culture seem likely to continue. She was a popularizer and a public figure who invited criticism and fought her enemies with enthusiasm, convinced always that God was on her side. Yet she was never a radical, as Garrison or the Grimke sisters were radical, nor was she, in any real sense, a reformer. Except by her sex--perhaps an important exception--she was not alienated from the society of the 1850's as Melville, Hawthorne, or Thoreau were alienated. The values she embraced were, or soon became, the central ones of her culture, and reactions to these values have varied since 1852 as the interests of literary critics and intellectual historians have shifted and changed.

Most of the interest in Harriet Stowe as a literary artist has been subordinate to interest in her as a spokesman for a movement or as a part of some particular development or trend. Studies of the author's language, for example, have appeared primarily in essays tracing the use of dialect or folklore in American literature; comments on her imagery seem to have been made exclusively by those who are interested in her relationship to the exegetical and rhetorical patterns of the Puritan sermon. This should not be surprising. Art in itself had little meaning to Mrs. Stowe, and although she sometimes worked hard on her books, she seemed to regard them primarily as vehicles for a moral message. Attempts to divorce them from an extra-literary context have been few and are perhaps bound to be only partly successful. The most fruitful approaches to Stowe and her works so far have been those which attempt to place the books within a multi-dimensional historical framework and to provide the reader with a rounded image of this surprisingly complex, often irritating, but finally representative American figure.

II

Although Harriet Beecher Stowe wrote and published fiction in various periodicals throughout the early years of her marriage and was, in fact, regarded as a lady of letters by her family, the first published commentary on her work of any length appeared in 1843 when her volume of sketches, The Mayflower, was praised, in terms of ten applied to her later work, for its "descriptive and dramatic power" and its high moral tone. She was hailed as one of a new group of Western writers.

Recognition, however, was not widespread. When Uncle Tom's Cabin appeared in serial form in the National Era in 1851, it seemed to many readers to have sprung from nowhere. Response to this book was immediate and passionate. Its popularity was so great that with-in a few weeks articles appeared commenting on its influence on popu-lar music and art, on the problems of literary piracy, and on its phenomenal sales. A number of magazines, rather than devoting time to its virtues or faults, simply announced that the qualities of the book were too well-known to need comment and recommended it to their readers. Of the longer reviews, many noted the book's faults of con-struction or style, but praised the book's characterization, quoted passages at length, and summarized the plot; other reviewers, like those mentioned above, were inspired by the novel to discuss the political issues it touched on or to comment on the proper function of fiction. A substantial minority admitted the book's virtues and power but felt that its effect was sure to be bad since the problems it presented could not be solved without major social change, and thus the emotion stirred up by the dramatic events could have no proper outlet.

The book's serious subject and the respectability of the Beecher name recommended it to religious readers who ordinarily regarded fiction as frivolous or inherently dangerous. Sectarian periodicals reviewed it favorably, a fact which increased phenomenally both the sales and the influence of the book and opened a market that would be exploited throughout the rest of the century. Although a few critics had reservations about the violence or vulgarity of the novel or about the attacks on the clergy contained in it, it was regarded as an exception to the general rule against fiction in a number of Protestant denominations and apparently stood on the shelf next to the Bible in many Northern homes.

Southern reaction to Uncle Tom's Cabin was relatively slow in coming, but grew during the 1850's when the book's impact in the North became evident. Like many of the other opponents of the book, influential Southern critics—John Thompson, George Holmes, and William Gilmore Simms, among others—accused Mrs. Stowe of dramatizing isolated incidents and of mistaking incidental abuses of power for the vices of a system. Attacks on her veracity drove the author to respond by publishing her sources in A Key to Uncle Tom's Cabin (1853), but this book, while it gave reinforcement to the opinions of convinced abolitionists, did nothing to change the minds of critics of the novel who merely repeated their accusations. Within a few years, more than sixteen fictional responses to Uncle Tom's Cabin had appeared (See Hayne, "Yankee in the Patriarchy," 1968.B3 and Appendix I), most of them defending the Southern system, but none very successful as fiction, a fact noted by the Southern Literary Messenger in 1856. Abroad, primed by Mrs. Stowe's shrewd sending of the book to such noted and sympathetic authors as Dickens, Macauley, and Charles Reade, praise for the book was at least as widespread as it was in the United States, although some historians and contemporary reviewers attributed this to already existing anti-American sentiment. George Sand's review for La Presse was widely quoted and testimonials from famous people were reprinted in the daily and monthly journals. Some of the comments were critical: many readers had doubts about the book's ultimate literary worth, but few denied it's power to arouse strong and lasting emotions. The London Times review, relatively critical and frequently reprinted in other publications, seemed to engender almost as much criticism as the book itself.

Mrs. Stowe's trip to Europe in 1854 was followed by the publication of her letters in Sunny Memories of Foreign Lands. Those critics that reviewed this book were, with a few exceptions, polite to the author, but gently chided her naiveté or regretted her lack of education and taste. The excited reception given to her in Britain and her near-meeting with Queen Victoria were, however, widely noted in the United States and generally approved.

More attention was given to the second anti-slavery novel, Dred (1856), which was inevitably compared to Uncle Tom's Cabin. Most readers were disappointed in the book, commenting that although some of the characters were memorable, the author's style was often verbose and careless, and the plot was disjointed and chaotic. A few noted that, despite its flaws, Dred gave a more acute picture of the social evils of the Southern system than Uncle Tom's Cabin and some preferred it for this reason to the earlier book, but it was not generally recommended and its attacks on the clergy were resented.

HARRIET BEECHER STOWE: A REFERENCE GUIDE

Throughout the 1860's Harriet Beecher Stowe remained a popular writer. Three of her New England novels--<u>The Minister's Wooing</u>, <u>The Pearl of Orr's Island</u>, and <u>Oldtown Folks</u>--were published in the decade from 1859 to 1869, as well as <u>Agnes of Sorrento</u>, numerous short stories, a number of essays on household or religious topics, and a book of biographical sketches. The New England books, historical studies with strong religious themes, evoked favorable but lukewarm responses: the literary skill evident in them pleased some but the theological disputes which formed their subject matter bored others. They were generally agreed to be weak in plot and exciting only to those who cared strongly about the doctrines of Samuel Hopkins or Jonathan Edwards. In some cases the author was criticized for exploiting an already worn-out genre.

Harriet Beecher Stowe supported the war when it came with enthusiasm, even repeating atrocity stories to her friends, and the high point of her social career came on Emancipation Day, January 1, 1862, when the audience at the Boston Music Hall arose spontaneously in tribute to her. After the war, when the disillusionments and disappointments of the Reconstruction period began, the cause with which she was associated in the public mind became less popular, and the decline in her reputation which had already begun was hastened in 1869 by what came to be known as the Stowe-Byron scandal.

Although there have been a number of speculations about the matter, no one really knows what led Mrs. Stowe to write "The True Story of Lady Byron" and insist that it be published in the <u>Atlantic Monthly</u>. The charge she made--that Byron's wife had left him because he had contracted and maintained an incestuous relationship with his sister--evoked an immediate and outraged response in the American and, especially, the British press. Mrs. Stowe was heaped with personal abuse and vilification far worse than any she had been subject to in 1852. She was accused of obscenity, sensationalism, greed, stupidity, and outright mendacity. The latter charge led her to expand the article into a book, <u>Lady Byron Vindicated</u> (1870), which, like the <u>Key</u>, did nothing to convince her opponents she was right. A very few publications supported her contention that the truth about an immoral life should be told, but the most charitable response most critics found possible was a suggestion that she had been duped or misled by Lady Byron and had then published on an unwise impulse.

The circulation of the <u>Atlantic</u> fell off substantially as a result of the Byron article and Mrs. Stowe's own reputation never fully recovered. The society novels she published in the 1870's were not well received. Her intentions were sometimes admired, but it was felt that her preaching was heavy-handed, that she did not really know the life she was describing, a charge that had been made by Southerners in the 1850's, and that her idea of polite language and behavior was ludicrous. Her last novel, <u>Poganuc People</u>, a memoir of her Connecticut girlhood that is often praised today, was granted only perfunctory recognition when it appeared.

INTRODUCTION

In the 1880's, Mrs. Stowe stopped writing and the work she had
done earlier was largely ignored. An occasional biographer stopped
by the Hartford home for an interview, but she seemed by this time a
creature from the remote past. Even the two biographies of her published in 1889, the more extensive one by her friend Annie Fields
brought out in 1897, and the Riverside edition of her complete works
in 1896 failed to evoke much excitement. The tone of her obituaries
in 1896 is eulogistic but dispassionate. The emotion that had once
surrounded her name had evaporated and Uncle Tom's Cabin, although
always granted a few lines in the textbooks of literary history that
were now being issued for use in schools, was treated with condescen-
sion as a literary curiosity, important in its time, but possessing
little artistic interest or merit. It was recommended reading, as
T. W. Higginson pointed out in an 1898 edition, primarily for those
who had no idea of what life in the 1850's or slavery had been like.

The centenary of Harriet Beecher Stowe's birth was marked by the
publication of a new biography by the author's son and grandson, a re-
working, for the most part, of material that had been published before.
Biographical sketches appeared in magazines, but little serious attention was given to her work until the publication of Rourke's profile
in Trumpets of Jubilee (1926). The energetic and rather imaginative
treatment given her here, with its emphasis on her frustrations and
unconscious outlets for them was questioned a few years later by
Catherine Gilbertson (Harriet Beecher Stowe, 1937.A1), but it pro-
vided a point of view that was expanded and sharpened by such later
critics and biographers as Edmund Wilson, John R. Adams, and Edward
Wagenknecht.

The twenties and thirties in general, however, were marked in
Stowe criticism by a growing consciousness of race and racial issues.
The idealization of Negroes that had been criticized earlier was now
condemned as stereotyping, a practice which not only confirmed and
made respectable racist feelings, but as William Braithwaite noted in
1925, retarded the development of more fully rounded black figures in
literature. A production of the play of Uncle Tom's Cabin was banned
in Connecticut in 1945. John Mason Brown noted the irony, but a
series of books and articles (Baldwin, Furnas, Gysin's To Master a
Long Good Night, 1946.B11) took increasingly strong stands against
the novel and what they felt to be its pernicious effect. The debate
continued into the nineteen sixties as various authors took modified
stands on the passivity of Tom and the values implicit in his action,
problems first noted by Garrison and the contributors to the Liberator
in 1852. "Uncle Tomism" and Stowe's attitude toward the figures she
created remain live and controversial issues.

Forrest Wilson's long biography of the author, still the most
detailed and thorough study of her life, came out in 1941. Although
generally regarded as a satisfactory and informative book, it has
little critical content. A more rigorous approach to the Stowe works
was taken by Charles Foster, Alice Foster and other disciples of Perry

Miller who sought to fit them into the theological traditions of New
England, a task sometimes accomplished only by ignoring or underplaying
the questions of social context that have ordinarily dominated studies
of the books. An often complementary re-evaluation of the New England
novels began at the same time: Edmund Wilson called attention to them
in his New Yorker reviews, and various scholarly articles and dissertations began to appear in the 1950's which examined their place in
the local color movement and explained their value as historical
documents.

The earlier view of Harriet Beecher Stowe as an anomalous and
embarrassing survivor of the sentimental tradition of female fiction
has become less common in the last fifteen years. Critics have begun
to speak of her as a realist who is closer to Twain and Cable than to
Lydia Sigourney, and they see in her works the close connections to
Faulkner and the Southern Gothic novel. An increasing number of
references to her role in the feminist controversies of the 1850's
and 60's found in essays by Ann Douglas, Gail Parker, Ellen Moers and
others suggest that another area of discussion is now being opened
for fresh examination and argument.

III

In the following guide to writings about Harriet Beecher Stowe,
I have tried to include all writings of significance which deal with
the author or her life. Brief references to her in longer articles,
historical surveys, textbooks, and so forth have been included when
they seemed interesting or representative of a widespread point of
view, but the volume of popular writing about Stowe, and particularly
about Uncle Tom's Cabin, has been so great that a substantial amount
of material has had to be discarded.

I have not included articles from daily newspapers. Much of
this material deals with the day to day movements of the Beecher or
Stowe families or has been reprinted from longer articles in magazines
or weekly journals. Lists of papers with relevant articles on particular subjects may be found in Wilson's bibliographical notes
(1941.A1), in Browne (1941.B4), Baender (1959.B1), and Lentricchia
(1966.B5). The New York Times Index for the years 1852-1896 contains
a number of references to her, as does the Subject Index of American
Periodicals, 1789-1870 compiled by New York University and found
there in the Elmer Holmes Bobst Library. Files of clippings containing obituary notices, programs, and so forth, can be found in the
Beecher collection of the Schlesinger Library, Radcliffe College; the
Beinecke Library, Yale University; and the Stowe-Day Memorial Library,
Hartford, Connecticut.

Some juvenile biographies of Mrs. Stowe have been included, but
children's versions of Uncle Tom's Cabin have been left out. Drama-
tizations of the novel, and of Dred, have also been excluded because

Introduction

they have nothing to do with Harriet Beecher Stowe, who, in fact, lost a good deal of money by refusing to sell the rights of her novel to an inquiring playwright. Articles about the "Tom shows" have been included when they discussed the author or the book as well as the play, or when they examined the relationship between the two. Information about the play and its history can be found in Birdoff, The World's Greatest Hit (1947.B1); Appendix III contains a selected list of articles on the topic.

Within a few years of its publication, Uncle Tom's Cabin had been translated into a large number of foreign languages, including Welsh and Icelandic. A list of translations can be found in Bullen's bibliographical introduction to the 1878 edition of Uncle Tom's Cabin (1878.B9), which was expanded for the Riverside edition of The Writings of Harriet Beecher Stowe (1896). Other useful lists of translations and of articles on Stowe in languages other than English can be found in Maclean (1910.A1), Lucas (1930.A1), Jackson (1953.B4), Woodress (1967.B7) among others (see Index), and in the MLA annual bibliographies.

Preparation of this guide would have been impossible without the helpful suggestions of E. Bruce Kirkham and the assistance of Anne S. MacFarland of the Stowe-Day Foundation. I am particularly grateful to the reference librarians of the New York Public Library for their patience, persistence, and help.

A Note on the Text

Items in Category A, Books, are independent publications, listed under their own names in major library catalogues, dealing entirely or in large part with the works or life of Harriet Beecher Stowe. In a few instances, primarily the years immediately following the publication of Uncle Tom's Cabin and during the Byron controversy of 1869-1870, the works so listed are not directly about Stowe but were inspired by her writing and refer throughout to her accusations and statements.

Books and articles referred to elsewhere that have not been located are identified by an asterisk. The source of the citation follows the entry; these sources are, with some exceptions, listed in the guide. They include:

> Browne, 1941.B4
> Bullen, 1878.B9
> Eichelberger, 1971.B5
> Gohdes, 1944.B1
> Jorgenson, 1952.A1
> Leary, 1954.B3
> Sabin, 1933.B5
> Poole's Index to Periodical Literature, I-VI
> Camerson, Kenneth. "Research Keys to the American Renaissance: Indexes to the Christian Examiner, North American Review and New Jerusalem Magazine," Hartford: Transcendental Books, 1967

Dissertations are listed under Shorter Writings.

Writings of Harriet Beecher Stowe

Prize Tale: A New England Sketch, 1834

An Elementary Geography, 1835

The Mayflower; or, Sketches of Scenes and Characters Among the Descendants of the Pilgrims, 1843

Uncle Tom's Cabin; or, Life Among the Lowly, 1852

A Key to Uncle Tom's Cabin, 1853

Uncle Sam's Emancipation, etc., 1853

Sunny Memories of Foreign Lands, 1854

Geography for My Children, 1855

Dred; A Tale of the Great Dismal Swamp, 1856

Our Charley and What To Do With Him, 1858

The Minister's Wooing, 1859

The Pearl of Orr's Island, 1862

Agnes of Sorrento, 1862

A Reply...In Behalf of the Women of America, 1863

The Ravages of a Carpet, 1865

House and Home Papers, 1865. Christopher Crowfield [pseud.]

Little Foxes, 1866. Christopher Crowfield [pseud.]

Stories About Our Dogs, 1865

Religious Poems, 1867

Queer Little People, 1867

Daisy's First Winter and Other Stories, 1867

The Chimney-Corner, 1868. Christopher Crowfield [pseud.]

Men of Our Times, 1868. Reissued as Lives and Deeds of Our Self-Made Men, 1872

Oldtown Folks, 1869

The American Woman's Home, 1969. With Catharine Beecher.

Lady Byron Vindicated, 1870

Little Pussy Willow, 1870

My Wife and I, 1871

Pink and White Tyranny, 1871

Sam Lawson's Oldtown Fireside Stories, 1872

Palmetto-Leaves, 1873

Woman in Sacred History, 1873. Reissued as Bible Heroines, 1878

We and Our Neighbors, 1875

Betty's Bright Idea, 1876. A similar collection was issued in London as Deacon Pitkin's Farm, 1875

Footsteps of the Master, 1876

Poganuc People, 1878

A Dog's Mission, 1881

Our Famous Women, 1884

The Writings of Harriet Beecher Stowe, 1896

Source: Blanck, Jacob, ed. Merle Johnson's American First Editions, 4th edition, revised and enlarged. Waltham, Mass.: Mark Press, 1965, pp. 481-84.

Writings about Harriet Beecher Stowe, 1843-1974

<u>1843 A BOOKS - NONE</u>

<u>1843 B SHORTER WRITINGS</u>

1   ANON. "The Mayflower," <u>Ladies' Repository and Gatherings of the West</u>, III (August), p. 255.
     This book is not substantial, but shows "an inventive mind," "great command of language," and "excellent morals."

2   ANON. "The Mayflower," <u>New Englander</u>, I (October), p. 556.
     Warmly praises the book's high moral tone and the author's descriptive and dramatic power, criticizing her only for using too many quotations and ornate, uncommon words.

<u>1852 A BOOKS</u>

*1   ANON. Slavery Past and Present; or Notes on <u>"Uncle Tom's Cabin."</u> London: Longman, Brown, Green, and Longmans.
     Cited in Sabin, 1933.B5.

2   ANON. <u>Uncle Tom in England; or, A Proof that Black's White</u>. New York: A. D. Failing.
     An "Echo, or Sequel" to <u>Uncle Tom's Cabin</u> in which the effects of education upon the characters of the novel are seen. <u>See also</u> Appendix I.

3   ANON. <u>Uncle Tom in England. The London Times on "Uncle Tom's Cabin." A Review</u>. New York: Bunce & Brothers.
     An eight page pamphlet reprinting the <u>Times</u>'s generally negative response to <u>Uncle Tom's Cabin</u>. Harriet Beecher Stowe's book is a "vehement and unrestrained argument in favour of her creed," which will "rivet the fetters" of slavery. Her characterization of the Negroes is good, but Tom's conversion of slaves is "audacious trash." In general, the blacks are too white, the whites too black. Widely reprinted and summarized.

1852

*4   EDWARDS, J. P. <u>Uncle Tom's Companions</u>.
          Cited in Sabin, 1933.B5.

5   HELPS, Sir ARTHUR. <u>A Letter on Uncle Tom's Cabin</u>. Cambridge:
          John Bartlett, 26 pp.
             A letter from a well-known British abolitionist, attesting
          to the essential truth of <u>Uncle Tom's Cabin</u> and the condi-
          tions of slavery depicted. Biblical arguments in support
          of slavery are attacked, but Harriet Beecher Stowe's com-
          parison of the slave and the English laborer condemned.

6   MURPHY, G. M. <u>The Slave Among Pirates, or "Uncle Tom's" Many
          Editors - A Satire</u>. London: W. Horsell.
             Satirical poem attacking publishers who pirated <u>Uncle
          Tom's Cabin</u>, dedicated to Harriet Beecher Stowe. Notes in
          closing that Thomas Bosworth had reportedly agreed to pay
          royalties to the author.

7   PRINGLE, EDWARD J. <u>Slavery in the Southern States</u>. Cambridge:
          J. Bartlett.
             <u>Uncle Tom's Cabin</u> contains many arguments against slavery,
          depicted in vivid scenes, but the author's zeal has over-
          taken her and the book will do great harm, arousing fanati-
          cism and rage. Exceptional abuses have been dwelt upon.

8   WADDELL, JAMES A. <u>"Uncle Tom's Cabin" Reviewed; or, American
          Society Vindicated from the Aspersions of Mrs. Harriet
          Beecher Stowe</u>. Raleigh, N. C.: Printed at the Office of
          the "Weekly Post."
             Extended comment on the problem of attacking a female
          writer, even one who, like Harriet Beecher Stowe, has sur-
          rendered her natural immunity. The author's literary
          talent is acknowledged, but the book is both untruthful
          and dangerous to the repute of the U. S. abroad. All
          assumptions of the book are attacked, especially the idea
          that man is responsible for the remote consequences of his
          actions.

<u>1852 B SHORTER WRITINGS</u>

1   AN ALABAMA MAN [WILLIAM BIRNEY]. "Some Account of Mrs.
          Beecher Stowe and her Family," <u>Fraser's Magazine</u>, XLVI
          (November), pp. 518-25.
             Biographical and descriptive sketch of Harriet Beecher
          Stowe and the Beechers, with special attention given to
          the family role in the Cincinnati riots. Reprinted as an
          introduction to <u>Uncle Sam's Emancipation</u> (1853.B1) and
          elsewhere. (Author identified by E. Bruce Kirkham.)

2   ANON. "Harriet Beecher Stowe," <u>North American Miscellany and
    Dollar Magazine</u>, IV, p. 328.
        The copyright premium of $10,300 on three months' sales
    of <u>Uncle Tom's Cabin</u> is the largest sum ever received from
    actual sales of a single work in so short a period of time.

3   ANON. "Introduction," <u>Uncle Tom's Cabin</u>. London: John Cassell,
    pp. ix-xiv.
        "No one can read <u>Uncle Tom's Cabin</u> and disbelieve the
    fall of man." Harriet Beecher Stowe emphasizes everywhere
    the spirit of Christianity and the influence of mother-
    love. One can only see "tyranny in absolute perfection"
    in "the vaunted land of the free."

4   ANON. "Negro Life in America," <u>Christian Observer</u>, LI (Octo-
    ber), pp. 695-710.
        <u>Uncle Tom's Cabin</u> is strongly recommended as "moral fic-
    tion," despite its slight offenses against delicacy, ap-
    proaches to profanity, and a "want of skill" in the organi-
    zation of the story. "She ought to have taken care that
    her book was such as might be read without hesitation to
    a family circle made up in part or in whole of women."

5   ANON. "Negro Life in America," <u>Christian Reformer</u>, 3 ser.,
    VIII, p. 472.
        Discussion of the Fugitive Slave law precedes review of
    <u>Uncle Tom's Cabin</u>. Plot summary and long excerpts from
    the novel. The author has pathos and humor at her command
    and displays Christian sympathies of "more than common
    purity and strength."

6   ANON. "The Queen's Dream. A Sequel to 'Uncle Tom's Cabin,'"
    <u>DeBow's Review</u>, XVI (November), pp. 95-105.
        A sketch attributed to the British correspondent of the
    New York <u>Herald</u>, answering <u>Uncle Tom's Cabin</u> by pointing
    out the hardships of free white men in commercial society.

7   ANON. "Uncle Tom's Cabin," <u>Athenaeum</u>, XXV (May), p. 574.
        Brief review. "The good done by books like this must be
    questioned," since emotions are stirred but no remedy for
    the evil is suggested.

8   ANON. "Uncle Tom's Cabin," <u>Athenaeum</u>, XXV (October), p. 1173.
        A review of works inspired by <u>Uncle Tom's Cabin</u> and
    announcement of the non-pirated edition.

9   ANON. "Uncle Tom's Cabin," <u>Baptist Magazine</u>, XLIV, p. 685.
        Brief note that this book is too popular to need exten-
    sive comment, but that the superior edition to date is
    Ingram, Cooke.

1852

10   ANON. "Uncle Tom's Cabin," <u>Baptist Reporter</u>, n.s. IX, p. 206.
        Brief comment: "If this book does not make Americans
        ashamed of themselves nothing done by man or woman can."

*11   ANON. "Uncle Tom's Cabin," <u>The Christian Inquirer</u>, II, p. 644.
        Cited in Bullen, 1878.B9.

12   ANON. "Uncle Tom's Cabin," <u>Christian Witness</u>, IX, p. 344.
        Harriet Beecher Stowe is a woman of a high order of in-
        tellect and fancy. Her book attacks the system, not the
        individual. A strongly favorable comment.

13   ANON. "Uncle Tom's Cabin," <u>The Critic</u> (London), XI (June),
        p. 293.
        Brief note. The novel is "a composition of average
        merit" which can be read and enjoyed only by the anti-
        slavery party.

14   ANON. "Uncle Tom's Cabin," <u>Dublin University Magazine</u>, XL
        (November), pp. 600-613.
        Applauds novel and its motive, and gives a brief history
        of slavery, as well as a plot summary and quotations from
        the novel. The scene is "too graphic to be unreal" but
        the "lower" characters are more interesting than the
        others.

*15   ANON. "Uncle Tom's Cabin," <u>Free Church Magazine</u>, n.s. I,
        p. 359.
        Cited in Bullen, 1878.B9

*16   ANON. "Uncle Tom's Cabin," <u>General Baptist Repository</u>, XXXI,
        p. 339.
        Cited in Bullen, 1878.B9.

17   ANON. "Uncle Tom's Cabin," <u>The Illustrated London News</u>, XXI
        (October 2), pp. 290-91.
        This book has "the stamp of truth" softened by beauty,
        and a "serviceable" fanaticism. The author has great
        skill in the delineation of character.

18   ANON. "Uncle Tom's Cabin," <u>Independent</u> (April 15), p. 62.
        A highly enthusiastic review in a paper for which Har-
        riet Beecher Stowe later wrote regularly. "The book is
        full of the intensest Truth; the <u>very</u> Truth, of facts and
        of ethics." Signed <u>S</u>.

19   ANON. "Uncle Tom's Cabin," <u>The Ladies' Repository</u>, XII (July),
        p. 279.
        A brief notice, commenting on the book's popularity.

20   ANON. "Uncle Tom's Cabin," The Literary Gazette (June 26),
        p. 513.
            A brief notice, recommending the novel; it "deserves
        popularity."

21   ANON. "Uncle Tom's Cabin," The Literary World, X (April 24),
        pp. 291-92.
            This is an odd book, "too potent and decidedly odorous"
        for the critic's taste. The incidents of the novel are
        "revolting and unjust," unfairly treated as daily occur-
        rences; the book is capable of producing "infinite mis-
        chief." The dialect humor is amusing but not specifically
        Negro.

22   ANON. "Uncle Tom's Cabin," Littell's Living Age, XXXIV
        (July 10), pp. 61-62.
            Summary of other reviews; Morning Post: the book is an
        exaggerated picture marked by genius and exhibiting a pe-
        culiar ability to see both sides of the issue; Southern
        Press: the novel is a caricature, focusing only on special
        cases; Tait's: this novel will be successful.

23   ANON. "Uncle Tom's Cabin," Littell's Living Age, XXXV (Octo-
        ber 16), pp. 97-111.
            Summary and excerpts from the Times review (1852.A3)
        and the Examiner: the genuine work of an American mind."
        Includes passages from the novel.

*24   ANON. "Uncle Tom's Cabin," Methodist New Connexion Magazine,
        3rd ser., XX.
            Cited in Bullen, 1878.B9.

*25   ANON. "Uncle Tom's Cabin," The Mother's Magazine.
            Cited in Bullen, 1878.B9

26   ANON. "Uncle Tom's Cabin," North American Miscellany and
        Dollar Magazine, IV, pp. 277-78.
            Excerpts from the novel.

27   ANON. "Uncle Tom's Cabin," Observer, New York (September 23).
            Review of novel in the context of the Parker-Beecher
        controversy; the book is "anti-ministerial" and anti-
        Christian, since ministers are portrayed in it as odious
        and contemptible creatures.

28   ANON. "Uncle Tom's Cabin," The Prospective Review, VIII,
        pp. 490-513.
            This book, with its lively moral sensibility, could only

have been written by a woman; it is marked by moderation, humour, and attention to the moral problems presented to the American people. St. Clare's comparison of slavery to the oppression of the English workers is discussed in detail.

29 ANON. "Uncle Tom's Cabin," Spectator, XXV (September 25), pp. 926-28.
    The book is effective because it avoids exaggeration and presents varied heroes and villains. Its weakest aspect is the characterization of Tom, whose virtues are consistent but unbelievable. Long excerpt included.

30 ANON. "Uncle Tom's Cabin," Tait's Edinburgh Magazine, XIX (June), p. 381.
    Brief notice. "Wherever there is a love of liberty and a hatred of oppression, there will this book be read." Later issues of the magazine list new editions.

31 ANON. "Uncle Tom's Cabin," Today. A Boston Literary Journal, II (July-December), pp. 9, 104, 215, 232, 328, 346.
    Various announcements about Uncle Tom's Cabin and related commercial matters, including publication and sales data, song about little Eva, German translation, English editions (nineteen to date), and piracy.

32 ANON. "Uncle Tom's Cabin," Westminster Review, LVIII (July), pp. 282-84.
    The book is remarkable for "its breadth of view...its genial charity" which traces evil to the system, not the individual. Its end is achieved with neither vulgarity nor exaggeration.

33 ANON. "Uncle Tom's Cabin and its Opponents," Eclectic Review, n.s. IV (December), pp. 717-744.
    Review of the novel and books inspired by it. Uncle Tom's Cabin, a "marvellous" book, is praised for its power but criticized for its comparison of slaves to English laborers. Attacks the Times review (1852.A3) and discusses the impact of the novel. Biographical sketch of Harriet Beecher Stowe included.

34 ANON. "Uncle Tom's Cabin - The Story of Eliza," Chambers's Edinburgh Journal, n.s. XVIII (September 4), pp. 155-58.
    Summary of the plot, with long excerpts.

35 ANON. "Uncle Tom's Cabin - The Story of Uncle Tom," Chambers's Edinburgh Journal, n.s. XVIII (September 18), pp. 187-90.

Summary of plot, with excerpts from the book. The plot
is weak, but Harriet Beecher Stowe's observation of character is good.

36 ANON. "X. Y. Z.," The Western Journal and Civilian, IX
      (November), pp. 133-39.
         Discusses the new political function of the novel.
      Uncle Tom's Cabin has literary merit and dramatic effective-
      ness but is pervaded with exaggeration. Harriet Beecher
      Stowe's comments on the Fugitive Slave law are attacked.
      Her book points to the "amalgamation of the races."

37 BACON, L. "The Literature of Slavery," New Englander, X
      (November), pp. 588-618.
         By bringing the facts of slavery to light, Harriet
      Beecher Stowe has done "what multitudes would much rather
      she had not done." The popularity of the book is analyzed
      and general accusations against it, especially those of
      untruthfulness, refuted.

38 BURRITT, ELIHU. "Introduction," Uncle Tom's Cabin. London:
      Partridge & Oakley, p. 40.
         An extravagant appreciation of the novel. The book has
      a special and heavenly mission; among other things, it
      must...open and inaugurate the Christian era of popular
      literature."

39 CARLISLE, the Earl of. "Introduction," Uncle Tom's Cabin.
      London: G. Routledge and Co.
         Calls for Englishmen to exert their moral influence to
      end slavery everywhere and sees Uncle Tom's Cabin as a
      weapon which can be used to make antislavery sentiment
      respectable wherever English can be read.

40 DICKENS, CHARLES. "North American Slavery," Household Words,
      VI (September 18), p. 1.
         Uncle Tom's Cabin is "not free from the fault of over-
      strained conclusions and violent extremes" yet is is "a
      noble work; full of high power, lofty humanity, the
      gentlest, sweetest, and yet boldest, writing." Its de-
      tails can be accepted as truth.

41 EASTMAN, MARY H. Aunt Phillis's Cabin or, Southern Life as
      It Is. Philadelphia: Lippincott, Grambo and Co.
         The fifteen page epilogue to this answer to Uncle Tom's
      Cabin responds directly to several of the points made by
      Harriet Beecher Stowe and questions the character of her
      heroes.

1852

42 ELLIS, S. E. "Uncle Tom's Cabin," Christian Examiner, LII
        (May), p. 451.
            Brief notice commending work and pointing out that it
        has more readers than the first two installments of Bleak
        House.

43 GARRISON, WILLIAM L. The Liberator (March 26).
            Finds the work strong, with "uncommon moral and philo-
        sophical acumen" displayed, but wonders whether Harriet
        Beecher Stowe believes in non-resistance for white men as
        well as black, and regrets the colonization sentiments
        expressed in the final chapter.

44 _____. The Liberator (September 17).
            Reply to a letter from H. C. Wright (1852.B55), defending
        the book as a strong but imperfect instrument, and objecting
        to Wright's misreading of the passages on Christianity.

45 HALL, S. C. (Mrs.) "Uncle Tom's Cabin," Sharpe's London Maga-
        zine, n.s. I, pp. 244-54.
            Contrasts Uncle Tom's Cabin with a fashionable book by
        Mrs. E. Oakes Smith. Former is a "fearless, yet womanly
        book" which powerfully depicts the "gigantic iniquity of
        American slavery." Includes extracts from the novel.

46 HART, JOHN S. The Female Prose Writers of America. Philadel-
        phia: E. H. Butler & Co., pp. 246-253.
            Brief biographical sketch preceding reprint of story
        from The Mayflower.

47 HELPS, ARTHUR. "A Letter on Uncle Tom's Cabin," Fraser's
        Magazine, XLVI (August), pp. 237-44.
            Reprint of 1852.A5.

48 HILL, ALICIA (with RICHARD WHATELY and SAMUEL HINDS). "Ameri-
        can Slavery and Uncle Tom's Cabin," North British Review,
        XVIII (February), pp. 235-58.
            Review of Uncle Tom's Cabin and related works. The
        former is an extraordinary book, all the more so because
        it has no love interest. Its power can be gauged by the
        wrathful answers it has received.

49 HOLMES, GEORGE F. "Uncle Tom's Cabin," Southern Literary
        Messenger, XVIII (October), pp. 630-38.
            Despite Harriet Beecher Stowe's virtues as a writer,
        she has placed herself "without the pale of kindly treat-
        ment" from Southerners by libeling and vilifying the
        Southern people and fomenting hatred. Holmes attacks her

ferninist designs and many of her techniques as well as the
content of the book, and comments at length on false asser-
tions about slavery, inconsistencies, etc.

50   KIRKLAND, CAROLINE M. (Mrs.)   North American Review, LXXVI
      (January), p. 112.
          Brief commendation of Uncle Tom's Cabin in longer article
      on American women writers.

51   NORTHCOTE, J. S.   "Uncle Tom's Cabin," The Rambler, X (October),
      pp. 413-24.
          Discussion, summary, and excerpts. The success of Uncle
      Tom's Cabin is due partly to subject, partly to treatment.
      It is artificial in plot and weak in style, but has many
      strong points.

52   SAND, GEORGE [Mme. DUDEVANT].   Review of Uncle Tom's Cabin,
      La Presse (December 17).
          The novel is defective according to the rules of French
      romance, but triumphant because of its faults. Harriet
      Beecher Stowe has genius rather than talent. Children are
      the true heroes of the book. (Reprinted in translation in
      "Introduction," Uncle Tom's Cabin. Boston: Houghton,
      Mifflin and Company (1878.B1); in Fields, Life and Letters
      of Harriet Beecher Stowe. Boston: Houghton, Mifflin and
      Company (1897.A1); and elsewhere. Widely quoted.)

53   SHERMAN, JAMES.   "Introduction," Uncle Tom's Cabin. London:
      H. G. Bohn.
          Uncle Tom's Cabin has taken its place as a standard work;
      piety and truthfulness are its chief charms. Review lists
      the number of slaves held by ministers in the United
      States, and calls for still more attention to this situa-
      tion.

54   THOMPSON, JOHN R.   "Uncle Tom's Cabin," Southern Literary
      Messenger, XVIII (December), pp. 721-31.
          Rejects the social role of fiction and asserts that
      Harriet Beecher Stowe has betrayed her sex. Loathsome
      misrepresentations fill the book. Thompson laments the
      lack of Southern writers and periodicals and the weakness
      of the responses to Uncle Tom's Cabin that have appeared.
      Attributes evils described in the novel to the human heart,
      not slavery, which, in fact, diminishes human misery. The
      book is filled with hypocrisy and sentimentality, with
      "poisonous vermin" and "putrescence," etc.

1852

55 WRIGHT, HENRY C. Letter to The Liberator (July 9), p. 3.
        Objects strongly to Uncle Tom's Cabin because it suggests
    that some compromise is possible among slaves, slave-owners,
    and the Christian church, and because of its sympathy with
    the colonization movement. The novel is a quietus to the
    consciences of the nation and a danger to abolitionists.
    See 1852.B43; 1852.B44.

1853 A BOOKS

1 ADAMS, F. C. Uncle Tom at Home. A Review of the Reviewers
    and Repudiators of Uncle Tom's Cabin by Mrs. Stowe.
    Philadelphia: W. P. Hazard.
        A defense of Uncle Tom's Cabin by a South Carolinian,
    primarily directed against the attacks from a Mr. P--- in
    "Slavery in the Southern States" and William Gilmore Simms.
    Gives numerous local incidents and examples to reinforce
    major points of the novel, and defends Harriet Beecher
    Stowe's dramatic and narrative structure.

2 NO ENTRY.

3 ANON. The Uncle Tom's Cabin Almanack or Abolitionist Memento.
    London: John Cassell.
        Almanac based on Uncle Tom's Cabin, with memoirs of
    noted abolitionists, pictures, a song about Uncle Tom,
    etc. No direct criticism of novel.

4 BRIMBLECOMB, NICHOLAS, Esq. [pseud]. Uncle Tom's Cabin in
    Ruins! Triumphant Defence of Slavery! in a Series of
    Letters to Harriet Beecher Stowe. Boston: Charles Waite.
        An extravagant defense of the "sublime" system of
    slavery, on the grounds that the slaves are, like all
    chattel, private property, attacking in detail all the
    main arguments and assumptions of the novel. Eva is an
    "impudent, meddlesome, and low-lived child," Legree is
    "thrifty, provident," etc. Possibly satire.

*5 CLARE, EDWARD. The Spirit and Philosophy of Uncle Tom's
    Cabin. London.
        Cited in Bullen (1878.B9), and Sabin (1933.B5).

6 DENMAN, THOMAS. Uncle Tom's Cabin, Bleak House, Slavery and
    Slave Trade. Seven Articles by Lord Denman, reprinted

from the "Standard"; with an article containing facts con-
nected with slavery, by Sir George Stephen, reprinted from
the "North-Hampton Mercury." London: Longman, Brown,
Green, and Longmans.

Open letter to Harriet Beecher Stowe. Review of <u>Bleak
House</u>, defending the Mrs. Jellybys of England; answer to
the <u>Times</u> review of <u>Uncle Tom's Cabin</u> (1852.A3), claiming
that slavery is a subject which demands passion and commitment; comments on Dickens's review in <u>Household Words</u>
(1852.B40). For Stephen article, <u>see</u> 1853.B30.

7 A Lady in New York [pseud.] <u>The Patent Key to Uncle Tom's
Cabin or Mrs. Stowe in England</u>. New York: Pudney & Russell.
   The preface to this long poem declares that the prompting
motive was defense of "the name of the Almighty Father,
when attacked by a set of raving maniacs, traitors to their
country and their God!" Poem attacks women's rights (and
men who fail to be stronger than women), abolitionism,
child labor, and those who deny racial inferiority. Attack
on English oppression of Ireland. Some praise for author's
skill.

8 STEARNS, E. J. <u>Notes on Uncle Tom's Cabin: Being a Logical
Answer to its Allegations and Inferences Against Slavery
as an Institution with a Supplementary Note on the Key, and
an Appendix of Authorities</u>. Philadelphia: Lippincott,
Grambo & Company.
   Lengthy attack on every aspect of the novel. Stearns includes newspaper reports of Harriet Beecher Stowe's English
trip, and suggests that book has aroused sentiment against
America rather than against slavery.

*9 THOMPSON, GEORGE. <u>American Slavery. A Lecture Delivered in
the Music Hall, Store Street, Dec. 13th, 1852. Proving
by Unquestionable Evidence the Correctness of Mrs. Stowe's
Portraiture of American Slavery in her Popular Work, Uncle
Tom's Cabin</u>. London.
   Cited in Bullen, 1878.B9.

10 WOODWARD, A. <u>A Review of Uncle Tom's Cabin; or, An Essay on
Slavery</u>. Cincinnati: Applegate & Co.
   An attack on <u>Uncle Tom's Cabin</u> and Harriet Beecher Stowe,
including discussion of the author's "vile aspersions of
Southern character," her wily ingenuity, hypocrisy, lust
for financial gain, etc., and an analysis of the impact of
the novel in England.

1853

1853 B SHORTER WRITINGS

   1   AN ALABAMA MAN [WILLIAM BIRNEY]. "Some Account of Mrs. Beecher
      Stowe and Her Family," <u>Uncle Sam's Emancipation; Earthly</u>
      <u>Care, A Heavenly Discipline and Other Sketches</u>. Philadel-
      phia: Willis P. Hazard.
         Reprint of 1852.B1.

 *2   ALPHA [pseud.]. "The War of the Fanatics," <u>Southern Eclectic</u>,
      II, p. 70.
         Cited in Browne, 1941.B4.

   3   ANON. "American Slavery and Emancipation by the Free States,"
      <u>Westminster Review</u>, LIX (January), pp. 125-67.
         A general discussion of the political problems presented
      by slavery with occasional reference to and quotation from
      <u>Uncle Tom's Cabin</u>.

   4   ANON. "Blackwood's Magazine," <u>United States Review</u>, XXXII,
      n.s. I (April), pp. 289-323.
         English support of Harriet Beecher Stowe and American
      abolitionism is attacked.

   5   ANON. "Editor's Table," <u>Southern Literary Messenger</u>, XIX
      (March), pp. 188-89.
         A note on the success in Paris of a garbled dramatization
      of <u>Uncle Tom's Cabin</u>.

 *6   ANON. "Freedom in England and Slavery in America," <u>Southern</u>
      <u>Eclectic</u>, II, pp. 279-89.
         Cited in Browne, 1941.B4.

   7   ANON. "A Key to Uncle Tom's Cabin," <u>Eclectic Review</u>, n.s. V
      (May), pp. 600-17.
         Praises and summarizes the contents of the <u>Key</u>, a "tri-
      umphant vindication of the novel."

   8   ANON. "A Key to Uncle Tom's Cabin," <u>Ladies' Repository</u>, XIII
      (June), p. 256.
         Brief note: this is a book that will not be easily laid
      aside.

   9   ANON. " A Key to Uncle Tom's Cabin," <u>Prospective Review</u>, IX,
      pp. 248-71.
         The <u>Key</u> is a "forcible and pertinent" reply to critics
      of the novel, and one which gives rise to many speculations
      about the slavery issue.

10   ANON. "A Key to Uncle Tom's Cabin," Westminster Review, n.s.
         III (July), p. 280.
            A brief notice describing the Key and its contents.

11   ANON. "Reception of Mrs. Beecher Stowe in London," United
         States Review, XXXII, n.s. I (May), p. 452.
            A satirical description of Harriet Beecher Stowe abroad,
         with the heroine in blackface, etc. "Who knows but Mrs.
         Beecher Stowe may one day become a second Pope Joan?"

12   ANON. "Those Dear Blacks," Bentley's Miscellany, XXXIII,
         pp. 92-101.
            An essay on the effect of Uncle Tom's Cabin on English
         social life, noting an increased sympathy with abolitionism,
         but questioning the motives of many fashionable sympathizers.

13   ANON. [CHARLES BRIGGS]. "Uncle Tomitudes," Putnam's Monthly,
         I (January), p. 97.
            Discussion of the remarkable success of Uncle Tom's
         Cabin. "It is a live book, and it talks to its readers as
         if it were alive." The primary defect of the novel is the
         obtrusive anti-slavery sentiment of the author, but the
         "constructive" ability of Harriet Beecher Stowe is admirable.
         Compares her to Cooper, Irving, etc. as a specifically
         American novelist. Author identiifed by Browne (1941.B4).

14   ANON. "Uncle Tom's Cabin," Church of England Magazine, XXXIV
         (June 4), p. 376.
            Notes that the Roman church fears the evangelical spirit
         of Uncle Tom's Cabin and has published a censored version
         of it.

*15   ANON. "Uncle Tom's Cabin," English Review, XVIII, p. 80.
         Cited in Poole's, IV.

16   ANON. "Uncle Tom's Cabin," The Friend (Philadelphia), XXVIII
         (First Month), pp. 159-60.
            There can be no exceptions to the rule against fiction,
         despite the opinions of the British Friend. Harriet
         Beecher Stowe's end may be worthy, but the book will do
         nothing to liberate slaves, and she should not be called
         a "conspicuous benefactor of the human race."

17   ANON. "Uncle Tom's Cabin," The Friend (Philadelphia), XXIX
         (Fifth Month), pp. 294-95.
            Continuation and development of the points made in
         earlier article (XXVIII-First Month, pp. 159-60: 1853.B16).

1853

*18   ANON. "Uncle Tom's Cabin," Local Preacher's Magazine, n.s. I.
          Cited in Bullen, 1878.B9.

 19   ANON. "Uncle Tom's Cabin," Sharpe's London Magazine, XVIII,
          n.s. II, p. 63.
             A note on the reception of the novel throughout the
          world, with a quotation from the comments of Frederika
          Bremer.

 20   ANON. "Uncle Tom's Cabin and Slavery in the Southern States
          by a Carolinian," New York Quarterly Review, I (January),
          pp. 470-78.
             Notes that Harriet Beecher Stowe work contains an equal
          amount of cariacature and truth. It shows narrative
          power, but idealization of the characters lessens the im-
          pact. Questions the utility of this kind of book. (May
          be target of F. C. Adams, Uncle Tom at Home, 1853.A1.)

 21   BEATTY, A. "The Evils of Slavery," The Western Journal and
          Civilian, X (August), pp. 319-28.
             Discusses "practical" plans for the abolition of slavery
          and the problems presented by the solutions suggested in
          Uncle Tom's Cabin.

 22   DIX, JOHN. "Mrs. Harriet Beecher Stowe, with Notices of Some
          of her family," Transatlantic Tracings. London: W.
          Tweedie, pp. 70-87.
             Discussion of Uncle Tom's Cabin as a publishing phenome-
          non, produced by new technology. It is a "live" book,
          which, despite its flaws, displays "the consumate art of
          the story-teller." No novel after Tom Jones displays
          superior "constructive ability" and there are many well-
          delineated characters. Article includes personal descrip-
          tions of Harriet Beecher Stowe and Henry Ward Beecher.

 23   ELLIS, S. E. "A Key to Uncle Tom's Cabin," Christian Examiner,
          LIV (May), pp. 504-05.
             Brief comment, defending publication of the Key, but
          warning that it will do "a vast deal of mischief."

 24   FISHER, S. G. "The Possible Amelioration of Slavery," North
          American Review, LXXVII (October), p. 466.
             Uncle Tom's Cabin is inferior to the works of Scott,
          Dickens, Currer Bell, and Hawthorne, but is unquestionably
          a work of genius, the power of which lies in its "highly-
          colored description of reality." Fisher defends at length
          the doctrine of racial inferiority and discusses the nature
          of private property.

25 HOLMES, G. F. "A Key to Uncle Tom's Cabin," Southern Literary
        Messenger, XIX (June), pp. 321-30.
            Strong attack on Harriet Beecher Stowe's coarseness
        and violation of principles of female delicacy. The Key
        is "an encyclopedia of slander" and the author "a pander
        to the prurient appetite of the public." Her proofs are
        irrelevant; it is the use to which her facts are put that
        is objectionable. Reiterates points from the Messenger
        review of the novel (1852.B54) and objects to the misuse
        of Christianity in it.

26 KER, LEANDER. Slavery Consistent with Christianity, with an
        Introduction embracing a Notice of the 'Uncle Tom's Cabin'
        Movement in England. Weston, Mo.: Finch and O'Gorman.
            The British believe more firmly in "all the absurd fic-
        tions and sickly sentiment contained in Uncle Tom's Cabin,"
        than in the Bible.

27 McCORD, LOUISA S. "Uncle Tom's Cabin," Southern Quarterly
        Review, n.s. VII (January), pp. 81-120.
            Abusive attack on Uncle Tom's Cabin and on Westminster
        Review. The book is gross, obscene, full of libels and
        falsehoods. Harriet Beecher Stowe does not know decent
        society or the language of the area she depicts. Offensive
        sexual undertones pervade the book. The heroes are
        mulatto, not Negro.

28 PATMORE, COVENTRY. "American Novels," North British Review,
        XIX (November), pp. 81-109.
            Praises Uncle Tom's Cabin, but comments at length on its
        one fault, the use of vulgar language. Contrasts it with
        The Scarlet Letter and The Blithedale Romance.

29 SIMMS, WILLIAM GILMORE. "A Key to Uncle Tom's Cabin," Southern
        Quarterly Review, n.s. VII (July), pp. 214-54.
            The Key, like the novel, "makes the simple...mistake, of
        charging upon an institution, what are the defects and
        vices of humanity at large." Harriet Beecher Stowe is a
        "woman-reasoner," whose process of thought is wholly sen-
        suous. The isolated facts presented, although true, to-
        gether make up a "wholesale lie." Specific incidents and
        characters are discussed at length.

30 STEPHEN, Sir GEORGE. "Uncle Tom's Cabin and The White Slave."
        Review from the "Northhampton Mercury," in Uncle Tom's
        Cabin, Bleak House, Slavery and Slave Trade. London:
        Longman, Brown, Green, and Longmans. (See 1853.A6.)
            Proves that the American novels in question are not

1853

exaggerations by comparing incidents from them with documents on slavery in the English colonies in the earlier
part of the century.

31   WARREN, SAMUEL. "Uncle Tom's Cabin and A Key to Uncle Tom's
      Cabin," Blackwood's Edinburgh Magazine, LXXIV (October),
      pp. 393–423.
         Notes the influence of Dickens in both the virtues and
      the faults of this work of a woman of genius. Laments the
      obvious preaching, but sees its necessity. The novel's
      chief fault is its want of "connectedness." Lengthy plot
      summary with many quotations.

1854 A BOOKS

1   HART, ADOLPHUS. Uncle Tom in Paris; or, Views of Slavery Out-
     side the Cabin. Together with Washington's Views of
     Slavery. Baltimore: Wm. Taylor & Company.
        Cited in Sabin, 1933.B5.

2   STEPHEN, Sir GEORGE. Antislavery Recollections; in a series
     of Letters, Addressed to Mrs. Harriet Beecher Stowe,
     written by Sir George Stephen, at her request.
        A narrative of the abolition of slavery in the British
     colonies, which, although addressed to Harriet Beecher
     Stowe, makes no direct mention of her or her books.

1854 B SHORTER WRITINGS

1   ANON. "Notes on Uncle Tom's Cabin," Southern Quarterly Review,
     XXV (January), pp. 248–49.
        Review of Stearns's book (1853.A8). This work is a
     "spirited and sensible rejoinder" to the novel, but one
     which will be ignored by those already resolved against
     the Southern cause.

2   ANON. "Southern Slavery and its Assailants – A Key to Uncle
     Tom's Cabin," DeBow's Review, XV (January), pp. 46–62.
        Discussion of the fallacies in the abolitionist arguments
     contained in the Key. The power to move readers in Harriet
     Beecher Stowe's novel is inherent in the incidents chosen
     and has little to do with the author's skill.

3   ANON. "Sunny Memories of Foreign Lands," Eclectic Review, C,
     n.s. VIII (September), pp. 327–41.
        Mrs. Stowe's impressions of Europe are "kindly and sym-
     pathetic," though not impartial. English observations are
     summarized, with many quotations.

4   ANON. "Sunny Memories of Foreign Lands," Freewill Baptist
        Quarterly, II (October), p. 475.
            It was hard to estimate the real talents of Harriet
        Beecher Stowe from Uncle Tom's Cabin. Here, despite the
        lack of profundity, she shows benevolent feeling, an
        ability to describe scenery effectively, and fearless in-
        dependence in the criticism of art.

5   ANON. "Sunny Memories of Foreign Lands," Graham's American
        Monthly Magazine, XLV (September), pp. 300-01.
            A book "modest in tone, and excellent in spirit."
        Harriet Beecher Stowe's comments on Murillo are nonetheless
        deplored and the inclusion of Charles Beecher's journal
        criticized.

6   ANON. "Sunny Memories of Foreign Lands," Knickerbocker, XLIV
        (September), pp. 297-301.
            These letters and observations are pleasant reading, al-
        though probably not spontaneous.

7   ANON. "Sunny Memories of Foreign Lands," Ladies Repository,
        XIV (September), p. 429.
            Brief note: these letters display a graceful style.

8   ANON. "Sunny Memories of Foreign Lands," New Englander, XII
        (August), p. 484.
            Brief descriptive comment.

9   ANON. "Sunny Memories of Foreign Lands," Putnam's Monthly
        (September), p. 651.
            Compliments Harriet Beecher Stowe's continued modesty in
        the midst of continental triumphs and notes that few
        Americans abroad took note of her. This book is a "highly
        respectable book of travels, but nothing more" from which
        Harriet Beecher Stowe's remarks on art, characteristic of
        the novice viewer, ought to have been omitted. Analysis
        of author's reaction to the upper classes in Britain.

10   ANON. "Uncle Tom's Cabin, Slavery, and the North American
        Review," Freewill Baptist Quarterly, II, pp. 23-41.
            Harriet Beecher Stowe's genius is proven by the universal
        popularity of Uncle Tom's Cabin, a book which, although
        dealing with vice, never debases or corrupts. The falla-
        cies in the North American Review's defense of slavery and
        of racial inferiority are pointed out and discussed.

11   AYTOUN, W. E. "Mrs. Stowe's Sunny Memories," Blackwood's
        Edinburgh Magazine, LXXVI (September), pp. 301-317.

1854

A long review of <u>Sunny Memories</u>, commending Harriet Beecher Stowe's "modest, unaffected, and sometimes naive observations," but lamenting her taste in literature and art as "either wholly uncultivated or radically bad," and criticizing her stand on women's rights and war. Notes her popularity with the British public.

12   BLYDEN, EDWARD W. Letter on colonization, etc., <u>The African Repository and Colonial Journal</u>, XXX (August), pp. 237-39.
        Cites the end of <u>Uncle Tom's Cabin</u> as an agreeable portent of growing interest in colonization.

13   ELLIS, SAMUEL E. "Sunny Memories of Foreign Lands," <u>Christian Examiner</u>, LVII (September), pp. 301-02.
        Brief comment, commending book.

14   PEABODY, A. P. "Sunny Memories of Foreign Lands," <u>North American Review</u>, LXXIX (October), pp. 423-41.
        Favorable review of <u>Sunny Memories</u> and analysis of the British class system. Harriet Beecher Stowe inherits an acute and vigorous pen from her father, but accuracy and finish are often lacking from her writing.

1855 A BOOKS - NONE

1855 B SHORTER WRITINGS

 *1   ANON. "Sunny Memories of Foreign Lands," <u>Metropolitan</u>, III, p. 148.
        Cited in Poole's II.

  2   PEABODY, A. P. "The Mayflower," <u>North American Review</u>, LXXXI (July), pp. 276-77.
        Brief review. These early tales contain fine passages of dialogue and scene-painting, and anticipate the success of <u>Uncle Tom's Cabin</u>.

  3   SENIOR, NASSAU W. "Slavery in the United States," <u>Edinburgh Review</u>, CI.
        A brief history of slavery in the United States, racism, etc. <u>Uncle Tom's Cabin</u> is a political pamphlet in the guise of a novel.

HARRIET BEECHER STOWE: A REFERENCE GUIDE

1856 A BOOKS

1   SENIOR, NASSAU W. <u>American Slavery: A Reprint of an Article</u> <u>on "Uncle Tom's Cabin," of which a Portion was Inserted in</u> <u>the 206th Number of the "Edinburgh Review"; and of Mr.</u> <u>Sumner's Speech of the 19th and 20th of May, 1856. With</u> <u>a Notice of the Events Which Followed that Speech.</u> London: T. Fellowes.
      A longer version of 1855.B3.

1856 B SHORTER WRITINGS

1   ANON. "Dred," <u>Christian Examiner</u>, LXI (November), pp. 474-75.
      Generally positive response to the novel. Reviewer is offended only by the monstrous and unnatural character of Dred.

2   ANON. "Dred," <u>DeBows Review</u>, XXI (December), p. 662.
      Brief comment: this book provides "another exhibition of abolition spite and spleen."

3   ANON. "Dred," <u>Eclectic Review</u>, CIV (October), p. 323.
      A "rather dismal" tale which, notwithstanding great and remarkable merits, "fails to excite and maintain a very profound interest."

4   ANON. "Dred," <u>Irish Quarterly Review</u>, VI (December), p. 776.
      This book does not come up to <u>Uncle Tom's Cabin</u> and was obviously written in haste. The characters talk much and do little. The novel shows the danger of making the Bible available to the common people and the low ebb of Christianity in the American South.

5   ANON. "Dred," <u>Ladies' Repository</u>, XVI (November), pp. 187-98.
      "Mrs. Stowe evidently cared more for the moral bearing of her book than for the plot or interest of the story." Brief description of plot and characters of the novel.

6   ANON. "Dred," <u>Littell's Living Age</u>, LI (November), pp. 546-52.
      Review reprinted from the <u>Examiner</u>: this book dwells more on the position of the master than that of the slave, but is still interesting and powerful, despite lengthy didactic passages. Plot summary and excerpts from the novel.

7   ANON. "Dred," <u>Monthly Religious Magazine</u>, XVI (October).
      Mrs. Stowe's badly named book has both absolute and relative excellence. It is flawed in construction and

1856

perhaps "too discouraging" in its views on reform, but is filled with a strong and righteous faith.

8   ANON. "Dred," New Quarterly Review, XX, pp. 346-66.
    The work is "full of power." The skill of some passages suggests that Mrs. Stowe had assistance. Grand qualities abound along with remarkable artistic defects.

9   ANON. "Dred," Tait's Edinburgh Magazine, n.s. XXIII (October), pp. 613-620.
    Discusses conditions of American slavery and summarizes plot of Dred, a book not inferior to Uncle Tom's Cabin. "The mechanism of the narrative is more complicated and the style is not less eloquent than that of its precursor." Defends the "evangelical Presbyterianism" of the author.

10 ANON. [W.R.A.]. "The Duty of Southern Authors," Southern Literary Messenger, XXIII (October), p. 242.
    The author calls for more and better responses to abolitionist propaganda. "The success of Uncle Tom's Cabin is an evidence of the manner in which our enemies are employing literature for our overthrow."

11 ANON. "Slavery," Dublin University Magazine, XLVIII (December), p. 675.
    Compares the author of Dred to Fanny Burney. Harriet Beecher Stowe is a "character-monger." The plot of the novel is weak; Dred himself is too strong for the novelist's powers. Extended discussion of the slavery question.

12 BARTLETT, D. W. "Harriet Beecher Stowe," Modern Agitators. New York: Miller, Orton & Mulligan, pp. 73-95.
    A brief biographical sketch of Harriet Beecher Stowe. Relationship between The Mayflower and Uncle Tom's Cabin is noted, with tale from the former and many passages from the latter included.

13 ELIOT, GEORGE. "Dred," Westminster Review, LXVI, n.s. X (October), pp. 571-73.
    Harriet Beecher Stowe has invented the Negro novel and bears comparison with Scott in her portrayal of racial conflict and "Hebraic Christianity." Her strongest point is her dramatic instinct; her weakness is a failure to show bad Negro characters.

14 FISHER, G. P. "Mrs. Stowe's New Novel," New Englander, XIV (November), pp. 515-526.
    Review of Dred. The story lacks unity, and the reader

loses interest when the author begins to argue rather than dramatize. Though generally inferior to Uncle Tom's Cabin, the novel does contain effective characters and passages and is superior to the earlier book in exposing the evils of the slave system. Despite its criticism of ministers, Dred is not anti-Christian.

15   GLEIG, C. E. S. "Dred," Blackwood's Edinburgh Magazine, LXXX (December), p. 693.
        The book is very uneven. Discusses the various ill-managed plots and their defects, and notes the book's vulgarity, dullness, repetition, and general failure as a work of "moral art." Comments on the futility of the ending.

16   GRAYSON, WILLIAM. "The Hireling and the Slave," I, The Hireling and the Slave, Chicora, and Other Poems. Charleston: McCarter & Co., Publishers, pp. 41-42.
        A substantial passage on Harriet Beecher Stowe, "a moral scavenger, with greedy eye," in a long poem defending slavery. A Key to Uncle Tom's Cabin is called a compilation of slanders and crimes. The motive for both books is avarice.

17   OLMSTED, FREDERICK L. A Journey in the Seaboard Slave States. New York: Dix and Edwards, p. 98, passim.
        Brief references are made throughout the book to Southern knowledge of and feelings about Uncle Tom's Cabin.

1857 A BOOKS

1   M'LEOD, DONALD. Donald M'Leod's Gloomy Memories in the Highlands of Scotland versus Mrs. Harriet Beecher Stowe's Sunny Memories in (England) a Foreign Land: or a Faithful Picture of the Extirpation of the Celtic Race from the Highlands of Scotland. Toronto: Thompson & Company.
        Documents the eviction of the Celts from the Sutherland estates and claims that the issue was "whitewashed" by Harriet Beecher Stowe in Sunny Memories.

1857 B SHORTER WORKS

1   SENIOR, NASSAU W. "American Slavery," Quarterly Review, CI (April), pp. 324-52; also Littell's Living Age, LIII (June), pp. 705-22.
        Review of Dred. This book is "more uniformly and

1857

intensely painful" than Uncle Tom's Cabin, and delineates
the moral degradation of the master more clearly. There
are problems in the characterization of Nina and Dred, and
in pacing. Discussion of the various ministers depicted
in the book, and many excerpts. Article ends with comments on Sumner, slavery, etc.

1858 A BOOKS - NONE

1858 B SHORTER WRITINGS

   1   ANON. "Dred," Christian Observer, LVII, p. 115.
         Brief notice of the novel.

   2   ANON. [A NEW ENGLAND LADY]. "Dred," Southern Literary Messen-
        ger, XXVII (October), pp. 284-86.
         Description of and attack upon the Beecher family, along
        with review of novel. Dred contains profanity, exhibits a
        want of female delicacy, and is filled with "libelous re-
        flections on the American ministry."

1859 A BOOKS - NONE

1859 B SHORTER WRITINGS

   1   ALLEN, W. F. "The Minister's Wooing," Christian Examiner,
        LXVII (November), p. 466.
         Brief notice of the novel.

   2   ANON. "The Minister's Wooing," Athenaeum, XXXIV (October 8),
        p. 459.
         Suggests comparing this book to Thackeray's The Vir-
        ginians. Regrets the attention given in this novel to
        slavery, a worn-out subject, and condemns Harriet Beecher
        Stowe's historical inaccuracy, as well as the "revolting
        spectacle of spiritual suffering" which marks the religious
        side of the book. Predicts that it will be read primarily
        for its love story.

   3   ANON. "The Minister's Wooing," The Englishwoman's Journal, IV
        (November), pp. 203-08.
         This book is worthy to take the place held by The Vicar
        of Wakefield in England, and is "instinct with the vigorous
        spiritual and mental life of the Puritan fathers." Lengthy
        excerpts included.

4   ANON. "The Minister's Wooing," <u>Saturday Review</u>, IX (October 22), pp. 483–85.
     Reviewer objects to the "gospel of vagueness and sentiment" which fills this novel. The subject is too solemn for treatment by a novelist, and the theological arguments embodied in the characters are not given their true weight nor subjected to rational judgment.

5   ANON. "The Works of Harriet Beecher Stowe," <u>Tait's Edinburgh Magazine</u>, n.s. XXVI (November), pp. 641–50.
     Review of the three novels published to date. <u>Dred</u> is praised highly and all three are commended for their lack of exaggeration and distortion in the portrayal of character and the management of plot. <u>The Minister's Wooing</u> has nothing dazzling in it, but has valuable qualities and fine details.

6   LUCAS, SAMUEL. "Stowe, Harriet Beecher: 'Dred,'" <u>Eminent Men and Popular Books</u>. London: Routledge, Warnes, & Routledge, pp. 207–230.
     Reprint of a review from <u>The Times</u> (September 18, 1856). An appreciation of individual characters. The book is "striking and remarkable," despite its exaggerations and literary flaws. Discussion of slavery and of whether such books tend to aid the cause of abolition.

1860 A BOOKS – NONE

1860 B SHORTER WRITINGS

1   ANON. "The Minister's Wooing," <u>Ladies Repository</u>, XX (January), p. 58.
     Reviewer found the book very dull reading, and filled with grave historical inaccuracies, impropriety, and doubtful theology.

2   ANON. "Two New Novels," <u>Scottish Review</u>, VIII (January), pp. 53–61.
     <u>Dred</u> suffers from self-consciousness; <u>The Minister's Wooing</u> is a fairer test of the author's powers. It suffers from an excessive number of didactic passages and from its tendency to provoke unnecessary controversy. Its purpose is uncertain, since plot and characterization are weak, but the analytic powers of the author and the vividness of her New England sketches give it charm.

1860

3   BACON, L. "The Minister's Wooing," <u>New Englander</u>, XVIII
        (February), p. 145.
            The novel is examined as an example of historical fiction
        and held up against "the truth of history." Although
        powerful and popular, it is inaccurate and contains many
        anachronisms.

4   JONES, J. H. "Mrs. Stowe and Her Critics," <u>University Quar-</u>
        <u>terly</u>, II (July), pp. 1-33.
            Review of <u>The Minister's Wooing</u>, a "quiet story," one
        "carved by the hand of genius." Many adjectives used to
        describe the felicitous characterizations and to defend
        Harriet Beecher Stowe against theological attack.

5   RHODES, M. J. "The Minister's Wooing," <u>Dublin Review</u>, XLVIII
        (May), pp. 190-228.
            This story has reality and freshness, but the writer
        has a noble heart which is unconsciously athirst for the
        Catholic faith. Long review, with many quotations used to
        prove Harriet Beecher Stowe's longing for the Roman church.

6   WARE, L. G. "The Minister's Wooing," <u>Christian Examiner</u>,
        LXVIII (January), pp. 113-24.
            "Not only in form, but intrinsically, this takes rank
        above the former books by the author." Reviewer applauds
        the vigorous free-thinking in the book, objecting only to
        the implausible happy ending.

<u>1861 A BOOKS - NONE</u>

<u>1861 B SHORTER WRITINGS</u>

1   ANON. "Mrs. Beecher Stowe's Wounded Feelings," <u>Saturday Re-</u>
        <u>view</u>, XII (September 14), pp. 262-63.
            Attack on Harriet Beecher Stowe, whose letter to Lord
        Shaftesbury calling for British intervention is "ladylike,"
        i.e., full of carelessness and hurt feelings. "Her pre-
        vious habits of mind have narrowed and warped her judg-
        ment," and she is in part responsible for the war--a con-
        flict which is <u>not</u> a "holy war" against slavery and one in
        which the British should not intervene.

2   ANON. "The Pearl of Orr's Island," <u>Eclectic Review</u>, s. VII,
        V (June), pp. 625-30.
            The <u>Pearl</u> is a sea-idyll, the "most perfect" of Mrs.
        Stowe's later works, a book one "can with confidence leave
        in the hands of a family of a daughter."

3   ANON. "The Pearl of Orr's Island," Englishwoman's Journal,
         VII (June), p. 275.
            This novel has "all the merit of The Minister's Wooing,"
         without the shadow of slavery. In it, the comic and
         pathetic are successfully blended.

4   JONES, J. H. "Mrs. Stowe and Her Critics," University
         Quarterly, III (January), pp. 93-115.
            Continuation of earlier article (1860.B4). Discusses
         doctrinal questions raised by The Minister's Wooing, and
         defends Harriet Beecher Stowe for her picture of Hopkins.
         She has presented to us, not a series of events, but "the
         secret spiritual life of his soul."

1862 A BOOKS - NONE

1862 B SHORTER WRITINGS

1   ANON. "Agnes of Sorrento and The Pearl of Orr's Island,"
         Christian Examiner, LXXIII (July), pp. 145-46.
            Reviewer wonders why, when the minor characters in these
         novels are so memorable, the heroines are so weak. Pre-
         fers The Pearl to Agnes, and points out the tediousness of
         repetition in the descriptive passages.

2   SMITH, C. C. "Agnes of Sorrento and The Pearl of Orr's
         Island," North American Review, XVC (July), p. 269.
            These are spirited and interesting novels, despite the
         author's lack of skill in controlling plot and delineating
         character. The Pearl of Orr's Island is superior, a story
         of "singular pathos and beauty."

1863 A BOOKS

1   CIVIS ANGLICUS [pseud.] A Voice from the Motherland, Answering
         Mrs. H. Beecher Stowe's Appeal. London: Trübner and Co.,
         39 pp.
            A detailed reply to Harriet Beecher Stowe's appeal of
         1863 for British support, affirming the continued hatred
         of slavery in the British Empire but defending English
         neutrality on the grounds that pressure to emancipate
         slaves was only a temporary by-product of an ill-conducted
         war to preserve the Union, that the North was split by
         corruption and faction, and the colored population ex-
         ploited, not really freed.

1863

1863 B SHORTER WRITINGS

1   ANON. "American Literature and the Civil War," Fraser's Maga-
         zine, LXVII (April), pp. 517-27.
            Several paragraphs of this general article are devoted
         to the nature and effect of Uncle Tom's Cabin by Catherine
         [sic] Beecher Stowe.

2   ANON. "Literature," Athenaeum, XXXVI (January 17), pp. 77-79.
            Comment on the effects of Uncle Tom's Cabin in the
         decade since it appeared ("with that bad book true progress
         ceased and reaction came") and on Harriet Beecher Stowe's
         recent appeal for English support. Accuses her of ingrati-
         tude and forgetfulness.

3   ANON. "Recent Novels of Harriet Beecher Stowe," Boston Re-
         view, III (January), pp. 82-94.
            Plot summaries and generally favorable comments about
         Agnes of Sorrento and The Pearl of Orr's Island. Agnes is
         charming, but written with less care. Many of the charac-
         ters of the two novels are alike. Reviewer condemns the
         author's denial of the doctrine of eternal punishment.

4   COBBE, FRANCES P. "Rejoinder to Mrs. Stowe's Reply to the
         Address of the Women of England," Atlantic Monthly, VII
         (April).
            Reprint of pamphlet published in London, affirming
         British abhorrence of slavery and support of freedom.

1864 A BOOKS - NONE

1864 B SHORTER WRITINGS

1   SENIOR, NASSAU W. "American Slavery," Essays on Fiction.
         London: Longman, Green, Longman, Roberts & Green,
         pp. 397-507.
            Full versions of articles on Uncle Tom's Cabin and Dred.

2   STEELE, Rev. GEORGE M. "Living Celebrities of New England,"
         Ladies' Repository, XXIV (September), pp. 535-39.
            Harriet Beecher Stowe is a literary artist, all of whose
         works have a "philanthropic bearing."

1866 A BOOKS - NONE

1866 B SHORTER WRITINGS

1   ANON. "Little Foxes," <u>Ladies' Repository</u>, XXVI (February),
      p. 123.
        Brief notice of publication.

1868 A BOOKS - NONE

1868 B SHORTER WRITINGS

1   ANON. "The Chimney Corner by Christopher Crowfield," <u>Nation</u>,
      VI (April 23), pp. 334-35.
        Mrs. Stowe's essays show much good sense and obviously
      fill a need, but she over-exalts housekeeping and women's
      practical work at the expense of their mental development
      and "the fact of personality" which "comes before the fact
      of sex." The pursuit of material comfort is a means, not
      an end.

2   DeFOREST, J. W. "The Great American Novel," <u>Nation</u>, VI
      (January 9), pp. 27-29.
        Survey of fiction notes that <u>Uncle Tom's Cabin</u> is the
      nearest approach to a panoramic novel Americans possess,
      despite its idealism and "village twaddle," but the other
      novels of Harriet Beecher Stowe are limited in scope.

3   PARKER, EDWIN POND. "Harriet Beecher Stowe," <u>Eminent Women of
      the Age</u>. Hartford: S. M. Betts & Co., pp. 296-331.
        Biographical sketch of Harriet Beecher Stowe with anec-
      dotes of her childhood, and comments on <u>Uncle Tom's Cabin</u>,
      <u>Dred</u> (lacks unity and simplicity), and <u>The Minister's
      Wooing</u>. The theology of the latter is defended.

1869 A BOOKS

1   ANON. <u>Byron painted by his Compeers</u>. London: S. Palmer.
        Various essays, memoirs, etc. of Byron's life, assembled
      to disprove the assertions of Harriet Beecher Stowe in
      "The True Story of Lady Byron." Conclusion notes that the
      facts contradict all the accusations of the novelist,
      whose preconceived ideas about incest would have shocked
      Lady Byron. Harriet Beecher Stowe will never again be ad-
      mitted into the private homes of Englishmen.

2   ANON. <u>Lord Byron's Defence in the Matter of the Stowe Scandal</u>.
      London: No. 183, Strand.

1869

An attack in verse on Harriet Beecher Stowe, signed "Byron": "Perchance she's some forlorn, neglected beauty,/ Or else--her husband doesn't do his duty." Suggests that the motive for her behavior is avarice.

3   ANON. The True Story of Lord and Lady Byron. London: T. Cooper & Company.
    The introduction to this collection of essays defending Byron and attacking Harriet Beecher Stowe and her charges, points out that "The True Story of Lady Byron" was not originally designed for English readers, and that it had been inspired by a particularly garish American edition of the Guiccioli book. Notes the Beecher family craving for notoriety.

4   AUSTIN, ALFRED. A Vindication of Lord Byron. London: Chapman & Hall.
    A defense of Lord Byron and Augusta Leigh, supporting the "hallucination theory," and condemning Harriet Beecher Stowe's treatment of the subject.

5   The Editor of Once a Week. The Stowe-Byron Controversy: a Complete Résumé of all that has been Written and Said upon the Subject, reprinted from "The Times," the Saturday Review:...together with an Impartial Review of the Merits of the Case.
    A résumé of public opinion, reprinting the substance of the Stowe article, letters to the newspapers attacking and supporting Harriet Beecher Stowe, etc. She is accused of carelessness, inconsistency, and lack of taste. The critic acquits her of a desire for notoriety, but finds the article rambling, the story novelistic, and the defense of Lady Byron gratuitous.

6   FLECK, DUDLEY. The Byron Mystery. London: Elliott.
    Re-examination of the facts of Byron's life in the light of the "farfetched assertions" of Harriet Beecher Stowe. Reviewer hopes she erred from ignorance, not malice.

7   OUTIS [pseud.] The 'True Story' of Mrs. Stowe. London: Mann Nephews.
    An attack on Mrs. Stowe, on Macmillan's, and on the general method of argument presented in "The True Story of Lady Byron," using parody, etc., to point out the errors in the charge and the logic of presentation.

28

1869 B SHORTER WRITINGS

1   AN AMERICAN [pseud.] "The Reverend Henry Ward Beecher and
     Mrs. Beecher Stowe," Cassell's Magazine, n.s. I, pp. 282-84.
        Biographical sketch of Harriet Beecher Stowe and her
     brother. The success of Uncle Tom's Cabin gave the author
     a craving for notoriety. The Byron disgrace is attributed
     to weakness. Harriet Beecher Stowe's essays are "perhaps
     more estimable" than her fiction.

2   ANON. "The American Woman's Home; on Principles of Domestic
     Science," Ladies' Repository, XXIX (October), pp. 316-17.
        A brief favorable review of the "estimable" book which
     elevates the employments that sustain the "sacred duties
     of the family state."

3   ANON. "The Byron Case," The Revolution (October 14), p. 236.
        Suggests that critics of the Byron article are hypocrites
     and would have been glad to reprint the article themselves.
     Suspects that the excitement is a covert attack on Harriet
     Beecher Stowe's anti-slavery views.

4   ANON. "The Byron Case," Saturday Review, XXVIII (September 11).
        Attacks the motives and taste of Harriet Beecher Stowe
     and comments on the articles and letters which have ap-
     peared to date.

5   ANON. "The Byron Controversy," The Woman's Advocate (Decem-
     ber), pp. 287-88.
        Letter, with comment, from a female Universalist minister
     to Harriet Beecher Stowe, applauding her conviction that
     truth must be told and citing the Byron article as a
     warning for young men.

6   ANON. "The Byron Horror," Nation, IX (August), p. 167.
        Defends the author's sincerity but suggests that her
     facts are wrong and hopes for more evidence.

7   ANON. "The Byron Mystery," Saturday Review, XXVIII (Septem-
     ber 4), p. 311.
        An attack on the Macmillan's article and on "a writer so
     inaccurate, and in other ways so positively repellent, as
     the authoress of Uncle Tom's Cabin"; her charges, however,
     are generally held to be true.

8   ANON. "The Byron Revelations," Independent (August 26), p. 1.
        The Byron article is "startling in accusation, barren in
     proof, inaccurate in dates, infelicitous in style."

1869

9   ANON. "The Byron Scandal," Athenaeum, LII (September 11),
       p. 336.
           The Byron revelations have caused a run on his books.
       Hopes to hear that Harriet Beecher Stowe has refused to
       take money for the story.

10   ANON. "The Byron Scandal," Independent (August 26), p. 1.
           Defends Harriet Beecher Stowe's ruthless defacement of
       a popular idol on the grounds that the public will be
       better off with the unwelcome knowledge than without it.

11   ANON. "The Byrons and Their Latest Biographer," St. James,
       XXV, pp. 133-36.
           Attack on Harriet Beecher Stowe's motives. She has
       pandered to the "lowest and most grovelling and sensual of
       appetites."

12   ANON. "The Case Stated," The Woman's Advocate (September),
       pp. 142-44.
           Comment on a Hearth and Home paper by Harriet Beecher
       Stowe entitled "What is and What is not the Point in the
       Woman Question." Rejoices in her lucid presentation and
       the temperate tone with which the history of the movement
       is recapitulated and the woman question "stripped of excess
       verbiage."

13   ANON. "Consistency, Thou Art a Jewel," The Woman's Advocate
       (October), pp. 192-93.
           Refuses to comment on the facts of the Byron case or the
       wisdom displayed by its author, but is delighted to see
       the Chicago Sun showing its true colors to the world by
       heaping obloquy upon an honored woman.

14   ANON. "Harriet Beecher Stowe," Lakeside, II (September),
       pp. 196-202.
           A sketch of the life and writings of Harriet Beecher
       Stowe. The Minister's Wooing is, in the literary sense,
       the finest work so far. Oldtown Folks suffers from lack
       of plot.

15   ANON. "Henry Ward Beecher and Harriet Beecher Stowe,"
       Harper's Weekly, XIII (October), p. 1.
           Biographical sketch of brother and sister, commenting
       on the absolute self-possession of Harriet Beecher Stowe.
       Their joint mission in life is "to agitate the human
       heart...to conflict against wrong."

1869

*16   ANON. "Lady Byron and Harriet Beecher Stowe," <u>Englishwoman's Domestic Magazine</u>, VII, p. 194.
        Cited in Poole's, I.

17   ANON. "Lady Byron's Story," <u>Harper's Weekly</u>, XIII (September 11), p. 579.
        Strong defense of the Harriet Beecher Stowe article, suggesting some difficulty with details, but supporting the revelation of truth, however unwelcome it may be.

18   ANON. "Lady Noel Byron and Mrs. Beecher Stowe. A Short Chapter of 'Ifs,'" <u>New Monthly Magazine</u>, CXLV (October), pp. 447-49.
        A general attack on Harriet Beecher Stowe's charges and level of taste.

19   ANON. "Let the Dead Rest," <u>Tomahawk</u>, V (September 11), p. 3.
        Whether the story is true or not, there is not the "faintest justification" for Mrs. Stowe's "repulsive eagerness" to publish it.

20   ANON. "Lord Byron and Mrs. Beecher Stowe," <u>Broadway</u>, III, pp. 167-85.
        Attack on Harriet Beecher Stowe and defense of Byron. Claims that defense on Lady Byron's reputation was only a pretense for publishing the scandalous story.

21   ANON. "Lord Byron Vindicated," <u>Fraser's Magazine</u>, LXXX (November), pp. 599-617.
        Résumé of the lives of Byron and his wife, disproving charges. The vagueness of the Stowe article suggests that perhaps she made the inference of incest and imagined that Lady Byron, who could not herself have made such charges, assented to it.

22   ANON. "Lord and Lady Byron," <u>Argosy</u>, VIII (October), pp. 274-289.
        Lengthy attack on the Byron article, pointing out improbabilities, inconsistencies, errors of fact, "A greater mistake was never made than to issue this paper."

23   ANON. "Oldtown Folks," <u>Every Saturday</u>, VIII (October 9).
        Review reprinted from <u>The Times</u>. Praises the unimpeachable realism of the book and sees its permanent value in the study of American religious opinion.

24   ANON. "Oldtown Folks," <u>Ladies' Repository</u>, XXIX (August), p. 157.

1869

> A brief comment on the novel, calling it the author's best book.

25 ANON. "Oldtown Folks," The Woman's Advocate (September), pp. 147–48.
> The novel is a "searching delineation of the Orthodoxy" of early New England. "The whole volume is aglow with sparkles of fancy and passages of deep human tenderness."

*26 ANON. "Some Thoughts in Connexion with Byron's Name," New Monthly Magazine, CXLV (November), pp. 558–562.
> Gohdes, 1944.B1.

27 ANON. "Stowe versus Byron," St. James's Magazine, XXV, n.s. IV (October), pp. 58–68.
> Harriet Beecher Stowe has been guilty of a "gross literary blunder" and is incapable of understanding Byron's life or poetry.

28 ANON. "Supposing it to be True," Nation, IX (September 9), p. 208.
> Attacks the Harper's Weekly defense of Harriet Beecher Stowe (1869.B17), but comments ironically on the outrage of the popular press which draws the line only at incest.

29 ANON. "The True Story of Mrs. Shakespeare's Life," Gentleman's Quarterly (December), pp. 63–73.
> A parody of the Byron article. Shakespeare murdered rival playwrights after purloining their plots. Alleged author, Harriet B. Cherstow, expects pecuniary profit for exposure of the crime.

30 ANON. "Was it a Mystification?" Nation, IX (September 2), p. 189.
> Suggests that Byron may simply have "mystified" or hoaxed his wife to try his power over her.

31 CURTIS, GEORGE. "The Editor's Easy Chair," Harper's, XXXIX (October), pp. 764–66.
> A defense of Harriet Beecher Stowe and the Byron article.

32 DENNETT, J. R. "Oldtown Folks," Nation, VIII (June 3), pp. 437–38.
> The book displays vigorous writing, but Harriet Beecher Stowe creates types rather than individuals and many of these are over-familiar "zoological specimens," unable to awake human interest.

32

33   GROVE, GEORGE. Introduction to "The True Story of Lady Byron's
     Life," Macmillan's Magazine, XX (September), p. 377.
          "The time has come" when the details of Byron's career
     "can no longer be concealed. This article will finally
     render justice" (Lady Byron).

34   HARTE, BRET. "Oldtown Folks," Overland Monthly, III (October),
     p. 390.
          Harriet Beecher Stowe's treatment of New England is more
     provincial than her material, which is itself rapidly
     losing whatever interest it once had.

35   HAYWARD, ABRAHAM. "The Byron Mystery," Quarterly Review,
     CXXVII (October), pp. 400-44.
          Summary and analysis of the controversy, including a re-
     view of Byron's life. Harriet Beecher Stowe's story is
     "principally a literary curiosity" which will be "flung
     aside with loathing and contempt" before the year is out.
     Reprinted in Littell's Living Age, CIII (November),
     p. 486 ff.

36   KINNEY, M. B. "Mrs. Stowe, Mrs. Somerville, and Mrs.
     Browning," Putnam's Monthly, XIII (June), p. 708.
          Description of a gathering of literati in Florence.

37   McCARTHY, JUSTIN. "Mrs. Stowe's Last Romance," Independent
     (August 26), p. 1.
          Attack on Byron article, which would have "delighted the
     taste of a Borgia family-circle." Finds the "sanctimonius
     imbecility of the manner in which Mrs. Stowe tries to re-
     gard her sickening task as a moral or religious duty" re-
     pellent, a kind of "prurient penitence."

38   MILLER, JOSIAH. Singers and Songs of the Church. London:
     Longmans, Green and Company, pp. 524-25.
          Brief biographical sketch.

39   MILES, GEORGE H. "The Atlantic Monthly: Its Charge against
     Byron," Southern Review, VI (October), pp. 477-78.
          Poem suggesting that Byron's afterlife should not be
     disturbed by a "libel borrowed from oblivion."

40   MOORE, REBECCA. "The Byron Scandal," The Revolution, IV
     (October 28), pp. 262-63.
          A letter from Manchester noting that the truth of the
     story is generally conceded in England. The sympathy of
     the press with Byron proves that Harriet Beecher Stowe was
     right to break the silence about his crimes.

1869

41 REDDING, CYRUS. "Lord Byron," New Monthly Magazine, CXLV
     (November), pp. 497-504.
        Long letter defending Byron, attacking both Lady Byron
     and Harriet Beecher Stowe, the latter as a "fiction-
     monger," unable to tell fact from fancy.

42 STANTON, ELIZABETH CADY. "The Moral of the Byron Case," Inde-
     pendent (September 9), p. 1.
        Suggests that the wrath of the press is a justification
     of the charge against Byron and that "Mrs. Stowe's fearful
     picture of the abominations of our social life, coming out
     simultaneously with John Stuart Mill's philosophy of the
     degradation of woman, will do much to rouse wise men to
     new thoughts on the social wrongs of the race."

43 WILBOUR, CHARLOTTE. "Harriet Beecher Stowe," The Revolution,
     IV (September 9), p. 149.
        Sympathizes with the wronged wife and notes that the
     conservative Harriet Beecher Stowe must have been shocked
     at the revelation made to her. Most critics of the story
     are hypocrites: incest and worse are common but seldom
     mentioned.

44 YOUMANS, __. "Mrs. Stowe's Mistake," Appleton's Journal, II
     (October 9), p. 247.
        Mrs. Stowe roused interest in Byron against her will and
     expectations because she misunderstood human nature.
     People wish to forget Byron's faults and she cannot coun-
     teract this movement.

1870 A BOOKS

1   MACKAY, CHARLES, ed. Medora Leigh; a History and an Auto-
     biography, with an introduction and a commentary on the
     charges brought against Lord Byron by Mrs. Beecher Stowe.
     New York: Harper & Brothers.
        Summarizes the story of the controversy and the contents
     of the Macmillan article, quotes Leigh letters and various
     defenses of Byron (pp. 1-21), then prints a biography of
     Augusta's daughter and an autobiography in which she claims
     Lady Byron told her Byron was her father. Recapitulates
     the entire story to exculpate the poet.

1870 B SHORTER WRITINGS

1   ANON. "The Byron Mystery and Mrs. Stowe," Saturday Review,
     XXIX (January 29), pp. 140-144.

Review of <u>Lady Byron Vindicated</u>, with summary and refu-
tation of theories held by other periodicals. Harriet
Beecher Stowe is attacked--"This is not the first time...
that her good intentions...have sown a crop only to be
watered with blood and tears"--but her charges are upheld.
The author is not always aware of the strength of her own
arguments. Reprinted in <u>Littell's Living Age</u>, CIV (March),
pp. 625-634.

2   ANON. "Lady Byron and Harriet Beecher Stowe," <u>American Bib-
liopilist</u>, II (February), p. 69.
      Notes the increased popularity of Byron works and re-
prints Byron anecdotes, along with the <u>Nation</u>'s comment
that the heroes of Harriet Beecher Stowe's novels resemble
the poet.

3   ANON. "Lady Byron and Mrs. Beecher Stowe," <u>New Monthly Maga-
zine</u>, CXLVI (February), pp. 217-19.
      An attack on Harriet Beecher Stowe's lack of generosity,
justice, etc.

4   ANON. "Mrs. Beecher Stowe's 'Vindication,'" <u>Argosy</u>, IX
(April 1), pp. 269-287.
      Repeats charges made in earlier <u>Argosy</u> article (1869.B22),
questions Harriet Beecher Stowe's capacity for rational
argument, and points out inconsistencies between article
and book.

5   ANON. Untitled. <u>The Woman's Journal</u>, I (January), p. 16.
      A comment on the household difficulties overcome by
Harriet Beecher Stowe during the composition of <u>Uncle
Tom's Cabin</u>.

*6   CHANDLER, P. W. "Lady Byron Vindicated," <u>New Jerusalem Maga-
zine</u>, XLII, p. 663.
      Cited in Cameron.

7   GODKIN, E. L. "Mrs. Stowe's 'Vindication of Lady Byron,'"
<u>Nation</u>, X (January 13), p. 24.
      Mrs. Stowe's publication was a misunderstanding of Lady
Byron's wishes. The present volume errs in using a
rhapsodical tone and presents no new evidence.

8   HAYWARD, ABRAHAM. "The Byron Mystery-Mrs. Stowe's Vindication," <u>Quarterly Review</u>, CXXVIII (January), p. 218.
      The prejudices of Harriet Beecher Stowe have led her to
see all facts through a "distorting medium." "She has
canonized the sinner, intending to deify the saint."

1870

9   HOWE, JULIA WARD. "Lady Byron Vindicated," The Woman's
       Journal, I (January), p. 20.
          The statements of Harriet Beecher Stowe are "bitter and
       partial" despite her understandable wish to vindicate her
       friend. The issue is "a quadrangular duel of women."

10   NEAL, JOHN. "Lady Byron," The Revolution, XI (January 20),
       pp. 36-37.
          Lady Byron Vindicated succeeds in justifying the earlier
       article. Reviewer notes and supports the main arguments
       of the book.

11   PAGET, J. "Lord Byron and his Calumniators," Blackwood's
       Edinburgh Magazine, CVII (January), pp. 123-38, 267-68.
          Strong attack on Harriet Beecher Stowe and her book:
       "all who would guard the purity of the home from pollu-
       tion, and the sanctity of the grave from outrage--have
       joined in one unanimous chorus of condemnation." Later
       note continues attack on the naiveté of Harriet Beecher
       Stowe.

12   REDDING, CYRUS. "Mrs. Stowe's Second 'True' Story," New
       Monthly Magazine, CXLVI (March), pp. 352-66.
          Violently negative response to Lady Byron Vindicated.
       Harriet Beecher Stowe's "zeal is without discretion, and
       stamped with unusual malignity." Among other things, she
       misuses scripture.

13   TWAIN, MARK [SAMUEL L. CLEMENS]. "Unburlesqueable Things,"
       Galaxy, X (July), p. 137.
          Short comment noting that the Byron scandal can not be
       burlesqued because incest is a "'situation' so tremen-
       dous" that burlesque cannot transcend it.

1871 A BOOKS - NONE

1871 B SHORTER WRITINGS

1   ANON. "The Beechers of Today," The Phrenological Journal and
       Life Illustrated, LII (January), p. 1ff.
          Portraits, mental and physical, of Harriet Beecher Stowe
       and the Beechers. All of them have genius, but their
       chief distinction lies in the ability to work hard.

2   ANON. "My Wife and I," Nation, XIII (November 16), pp. 324-25.
          The book is weak because of an over-attention to domestic
       details. It is not a novel but a guide to young house-
       holders.

3   ANON. "My Wife and I," Saturday Review, XXXII (December 30),
        p. 860.
            Brief review. The book is "cleverly written," but "as
        for ourselves, we would as soon have the present sewer
        question discussed in a novel as women's position in the
        world."

4   ANON. "Pink and White Tyranny," Ladies Repository, XXXI
        (September), p. 234.
            Brief favorable notice of the novel.

5   ANON. "Pink and White Tyranny," Nation, XIII (August 10),
        p. 94.
            This didactic novel fails both as a record of observa-
        tion and as a moral weapon because of its exaggeration of
        the manners of the day.

6   ANON. "Pink and White Tyranny," Overland Monthly, VII (Sep-
        tember), pp. 288-89.
            The handling of the society material in this book is
        feeble and the moral pushed too hard.

7   ANON. "Pink and White Tyranny," Saturday Review, XXXII
        (July 1), pp. 24-25.
            Despite the commendable moral--that the right of divorce
        will injure women more than men--and the familiarity of
        the type of American girl it portrays, this book is dull
        and weak, the heroine stupid, and the society depicted
        vulgar.

8   HOWELLS, WILLIAM DEAN. "Pink and White Tyranny," Atlantic
        Monthly, XXVIII (September), pp. 377-78.
            Pink and White Tyranny is a sermon with a forced moral,
        although a readable book. The characters are "overcharged"
        with their peculiar qualities, which "weakens the ethical
        effect."

1872 A BOOKS - NONE

1872 B SHORTER WRITINGS

1   ANON. "My Wife and I," Godey's Ladies Book, LXXXIV (January),
        p. 98.
            An admirable book, where "all that relates to the joint
        interests of men and women has been thrown into the arena
        as an open question."

1872

2   ANON. "My Wife and I," Harper's Magazine, XLIV (February),
        pp. 462-63.
            There are two main faults in this book: the woman's voice
        is apparent in the male narrator and the characters and
        situations are exaggerated throughout. Yet it is a
        "courageous and outspoken" novel, "admirable in several
        particulars."

3   ANON. "Oldtown Fireside Stories," Princeton Review, n.s. I
        (July), p. 603.
            A very brief comment describing the stories as "racy."

4   HOWELLS, WILLIAM DEAN. "My Wife and I," Atlantic Monthly, XXIX
        (January), pp. 110-11.
            The purpose of this book is good, but it is not Mrs.
        Stowe's best work; it lacks all "fineness of touch and
        mellowness of tone."

5   _____. "Sam Lawson's Oldtown Fireside Stories," Atlantic
        Monthly, XXIX (March), pp. 365-66.
            Contrasts this book with Eggleston's A Hoosier School-
        master. Praises Harriet Beecher Stowe's skill in recording
        the voice of an already vanished community, in a form which
        embodies "the naturalness of first-rate art."

6   PERRY, THOMAS S. "American Novels," North American Review,
        CXV (October), p. 370.
            Comments on Pink and White Tyranny and My Wife and I in
        a general survey of fiction. These are ignoble and
        cynical novels. Harriet Beecher Stowe has "overshot her
        mark" by using cariacature unnecessarily. Praises Sam
        Lawson stories.

1873 A BOOKS - NONE

1873 B SHORTER WRITINGS

1   ANON. "Palmetto Leaves," Athenaeum, LIX, no. 2381 (June 14),
        p. 759.
            Brief review. This is a pleasant and lively book which
        touches on the condition of the Negroes in the South.

2   ANON. "Palmetto Leaves," Overland Monthly, X (June), p. 583.
            The book contains sly humor, keen observation, and is
        "readable and interesting."

3   ANON. "Palmetto Leaves," <u>Saturday Review</u>, XXXV (May 24),
      p. 697.
        A very brief notice.

4   PHELPS, F. "Pink and White Tyranny," <u>New Jerusalem Magazine</u>,
      XLIV, p. 248.
        Summary of plot. This is an interesting story, the main
      flaw of which is that the reformation of the main character
      is indicated but not shown, and hence cannot help others.

<u>1875 A BOOKS - NONE</u>

<u>1875 B SHORTER WRITINGS</u>

1   ANON. "We and Our Neighbors," <u>Athenaeum</u>, LXIII, no. 2477
      (April 17), pp. 519-20.
        Reviewer is critical of the author's grammar and "verbal
      flourishes," but feels that the book can be read with
      "harmless enjoyment." Comments on Harriet Beecher Stowe's
      advocacy of "inter-sexual friendship."

2   ANON. "We and Our Neighbors," <u>Atlantic</u>, XXXVI (August), p. 248.
        Although the New England novels proved the strength of
      Harriet Beecher Stowe's talent, this book, like <u>My Wife</u>
      <u>and I</u>, is filled with uninteresting talk by vulgar people
      and "seems to have very little excuse for being."

3   ANON. "We and Our Neighbors," <u>Harper's</u>, LI (July), p. 298.
        This novel displays some force and originality, but lacks
      unity and finish.

4   ANON. "We and Our Neighbors," <u>Overland Monthly</u>, XV (Septem-
      ber), p. 301.
        This is a "sound, interesting, well-flavored story."

5   DUYCKINCK, EVART. "Harriet Beecher Stowe," <u>Cyclopaedia of</u>
      <u>American Literature</u>, II. New York: Charles Scribner &
      Co., pp. 522-530.
        Biographical sketch of Harriet Beecher Stowe and descrip-
      tion of her major works, with excerpts from <u>Uncle Tom's</u>
      <u>Cabin</u>, <u>Oldtown Fireside Stories</u>, etc.

6   JAMES, HENRY. "We and Our Neighbors," <u>Nation</u>, XXI (July 22),
      p. 61.
        Brief review. The book is filled with an "atmosphere of
      dense back-stairs detail," and the subject of the novel is
      elusive. The language of conversation is "an amalgam of

1875

>rural Yankee dialect, Southern negro jargon and the style
>of the paragraphs in the Home Journal."

1877 A BOOKS - NONE

1877 B SHORTER WRITINGS

1   RICE, C. DUNCAN. "Introduction," "Uncle Tom's Story of his
     Life": An Autobiography of Josiah Henson, from 1789 to
     1876. With a Preface by Mrs. H. B. Stowe, and an Intro-
     ductory note by G. Sturge and S. Morley. London: Frank
     Cass & Company Limited. 2nd edition.
          Rice notes that the connection between Henson and Uncle
     Tom is dubious and vague, despite the fact that the
     original introduction insists that the relationship can
     be "most satisfactorily established."

1878 A BOOKS - NONE

1878 B SHORTER WRITINGS

1   ANON. "Introduction," Uncle Tom's Cabin. Boston: Houghton,
     Mifflin and Company, pp. vii-xxxvii.
          Biographical sketch of Harriet Beecher Stowe. Uncle
     Tom's Cabin originated with a vision of the death of Tom,
     after which the book was "imposed" upon the author from
     above. History of early editions and of the book's im-
     mediate and immense popularity. Includes Harriet Beecher
     Stowe's correspondence with Dickens, Macauley, et al., and
     George Sand's critique. This introduction was reprinted
     in many later Houghton, Mifflin editions of Uncle Tom's
     Cabin and in The Writings of Harriet Beecher Stowe, Cam-
     bridge: Riverside Press (1896), I.

2   ANON. "Poganuc People," Athenaeum, LXX, no. 2654 (Septem-
     ber 7), pp. 303-04.
          This book is a sketch of country life rather than a
     novel, but it gives the reader "a pleasant feeling of
     fresh air."

3   ANON. "Poganuc People," Atlantic Monthly, XLII (October),
     p. 430.
          Thin and quiet "mildly affecting reminiscences" of a
     New England Mrs. Stowe knew thoroughly. Reviewer questions
     the worth of Harriet Beecher Stowe's dialect reproduction
     but values the historical record provided by the book.

4   ANON. "Poganuc People," Harper's, LVII (August), p. 467.
        This is a far better book than some of the novelist's
        later ones, but it lacks the dramatic element.

5   ANON. "Poganuc People," Library Table, IV (June 8), p. 283.
        This novel is a feeble imitation of Oldtown Folks.
        There is nothing really bad in it but nothing strikingly
        good either; in fact, "there is not a single chapter that
        the cultured mind can follow word for word."

6   ANON. "Poganuc People," Nation, XXVII (August 22), p. 118.
        A brief comment: The public in general is tired of these
        "sweet-cider" sketches, and their publication is "uninten-
        tionally pathetic."

7   ANON. "Poganuc People," Rose-Belford's, I (July), pp. 122-23.
        This is a book with "fine scope for Mrs. Stowe's peculiar
        powers" which will attract readers.

8   ANON. "Poganuc People," Sunday Afternoon, II (August), pp. 189-
        90.
        "As faithful as a Dutch genre picture," this is a novel
        from which one can learn and which will become a classic.

9   BULLEN, GEORGE. "Bibliography," Uncle Tom's Cabin. Boston:
        Houghton, Osgood and Company, pp. xxxix-lviii.
        A list of the contents of the British Museum collection
        of works relating to Uncle Tom's Cabin in three parts:
        complete texts of work; translations; and critical notices,
        English and foreign. Notes also juvenile and dramatic
        versions of book, as well as editions not yet obtained by
        library. Reprinted, with additions and revisions, in later
        Houghton Mifflin editions of Uncle Tom's Cabin and in The
        Writings of Harriet Beecher Stowe. Cambridge, Mass.:
        Riverside Press, 1896.

1879 A BOOKS - NONE

1879 B SHORTER WRITINGS

1   ANON. "Uncle Tom's Cabin," Atlantic Monthly, XLIII (March),
        pp. 407-08.
        Praises simplicity and frankness of Harriet Beecher
        Stowe's preface to the new edition. There are glaring
        errors of taste and fact in the novel, but never any of
        heart. "Here is an American novel as great in its way as
        Longfellow's Evangeline or Hawthorne's Scarlet Letter, and

1879

> probably greater, upon the whole, than any other novel of
> our time."

2 ANON. "Uncle Tom's Cabin," Harper's, LVIII (February), p. 467.
   A brief comment on the edition, not its contents.

3 ANON. "Uncle Tom's Cabin," Rose-Belford's, II (Jaunary),
   pp. 123-25.
   A brief comment on the immense popularity of the novel,
   taking note of the new edition.

1882 A BOOKS - NONE

1882 B SHORTER WRITINGS

1 ANON. "Harriet Beecher Stowe (In Celebration of her 70th
   Birthday)," The Critic (July 1), p. 176.
   Brief tribute to Harriet Beecher Stowe's "characteristi-
   cally American" genius.

2 ANON. "Mrs. Stowe's Birthday," Literary News (July), pp. 197-
   98.
   Description of the Atlantic birthday party, with excerpts
   from Holmes's and Whittier's poems. Includes reprint of
   Boston Traveller article on Harriet Beecher Stowe, praising
   Uncle Tom's Cabin and the New England novels.

3 BOLTON, SARAH K. "Harriet Beecher Stowe," Famous American
   Authors. New York: Thomas Y. Crowell Company, pp. 194-201.
   Biographical sketch with anecdotes of the later years of
   Harriet Beecher Stowe, showing that she was a "true home
   woman" and a devoted mother.

4 HOLMES, OLIVER WENDELL. "At the Summit: Verses to Harriet
   Beecher Stowe," Atlantic Monthly, L (August), p. 164.
   Poem honoring Harriet Beecher Stowe on the occasion of
   her seventieth birthday.

5 HOUGHTON, H. O. and OTHERS. "Birthday. The Party to Harriet
   Beecher Stowe," Atlantic Monthly, L (August), supplement.
   Includes guest list; birthday tributes by Houghton,
   Henry Ward Beecher, and others; letters of congratulation
   and tribute.

6 NICHOL, JOHN. American Literature: An Historical Sketch.
   Edinburgh: Charles & Adam Black. (Reprinted 1972, Free-
   port, N. Y.: Books for Libraries Press.)

Uncle Tom's Cabin, despite the mediocrity of its style,
has some conspicuous merits: it seems to be a precise,
though somewhat crude, résumé of observations on the black
world. Nichol criticizes all the later works, especially
Lady Byron Vindicated, but notes the additional importance
of Uncle Tom's Cabin as juvenile literature.

1883 A BOOKS - NONE

1883 B SHORTER WRITINGS

1　ABBOTT, LYMAN. Henry Ward Beecher: A Sketch of his Career.
New York: Funk & Wagnalls.
　　Little exclusively about Harriet Beecher Stowe, but many
quotations from her works and letters, as well as general
description of Beecher family life.

2　FORMAN, W. H. "Uncle Tom's Cabin," Manhattan, I (January),
p. 28.
　　Interview with John P. Jewett, Harriet Beecher Stowe's
first publisher, who discusses the background of the
Josiah Henson debate and describes his role in the publication of Uncle Tom's Cabin.

3　HANAFORD, PHEBE COFFIN. "Literary Women," Daughters of America; or Women of the Century. Boston: B. B. Russell,
pp. 221-23.
　　Brief biographical sketch.

4　PARTON, JAMES. "Mrs. H. B. Stowe and Uncle Tom's Cabin,"
Noted Women of Europe and America. Hartford: Phoenix
Publishing Co., pp. 73-77.
　　Brief comments on the writing and publication of Uncle
Tom's Cabin.

1884 A BOOKS - NONE

1884 B SHORTER WRITINGS

1　COOKE, ROSE TERRY. "Harriet Beecher Stowe," Our Famous Women.
Edited by E. S. P. Ward. Hartford: A. D. Worthington &
Co., pp. 581-601.
　　Biographical essay on Harriet Beecher Stowe. The empha-
sis of the chapter is on Uncle Tom's Cabin, but each of
the major works is discussed.

1884

2   DERBY, J. C. "Harriet Beecher Stowe," <u>Fifty Years Among
       Authors, Books, and Publishers</u>. New York: G. W. Carleton,
       pp. 452-460.
          Memoir of Harriet Beecher Stowe, including conversations
       with and about her. Claims that the characters in her
       fiction were suggested by people in her own household.

1885 A BOOKS - NONE

1885 B SHORTER WRITINGS

1   ANON. "Harriet Beecher Stowe," <u>Book News</u>, III (August),
       pp. 288-89.
          Biographical sketch and list of published books.

*2   ANON. "Uncle Tom's Cabin," <u>Cottage Hearth</u>, XI (November),
       p. 360.
          Cited in Eichelberger, 1971.B5.

3   ANON. "Uncle Tom's Cabin," <u>Critic</u>, VII, n.s. iv (October 3),
       p. 160.
          An appreciation of the new edition of <u>Uncle Tom's Cabin</u>,
       recommending that the book be re-read.

4   ANON. "Uncle Tom's Cabin: Is it a Novel?" <u>Andover Review</u>, IV
       (October), pp. 363-67.
          An attempt to assess the book as a work of art: although
       "modern" literary critics may reject it as a mere politi-
       cal pamphlet, <u>Uncle Tom's Cabin</u> has artistic merits which
       co-exist happily with its moral and ethical purpose.

*5   HAYNE, PAUL H. Poem to Harriet Beecher Stowe in the Papers of
       Paul Hamilton Hayne, unpublished, Duke University Library,
       p. 284.
          Letter to a friend, February 4, 1885, ridiculing the
       Harriet Beecher Stowe birthday celebrations with a poem
       attacking her. Cited in Browne, 1941.B4.

1886 A BOOKS - NONE

1886 B SHORTER WRITINGS

1   RICHARDSON, CHARLES. <u>American Literature</u>. New York: G. P.
       Putnam's Sons, pp. 410-12.
          Harriet Beecher Stowe would have a respectable place in
       literary history even without <u>Uncle Tom's Cabin</u>. That

novel is far from faultless, but in it she "strongly
seizes a significant theme, treats it with immediate
originality and inevitable effect."

2   TWICHELL, JOSEPH H.   "Mrs. Harriet Beecher Stowe in Hartford,"
     Critic, IX (December 18), pp. 301-02.
          A description of Harriet Beecher Stowe in her old age,
     of her daily life and her Hartford home.

1887 A BOOKS - NONE

1887 B SHORTER WRITINGS

1   ALLEN, JAMES L.   "Mrs. Stowe's 'Uncle Tom' at Home in Ken-
     tucky," Century, XXXIV (October), pp. 852-67.
          A description of pre-war conditions in Kentucky, with
     some reference to situations depicted in Uncle Tom's
     Cabin.

2   BEERS, HENRY A.   An Outline Sketch of American Literature.
     New York: Chautauqua Press, pp. 229-30.
          Uncle Tom's Cabin is a great book, the New England novels
     have a mild interest for the reader, but the other Harriet
     Beecher Stowe novels are "beneath criticism."

1888 A BOOKS

1   FAIRFIELD, ABBIE H.   Flowers and Fruit from the Writings of
     Harriet Beecher Stowe.   Boston: Houghton, Mifflin and
     Company.
          Brief excerpts from the writings of Harriet Beecher
     Stowe, classified by subject.   No criticism or secondary
     material.

1888 B SHORTER WRITINGS

1   ANON.   "Harriet Beecher Stowe," Ladies Home Journal, V (Novem-
     ber), p. 2.
          Biographical sketch, with emphasis on the writing of
     Uncle Tom's Cabin.   Jewett's comments (1883.B2) included.

2   BEECHER, WILLIAM E. and Reverend SAMUEL SCOVILLE.   A Biography
     of Henry Ward Beecher.   New York: L. Webster and Company.
          Quotations from the works and letters of Harriet Beecher
     Stowe, but little directly about her.   Attempts to explain
     the Parker incident of 1852 (pp. 259-60).

1888

3 DICKINSON, GIDEON. <u>The Wanderer, or, Life's Pilgrimage</u>.
Boston: H. H. Clark & Co., pp. iii-xxvi.
The lengthy introduction to this poem is entirely given
over to an attack on Harriet Beecher Stowe's Byron book
and vilification of the character of Henry Ward Beecher.

4 WILLARD, FRANCES E. "Harriet Beecher Stowe at Home," <u>Chautau-</u>
<u>quan</u>, VIII (February), pp. 287-88.
Description of a Hartford meeting between Willard and
the elderly Harriet Beecher Stowe.

1889 A BOOKS

1 McCRAY, FLORINE THAYER. <u>The Life-Work of the Author of Uncle</u>
<u>Tom's Cabin</u>. New York: Funk & Wagnalls.
Not in intent a biography, but a description of the works
of Harriet Beecher Stowe with "running commentary," including the main facts of the novelist's life. Written
with cooperation of the family, but approval was later
withdrawn by Harriet Beecher Stowe. Criticism of the
novels is broad and emotional; the author rejects aesthetic
and technical standards: "<u>Uncle Tom's Cabin</u> is full of
thought which is deeper than speech. It glows with feeling
which is deeper than thought." Contains some information
not in the C. E. Stowe biography (1889.A2).

2 STOWE, CHARLES EDWARD. <u>The Life of Harriet Beecher Stowe</u>.
Boston & New York: Houghton, Mifflin and Company.
The authorized biography, written by the author's
youngest child during his mother's lifetime with her
approval and supervision. Includes illustration and many
letters--some apparently edited or abridged without com-
ment--to and from Mrs. Stowe. Presents the image of herself Harriet Beecher Stowe wished to preserve and was
described by some contemporaries as an autobiography.
Primary source for many later biographers.

1889 B SHORTER WRITINGS

1 ANON. "Harriet Beecher Stowe," <u>Literature</u>, II (February 16),
pp. 288-301.
Reprint of an article from <u>Literary News</u>, along with
"The Story of Uncle Tom's Cabin," critical comment on the
later novels (Harriet Beecher Stowe excels in the description of character and scenery) and excerpts from her works.

2   ANON. "The Life of Harriet Beecher Stowe," <u>Nation</u>, XLIX
          (November 7), p. 377.
              Review of Stowe biography, generally negative. The
          treatment of the subject is poor and the book contains
          many mistakes.

3   BEADLE, J. H. "Harriet Beecher Stowe," <u>Literature</u>, II
          (February 16), pp. 287-88.
              Biographical sketch of Harriet Beecher Stowe, noting the
          genius of her first novel but also pointing out the
          "errors" in it.

4   McCRAY, FLORINE THAYER. "Mrs. Stowe's Biographers," <u>Critic</u>,
          XVI (November 16), p. 244.
              Author wishes to absolve herself from responsibility for
          the simultaneous publication of her biography and that of
          C. E. Stowe.

5   MILLER, OLIVE THORNE. "The Life of Harriet Beecher Stowe,"
          <u>Epoch</u>, VI (December 27), p. 760.
              This biography (Stowe) is one of the most fascinating
          books of the season.

*6   MUNROE, KIRK. "Harriet Beecher Stowe," <u>Lives and Deeds of Our
          Self-Made Men</u> by Harriet Beecher Stowe.
              Cited in Wilson, 1941.A1, p. 656.

7   SMYTH, ALBERT H. <u>American Literature</u>. Philadelphia: Eldredge
          & Brothers.
              Brief biographical sketch of Harriet Beecher Stowe. Her
          work is divided into three categories: slavery books, New
          England books (superior to the former in style) and practi-
          cal or household works.

8   TWICHELL, JOSEPH H. "Harriet Beecher Stowe," <u>Authors at Home</u>.
          Edited by J. L. and J. B. Gilder. New York: Cassell &
          Company, Ltd., pp. 315-322.
              Reprinted from <u>Critic</u>, IX, December 18, 1886. (1886.B2)

1890 A BOOKS - NONE

1890 B SHORTER WRITINGS

*1   ALLEN, ELEANOR P. "Harriet Beecher Stowe," <u>Lippincott's
          Magazine</u>, XLVI, pp. 261-72.
              Unlocatable. Cited in Adams, 1963.A1, p. 256.

1890

2 ANDERSON, EDWARD PLAYFAIR. "Harriet Beecher Stowe," <u>Dial</u>, X
        (April), p. 336.
            Review of the Stowe <u>Life</u>. Biographical sketch. The
        Stowe book is adequate, but there is critical and bio-
        graphical work still to be done. The New England stories
        are the chief literary achievements of Harriet Beecher
        Stowe.

3 ANON. "The Author of Uncle Tom's Cabin," <u>Leisure Hour</u>, XXXIX
        (March), p. 307.
            Review of Stowe <u>Life</u>, and biographical sketch. This an
        "autobiography," one "rich in interesting details."

4 ANON. "Harriet Beecher Stowe," <u>London Quarterly Review</u>, LXXIV
        (April), pp. 28-42.
            Review of Stowe biography. Finds biographical sources
        for fictional characters and themes, and summarizes the
        main events of Harriet Beecher Stowe's life.

5 ANON. "Harriet Beecher Stowe," <u>Saturday Review</u>, LXIX
        (March 15), p. 324.
            Biographical sketch of Harriet Beecher Stowe and review
        of Stowe <u>Life</u>.

6 ANON. "The Life of Harriet Beecher Stowe," <u>Athenaeum</u>, XCV
        (January 11), pp. 41-42.
            Review of Stowe <u>Life</u>. An interesting and instructive
        book, "in all but form an autobiography." Reviewer com-
        ments on the naiveté of Harriet Beecher Stowe and quotes
        several of her letters.

7 ANON. "The Life of Harriet Beecher Stowe," <u>Blackwood's
        Edinburgh Magazine</u>, CXLVII (March), pp. 408-412.
            Review of Stowe <u>Life</u>. This biography is not very inter-
        esting. Reviewer assesses Harriet Beecher Stowe's talent
        and her "ingenuous" personality.

8 ANON. "The Life of Harriet Beecher Stowe," <u>Spectator</u>, LXIV
        (February 22), pp. 266-68.
            Review of Stowe <u>Life</u>. Biographical sketch of Harriet
        Beecher Stowe who appears to be a "healthy-minded, genial
        woman."

*9 ANON. "Mrs. Stowe's Decline." Unidentified clipping. <u>Random
        Papers</u>, XXXVII. Litchfield Historical Society, p. 137.
            Cited in Wilson, 1941.A1, p. 657.

10 CHADWICK, J. W. "The Life of Harriet Beecher Stowe," Nation,
     L (January 9), p. 34.
         Review of Stowe Life. This biography is not the defini-
     tive book on Harriet Beecher Stowe since it lacks critical
     evaluation. Summary of life, pointing out that Harriet
     Beecher Stowe had been neither intellectually nor morally
     prepared for her anti-slavery writings, but that the suc-
     cess of Uncle Tom's Cabin liberated her talents.

11 LEWIN, WALTER. "The Life of Harriet Beecher Stowe," Academy,
     XXXVII (March 8), pp. 162-63.
         Review of Stowe Life. Biographical summary, noting that
     Harriet Beecher Stowe was an "emotional rather than an
     inspired woman," erring in judgment but cheerful, pious,
     and brave.

12 LOWELL, JAMES RUSSELL. "Advice to Mrs. Stowe (From an old
     Letter)," Critic, XVII (July 5), p. 11.
         Quotation from an undated letter from Lowell to Harriet
     Beecher Stowe, advising her to follow nature and her
     instincts in writing.

13 McCRAY, FLORINE THAYER. "Uncle Tom's Cabin and Mrs. Stowe;
     Extracts from the Life Work of the Author of Uncle Tom's
     Cabin," Magazine of American History, XXIII (January),
     pp. 16-22.
         Extracts from McCray's book, with many descriptions of
     Harriet Beecher Stowe's Hartford days and quotations from
     her letters.

14 SYMINGTON, A. MacLEOD. "Harriet Beecher Stowe," Sunday Maga-
     zine, XIX, p. 614.
         Review of Stowe Life. Biographical sketch and general
     comment.

15 TEETOR, H. D. "The Origin of Uncle Tom's Cabin: Reminiscences
     of Harriet Beecher Stowe in Cincinnati," Magazine of
     Western History, XII (May), p. 24.
         Discusses the Ohio sources of characters and incidents
     in Uncle Tom's Cabin.

16 TUCKERMAN, C. K. "Sir John Bowring and American Slavery,"
     Magazine of American History, XXIII (March), pp. 232-36.
         Recounts the reaction of a famous English radical to
     Uncle Tom's Cabin.

1891 A BOOKS - NONE

1891

1891 B SHORTER WRITINGS

1 MATTHEWS, BRANDER. "Uncle Tom's Cabin," Cosmopolitan, XII
        (March), pp. 637-38.
            Praises the story and admires the pictures of the new
        edition.

2 REPPLIER, AGNES. Points of View. Boston & New York: Houghton,
        Mifflin & Company, pp. 75-77.
            Suggests that Uncle Tom's Cabin made slavery seem to
        her an attractive institution, one that bred heroic and
        virtuous individuals.

3 THAYER, WILLIAM. Success and its Achievers Illustrated.
        Boston: A. M. Thayer & Co., p. 509.
            Anecdotes about the Beecher family used to illustrate
        the value of conversation in the home.

*4 THOMPSON, MAURICE. "Harriet Beecher Stowe," Independent
        (July).
            Cited in Wilson, 1941.A1, p. 656.

1892 A BOOKS

1 CORLEY, DANIEL B. A Visit to Uncle Tom's Cabin. Chicago:
        Laird & Lee.
            Description of a visit to Natchitoches Parish, Louisiana,
        supposed site of Legree plantation and cabin of Uncle Tom.
        Subsequent removal of cabin for reconstruction at Chicago
        World's Fair described. Letters and documents included
        attesting to the local belief that Robert McAlpen, one-
        time owner of the plantation, was the model for Legree.

1892 B SHORTER WRITINGS

1 ANON. "Uncle Tom's Cabin," Spectator, LXVIII (March 26),
        pp. 434-36.
            Comments on the new edition of the novel, on its in-
        fluence in the 1850's, and the English reception of it.
        Notes the characteristic comments from Macauley, Dickens,
        et al. quoted in the reprinted "Introduction."

2 HAWTHORNE, JULIAN and LEONARD LEMMON. American Literature:
        A Textbook for the Use of Schools and Colleges. Boston:
        D. C. Heath & Co., pp. 87-88.
            From a literary point of view, the merit of Uncle Tom's

Cabin is not great; even the best of Harriet Beecher
Stowe's novels can hardly be regarded as sound literature.

1893 A BOOKS - NONE

1893 B SHORTER WRITINGS

1   BURNETT, FRANCES HODGSON. The One I Knew Best of All. New
     York: Charles Scribner's Sons, pp. 237-38.
        Author describes her romantic childhood impressions of
     the Civil War, as filtered through Uncle Tom's Cabin.

2   JOHNSTON, Reverend B. "Lives Worth Living," Youth, XVII
     (May), pp. 71-72.
        Brief biographical sketch of Harriet Beecher Stowe,
     emphasizing the womanly attainment of virtue she repre-
     sents. Information taken from the C. E. Stowe biography
     (1889.A2).

3   RHODES, J. F. History of the United States from the Compromise
     of 1850, I. New York: Harper & Brothers, pp. 363-65.
        Mrs. Stowe used her facts, essentially accurate ones,
     with "the intuition of genius," her most conspicuous
     failure being in the portrayal of the upper classes.

4   SHOUP, F. A. "'Uncle Tom's Cabin' Forty Years After,"
     Sewanee Review, II (November), pp. 88-104.
        Article on Uncle Tom's Cabin by a Southerner, who defends
     Harriet Beecher Stowe and claims that she was fair, but
     feels Tom's virtues were the result of slavery. Harriet
     Beecher Stowe represented her own emotions in Tom, not
     those of a slave. Comments on the unhappy results of
     emancipation.

5   VIZETELLY, HENRY. Glances Back Through Seventy Years. London:
     K. Paul, Trench, Trübner & Co. Ltd.
        Reprinted material from a letter to the Literary World*,
     correcting misapprehensions about the first English edition
     of Uncle Tom's Cabin. Vizetelly earned only about $500
     from the proceedings. He notes the subsequent economic
     failure of A Key to Uncle Tom's Cabin. [*Unlocated.]

1894 A BOOKS - NONE

1894

1894 B SHORTER WRITINGS

1   GARRISON, W. P. and F. J. William Lloyd Garrison: The Story
        of his Life Told by his Children, III. Boston and New
        York: Houghton, Mifflin and Company, pp. 360-64.
            Discusses the reactions of Garrison and Wendell
        Phillips to Uncle Tom's Cabin and quotes at length from
        Garrison's review (1852.B43). A series of letters from
        Harriet Beecher Stowe objecting to the Liberator's stand
        on religion are included (pp. 395-401).

2   NORTON, C. E., ed. The Letters of James Russell Lowell, II.
        Cambridge: The Riverside Press.
            Letter to E. L. Godkin, saying that the article in the
        Quarterly Review (1869.B35) settles the Byron matter and
        declines further comment on it.

1895 A BOOKS - NONE

1895 B SHORTER WRITINGS

*1   ANON. _____, The Andover Magazine, I.
        Cited in Wilson, 1941.A1, p. 649.

2   KIMBALL, A. R. "Hartford's Literary Corner," Outlook, LI
        (June), pp. 903-06.
            Describes the Nook Farm area and comments on Harriet
        Beecher Stowe's current state of health.

3   McDOWELL, G. S. "Harriet Beecher Stowe at Cincinnati and
        Sources for Characters in Uncle Tom's Cabin," New England
        Magazine, n.s. XII (March), pp. 65-70.
            Description of Harriet Beecher Stowe's Cincinnati years,
        including sketch of her house and notes on sources of
        characters and incidents in Uncle Tom's Cabin.

1896 A BOOKS

1   HOOKER, ISABELLA BEECHER. A Brief Sketch of the Life of
        Harriet Beecher Stowe, by her Sister. Hartford: Privately
        printed.
            A cursory summary of the life of Harriet Beecher Stowe,
        containing no new information.

1896 B SHORTER WRITINGS

1   ANON. "Harriet Beecher Stowe," Athenaeum, CVIII (July 4),
     p. 36.
          Obituary note. Praises the New England novels and views
     the Byron incident as "the solitary mistake in a good
     woman's life."

2   ANON. "Harriet Beecher Stowe," Critic, XXIX (July 11),
     pp. 27-29.
          Standard obituary. Quotes Holmes's birthday poem
     (1882.B4) and earlier Critic article (1882.B1).

3   ANON. "Harriet Beecher Stowe," Outlook, LIV (July 11),
     pp. 49-50.
          Obituary essay, with description of Harriet Beecher
     Stowe, biographical sketch, and comments about her from
     writers of her generation.

4   ANON. "Harriet Beecher Stowe," Spectator, LXXVII (July 4),
     p. 3.
          Obituary notice. Harriet Beecher Stowe was "the most
     effective female philanthropist who ever lived," an
     amazing fact since she was "neither a great woman nor a
     great artist" and her books subsequent to Uncle Tom's
     Cabin are "scarcely third rate."

5   ANON. "Harriet Beecher Stowe," Peterson's Magazine, n.s. VI
     (July), p. 824.
          Standard obituary notice and comment.

6   ANON. "An Interview with Harriet Beecher Stowe," Outlook, LIV
     (August 22), p. 347.
          Letter recalling an interview with Harriet Beecher Stowe,
     who had refused to write a temperance novel because she
     felt there could be no "bright side" to such a story.

7   ANON. "The Late Mrs. Beecher Stowe," Illustrated London News,
     CIX, no. 2986 (July 11), pp. 46-47.
          Standard obituary notice and biographical sketch, with
     photographs of the Hartford house and other illustrations.

8   ANON. "The Late Mrs. Beecher Stowe," Sketch (July 8), p. 424.
          Standard obituary tribute.

9   ANON. "A Short Biography of the Author of 'Uncle Tom's
     Cabin,'" The Peterson Magazine, n.s. VI (August), p. 824.
          Brief biographical sketch.

1896

10   ANON. "The Writings of Harriet Beecher Stowe," New York Times
     Saturday Supplement (November 14), p. 4.
          A short comment on the Riverside edition, calling Uncle
     Tom's Cabin a book of "historical rank."

11   ANTHONY, S. B. "Mrs. Stowe," Outlook, LIV (August 1), p. 213.
          Comment from feminist Anthony, quoting House and Home
     Papers (1865) on women and suffrage and claiming that
     Harriet Beecher Stowe was in accord with her sister Isa-
     bella on the issues.

12   BURTON, RICHARD. "The Author of Uncle Tom's Cabin," Century,
     LII n.s. XXX (September), pp. 698-704.
          Standard biographical sketch of Harriet Beecher Stowe,
     which mentions rumors that Lewis Clark of Lexington was
     the model for George Harris. Notes the importance of the
     later works in the history of American fiction.

13   _____. "Mrs. Stowe at Eighty-Five," Ladies Home Journal, XIII
     (June), pp. 3-4.
          Description of Harriet Beecher Stowe's home and person,
     with photographs taken for the article and some biographi-
     cal information.

14   NO ENTRY.

15   COOKE, GEORGE WILLIS. "Harriet Beecher Stowe," New England
     Magazine, n.s. XV (September), pp. 3-18.
          Review of the life and work of Harriet Beecher Stowe.
     Finds merit in Uncle Tom's Cabin and the New England
     novels. Author gave too little attention to aesthetics
     but was nonetheless effective. Compares Uncle Tom's Cabin
     to work of Turgenev, and discusses Harriet Beecher Stowe
     as a "womanly" novelist who emphasized feeling, domesticity,
     etc. in her works.

16   DIDIER, EUGENE L. "Harriet Beecher Stowe," Chautauquan, XXIII
     (July), pp. 389-91.
          Biographical sketch.

17   FIELDS, ANNIE. "Days with Mrs. Stowe," Atlantic Monthly,
     LXXVIII (August), pp. 145-156.
          Biographical sketch, description of Harriet Beecher
     Stowe's person, and memoir of the author's long friendship
     with her. Points out that Harriet Beecher Stowe was not a
     "student of literature." Describes her friendship with
     George Eliot, her relationship with Henry Ward Beecher,
     and her life in Hartford. Reprinted in Fields, Authors

and Friends. Boston & New York: Houghton, Mifflin &
Company, pp. 157-226; and in Bookman, III (August),
pp. 487-90.

18 HIGGINSON, T. W. "Harriet Beecher Stowe," Nation, LXIII
(July 9), pp. 24-26.
Obituary notice, summarizing the life of Harriet Beecher
Stowe and evaluating her work. Uncle Tom's Cabin is not
likely to be judged a great or lasting work, but it
appeared at a favorable time. The later books are weaker,
often thin. The Byron incident remains inexplicable.

19 HOWARD, JOHN R. "Harriet Beecher Stowe, a Sketch; with
personal recollections by E. E. Hale, J. W. Howe, and
others," Outlook, LIV (July 25), pp. 138-43.
Biographical sketch by a family friend, including
various tributes.

20 MORSE, JAMES HERBERT. "Harriet Beecher Stowe," Critic, XXIX
n.s. XXVI (July 4), pp. 1-2.
Biographical sketch of Harriet Beecher Stowe. Uncle
Tom's Cabin shows her "best art." Quotes Longfellow's
journal on the effect of the book.

21 _____, ed. The Life and Letters of Oliver Wendell Holmes,
I, II. Boston: Houghton, Mifflin, and Company, pp. i,
179; ii, 183-4, 209, 228.
Various letters to Motley and Harriet Beecher Stowe,
commenting on the Byron scandal and the unexpected excitement it had generated. Connects it with the Beecher-
Tilton scandal in 1874.

22 PHELPS, ELIZABETH S. (WARD). "Reminiscences of Harriet
Beecher Stowe," McClure's Magazine, VII (June), p. 3.
A memoir recounting Harriet Beecher Stowe's days in
Andover (a place too thoroughly masculine to appreciate
her), life in her Florida home, and the Birthday dinner
of 1882.

23 WALLIS, S. T. "The Life of P. T. Barnum and Sunny Memories of
Foreign Lands by Harriet Beecher Stowe," Writings, II.
.Baltimore: J. Murphy & Company, pp. 69-84.
These two volumes are revelations of their era. The
Harriet Beecher Stowe work is an unconscious portrait of
the author as humbug. Sunny Memories represents "mediocrity beyond redemption" and Uncle Tom's Cabin would have
made no mark had its heroes been white. "Transgressors
like Mrs. Stowe are harmless only when laughed at."

1896

24   WARD, JULIUS H.   "Harriet Beecher Stowe," Forum, XXI (August),
         pp. 727-34.
            Biographical sketch with critical comments. Uncle Tom's
         Cabin was written, like most great books, "under the
         dominant sense of a higher power." Later works are ad-
         mired, and Harriet Beecher Stowe compared to George Eliot.

25   WARNER, CHARLES D.   "Introduction," The Writings of Harriet
         Beecher Stowe, I. Cambridge: The Riverside Press.
            Biographical sketch describes the background of Harriet
         Beecher Stowe's life, her constant religious concern, and
         her later years.

26   _____. "The Story of Uncle Tom's Cabin," Atlantic Monthly,
         LXXVIII (September), pp. 311-21.
            Analysis of the success of Uncle Tom's Cabin, praising
         its construction, character drawing, pathos, ahd humor,
         and attempting to place it in its historical context.
         Reprinted in The Writings of Harriet Beecher Stowe, I.
         Cambridge: The Riverside Press.

27   WATERLOO, STANLEY.   "Harriet Beecher Stowe," Famous American
         Men and Women. Chicago: Wabash Publishing House, p. 38.
            Brief biographical sketch with photograph of Harriet
         Beecher Stowe in old age.

28   WRIGHT, HENRIETTA.   "Harriet Beecher Stowe," Children's Stories
         in American Literature. New York: Charles Scribner's Sons,
         pp. 188-202.
            A biography of Harriet Beecher Stowe for children.

1897 A BOOKS

1   FIELDS, ANNIE.   The Life and Letters of Harriet Beecher Stowe.
         Boston and New York: Houghton, Mifflin & Company.
            Full length biography, including personal memories of
         the author, etc. Most of the early material is taken from
         Harriet Beecher Stowe's memoirs of her childhood years and
         letters of the period, many printed here for the first
         time. Reviews of Uncle Tom's Cabin are included.

1897 B SHORTER WRITINGS

1   ANON. "The Life and Letters of Harriet Beecher Stowe,"
         Academy, LIII (February), pp. 169-70.

Review of Fields biography, and comment on the life of
Harriet Beecher Stowe: her effectiveness was due in part
to her lack of profundity.

2 ANON. "The Life and Letters of Harriet Beecher Stowe,"
   London Quarterly, XC (July), pp. 326-35.
      A compact "redaction" of the Fields book. The reviewer
   evaluates the work of Harriet Beecher Stowe, comments on
   her sympathetic nature, and compares her method of writing
   Uncle Tom's Cabin with the practice of Charlotte Brönte:
   both women were "possessed" by an overpowering imaginative force.

3 ANON. "The Life and Letters of Harriet Beecher Stowe," New
   York Times Saturday Supplement (November 27), pp. 2-3.
      Review of Fields biography. Sketch of the life of
   Harriet Beecher Stowe, with quotations from the letters
   included in the book.

4 FOLEY, P. K. American Authors, 1795-1895. A Bibliography of
   First and Notable Editions Chronologically Arranged with
   Notes. Boston: The Publishers Printing Company, pp. 278-81.
      A list of the published works of Harriet Beecher Stowe.

5 LEE, GERALD S. "The Writings of Harriet Beecher Stowe," Critic,
   XXX n.s. XXVII (April 24), pp. 281-83.
      Review of the Writings. One can criticise Uncle Tom's
   Cabin only from a journalistic point of view. Its story
   was the great theme of her life, and its virtues became the
   faults of her other tales. Speculates about the Beecher
   family and the effect of publicity upon Harriet Beecher
   Stowe.

6 MERRIAM, GEORGE S. Introduction to excerpts from Uncle Tom's
   Cabin and The Minister's Wooing. Warner's Library of the
   World's Best Literature, XXXV. New York: The International
   Society, pp. 14067-14073.
      Biographical sketch. Uncle Tom's Cabin is a "deeply
   religious book" in close accord with the great philanthropic
   movements of its age. The Minister's Wooing marks the peak
   of Harriet Beecher Stowe's writing. Her work lacks finish,
   but she has a "free, strong touch, not unlike Walter
   Scott's."

7 PHELPS, ELIZABETH S. (WARD). "Harriet Beecher Stowe," Chapters from a Life. Boston & New York: Houghton, Mifflin &
   Company, pp. 131-40.
      Reprinted from McClure's Magazine, VII (June), 1896.
   (1896.B22)

1898

<u>1898 A BOOKS – NONE</u>

<u>1898 B SHORTER WRITINGS</u>

1   ANDERSON, JOHN PARKER. Description of Harriet Beecher Stowe
        exhibit in Kate Brannon Knight, <u>History of the Work of</u>
        <u>Connecticut Women at the World's Columbian Exposition,</u>
        <u>Chicago 1893</u>. Hartford: Case, Longwood, & Brainard Co.,
        pp. 107–23.
            List of objects in Stowe exhibit (busts, etc.); includes
        also abstracts of letters and Bullen bibliography (revised)
        from the 1878 edition of <u>Uncle Tom's Cabin</u>.

2   DUNBAR, PAUL L. "Harriet Beecher Stowe," <u>Century Magazine</u>,
        LVII (November), p. 61.
            A short poem in honor of Harriet Beecher Stowe.

3   GRISWOLD, HATTIE T. "Harriet Beecher Stowe," <u>Personal Sketches</u>
        <u>of Recent Authors</u>. Chicago: A. C. McClurg, pp. 168–90.
            Biographical essay with some reprinted letters and
        general comments on the Beecher family.

4   GUERRY, WILLIAM A. "Harriet Beecher Stowe," <u>Sewanee Review</u>,
        VI, pp. 335–344.
            A sympathetic biographical sketch, pointing out the im-
        portance of the author's background and character in the
        writing of <u>Uncle Tom's Cabin</u>, but noting that her sources
        were often questionable.

5   HIGGINSON, THOMAS W. "Introduction," <u>Uncle Tom's Cabin</u>. New
        York: D. Appleton & Company, pp. iii–xiv.
            An informative and critical introduction written for a
        generation with little first-hand knowledge of slavery.
        Values <u>Uncle Tom's Cabin</u> above the later works, although
        of the New England novels he comments that "if there was
        tediousness, it may have been partly in the theme."

6   WEEKS, STEPHEN B. <u>Anti-Slavery Sentiment in the South</u>.
        Washington, D. C.: Southern History Association, pp. 87–
        130.
            Article on emancipation societies and individuals holding
        strong anti-slavery views in the South, primarily before
        1832. Little specifically about Harriet Beecher Stowe but
        includes a letter from her to Rev. Daniel Goodloe of North
        Carolina.

7   WOLFE, THEODORE F. <u>Literary Haunts and Homes</u>. Philadelphia:
        J. B. Lippincott Company, pp. 200–03.

A description of the two Hartford homes of Harriet Beecher Stowe.

1900 A BOOKS - NONE

1900 B SHORTER WRITINGS

1   WENDELL, BARRETT. A Literary History of America. New York:
     Charles Scribner's Sons. (Reprinted by Greenwood Press,
     1968), pp. 352-56.
          Brief biographical sketch. Uncle Tom's Cabin is care-
     lessly written but a "remarkable piece of fiction" with
     characters that have "a pervasive vitality." Harriet
     Beecher Stowe's best book is Oldtown Folks.

1901 A BOOKS - NONE

1901 B SHORTER WRITINGS

1   DODGE, H. AUGUSTA, ed. Gail Hamilton's Life in Letters.
     Boston: Lee & Shepard, pp. 594, 782-83.
          Incidental mention of Harriet Beecher Stowe with some
     descriptive material.

2   HOWELLS, WILLIAM DEAN. Literary Friends and Acquaintances.
     New York: Harper & Brothers Publishers, pp. 118, 138-39.
          Comment on Uncle Tom's Cabin: a work appealing primarily
     to the ethical, not the artistic, sense. Description of
     editorial problems in Harriet Beecher Stowe's written
     texts (errors of syntax, diction, spelling, etc.) and of
     Howells's meeting with the author. Describes an overheard
     conversation between Harriet Beecher Stowe and Holmes.

3   NEWCOMER, ALPHONSO G. American Literature. Chicago: Scott,
     Foresman and Company.
          Uncle Tom's Cabin is a romance rather than a novel, and
     is now "more a historical document than a living force."

1902 A BOOKS - NONE

1902 B SHORTER WRITINGS

*1   ROGERS, J. M. "Uncle Tom's Cabin in Kentucky." Era, X (Sep-
     tember), pp. 262-68.
          Cited in Leary, 1954.B3.

1903

1903 A BOOKS - NONE

1903 B SHORTER WRITINGS

    1   GEISSINGER, J. A. "Where Eliza, of Uncle Tom's Cabin Fame,
           Took her Flight," Ladies Home Journal, XX (September),
           p. 7.
             Description of Ripley, Ohio and the Parker family, sup-
           posed sources for the story of Eliza crossing the ice.

    2   MAURICE, A. B. "Famous Novels and Their Contemporary Critics,"
           Bookman, XVI (March), pp. 23-30.
             Quotes at length from a large number of early reviews
           of Uncle Tom's Cabin, representing widely varying points
           of view.

    3   WEED, GEORGE L. "The True Story of Eliza," Independent, LV
           (September 17), pp. 224-26.
             Tells the story of Eliza as it had been told to him by
           a school friend.

1905 A BOOKS - NONE

1905 B SHORTER WRITINGS

    1   BEACH, SETH C. "Harriet Beecher Stowe," Daughters of the
           Puritans. Boston: American Unitarian Association,
           pp. 209-47.
             Biographical essay, emphasizing the role of New England
           theology and of the Beecher family habits and traditions
           in the life and writings of Harriet Beecher Stowe.

    2   HOOKER, ISABELLA BEECHER. "The Last of the Beechers: Memories
           on my Eighty-third Birthday," Connecticut Magazine, IX,
           pp. 286-98.
             Memoir of Isabella Hooker's life, with some references
           to sister Harriet.

    3   HOWE, JULIA WARD. "Harriet Beecher Stowe," Reader, V (March),
           pp. 613-17.
             Biographical sketch with personal reminiscences and
           comment by Howe that she was not much struck by Uncle
           Tom's Cabin in its serial form, having noted its many
           faults of style.

1907 A BOOKS - NONE

1907 B SHORTER WRITINGS

1   MacTAVISH, NEWTON. "The Original Uncle Tom," Canadian Magazine,
        XXX, pp. 25-29.
        Biographical sketch of Josiah Henson.

1910 A BOOKS

1   MacLEAN, GRACE EDITH. Uncle Tom's Cabin in Germany. New York:
        D. Appleton.
        Discusses the widespread influence of Uncle Tom's Cabin
        and other works by Harriet Beecher Stowe in nineteenth-
        century Germany, with lists of translations, reviews, stage
        versions, literary works inspired by the novel, etc. In-
        cludes a biographical sketch of Harriet Beecher Stowe and
        an essay on the importance of Uncle Tom's Cabin in the in-
        ternational anti-slavery movement. Dissertation: Univer-
        sity of Heidelberg, 1910.

1910 B SHORTER WRITINGS

1   ANON. "Introduction," Uncle Tom's Cabin. Chicago: M. A.
        Donohue & Company, pp. 1-50. (Dated 191-).
        The story of Henry Ward Beecher's slave auctions; un-
        signed biographical sketch of Harriet Beecher Stowe; a
        history of Uncle Tom's Cabin, with the Fugitive Slave law
        seen as the immediate inspiration; and a key to the
        characters of the novel (with reference to A Key to Uncle
        Tom's Cabin).

2   ERSKINE, JOHN. "Harriet Beecher Stowe," Leading American
        Novelists. New York: H. Holt & Company, pp. 274-323.
        (Reprinted Freeport, N. Y.: Books for Libraries Press,
        1966, 1968.)
        A critique of the major novels and a biographical sketch.
        Erskine sees Harriet Beecher Stowe's talent as a combina-
        tion of realism and idealism, the latter an inheritance
        from Puritan theology. He notes the accuracy of her por-
        traits of Negro character, but questions her assumption
        that slavery had caused the "shortcomings" of the race.

3   MacLEAN, GRACE EDITH. "Uncle Tom's Cabin in Germany." Ph.D.
        Dissertation, University of Heidelberg. (See 1910.A1)

1911

<u>1911 A BOOKS</u>

1   STOWE, CHARLES EDWARD and LYMAN BEECHER STOWE. <u>Harriet Beecher</u>
    <u>Stowe: The Story of Her Life</u>. Boston and New York:
    Houghton, Mifflin & Company.
        A memorial biography by the son and grandson of Harriet
    Beecher Stowe which aims to tell of the novelist "not so
    much what she did as what she was, and how she became what
    she was." Includes some material from the Fields <u>Life and</u>
    <u>Letters of Harriet Beecher Stowe</u> (1897.A1) but does not go
    beyond earlier biographies.

2   TERRELL, MARY CHURCH. <u>Harriet Beecher Stowe: An Appreciation</u>.
    Washington, D. C.: Murray Brothers Press. Pamphlet.
        Admiring comments about Harriet Beecher Stowe, with
    emphasis on the power and success of <u>Uncle Tom's Cabin</u>,
    and on the philanthropy of its author toward the "Colored-
    American."

<u>1911 B SHORTER WRITINGS</u>

1   ANON. "Building Uncle Tom's Cabin," <u>Bookman</u>, XXXIII (July),
    pp. 346-47.
        Review of the C. E. and L. B. Stowe biography. Summa-
    rizes passages from the book, noting that <u>Uncle Tom's</u>
    <u>Cabin</u> was to have been a work of "pacification," and
    listing the sources of Legree, Eliza, etc.

2   ANON. "Harriet Beecher Stowe: The Story of Her Life," <u>Bookman</u>
    (London), XLI (December), p. 6.
        Review of new biography. This is a leisurely book that
    suggests a novel.

3   ANON. "Harriet Beecher Stowe: The Story of Her Life," <u>Nation</u>,
    XCIII (August 17), p. 143.
        Review of Stowe biography, with quotations from this
    "charming and affectionate book," and some general com-
    ments on Harriet Beecher Stowe.

4   ANON. "Moving Novel Sixty Years After: Uncle Tom's Cabin,"
    <u>Outlook</u>, XCVIII (July), pp. 286-87.
        Biographical sketch with critical commentary. Harriet
    Beecher Stowe lived in an atmosphere where art had a sub-
    ordinate place, but created a novel which stirred the
    country. Like Turgenev's similar book, it is of greater
    significance in history than in literature.

5   ANON. "The Novel that Overruled the Supreme Court," Current
      Literature, LI (August), pp. 208-10.
         Inspired by the Stowe biography, this essay emphasizes
      the moderate nature of the views expressed in Uncle Tom's
      Cabin, and notes its importance in breaking down the tra-
      ditional prejudices against fiction and the theater.

6   ANON. "Uncle Tom's Cabin: The Most Influential Novel Ever
      Written," Nation, XCII (June), pp. 619-20.
         Remarks on the continuing influence and power of the
      novel. Despite its lack of art, it touched the emotions
      of a generation or more of readers.

7   CAIRNS, WILLIAM B. "'Uncle Tom's Cabin' and its Author,"
      Dial, L (June 16), pp. 465, 469-70.
         Notes the centennial celebration of Harriet Beecher
      Stowe's birth. Finds the new Stowe biography "unsympa-
      thetic" and suggests that an analysis of Harriet Beecher
      Stowe's character—her lack of social distinction, her
      emotional nature and its manifestations, etc.—is still to
      be made.

8   FIELDS, ANNIE, ed. The Letters of Sarah Orne Jewett. Boston
      and New York: Houghton, Mifflin & Company, pp. 46-47.
         Jewett writes that she was influenced by Stowe's New
      England novels. The Pearl of Orr's Island is "classical-
      historical," though "an incomplete piece of work."

9   HILLIS, N. D. "The Beecher Family," Munsey's Magazine, XLVI
      (November), pp. 191-201.
         The Beechers were to America what the Arnolds were to
      nineteenth-century England. Includes a brief biography of
      Harriet Beecher Stowe and a description of the writing and
      impact of Uncle Tom's Cabin.

10 JERROLD, WALTER. "The Author of 'Uncle Tom': Some Centenary
      Notes." Bookman (London), XL (September), pp. 241-45.
         An attempt to estimate the place of Harriet Beecher
      Stowe in the history of nineteenth-century letters. She
      was a writer who touched the imagination of her generation.

11 MACKAY, CONSTANCE D. "The Harriet Beecher Stowe Centenary,"
      New England Magazine, n.s. XLIV (June), pp. 345-60.
         Biographical sketch, with particular attention given to
      the Brunswick years.

12 SCUDDER, HORACE E. "Harriet Beecher Stowe," Encyclopaedia
      Britannica, 11th edition, XXV. Cambridge: Cambridge

1911

        University Press, pp. 972-73.
        Biographical sketch. Reprinted in later editions.

13   SANBORN, F. B. "Mrs. Stowe and Her Uncle Tom," <u>Bibliotheca</u>
      <u>Sacra</u>, LXVIII (October), pp. 674-83.
        An address given on the 100th anniversary of Harriet
      Beecher Stowe's birth, praising the moral force of <u>Uncle</u>
      <u>Tom's Cabin</u>.

14   STOWE, C. E. "Harriet Beecher Stowe: Friend of the South,"
      <u>Outlook</u>, XCVIII (June 10), pp. 300-03.
        Stowe reports that Harriet Beecher Stowe did not mean to
      arouse the South and was surprised at the effect of <u>Uncle</u>
      <u>Tom's Cabin</u>. She remained a friend of Southerners and
      after the war "raised her voice in protest against giving
      the ballot to former slaves."

15   _____. "How My Mother Wrote Uncle Tom's Cabin," <u>Ladies Home</u>
      <u>Journal</u>, XXVIII (June), p. 9.
        Biographical and background sketch, emphasizing the un-
      self-conscious personality of Harriet Beecher Stowe.

16   _____ and L. B. STOWE. "The Girlhood of Harriet Beecher
      Stowe," <u>McClure's Magazine</u>, XXXVII (May), pp. 28-40.
        An anecdotal history of Harriet Beecher Stowe's early
      years, describing, among other things, her escape from
      Calvinist theology.

17   _____ and L. B. STOWE. "How Mrs. Stowe Wrote Uncle Tom's
      Cabin," <u>McClure's Magazine</u>, XXXVI (April), pp. 604-21.
        Description of the sources of incidents and characters
      in <u>Uncle Tom's Cabin</u>, including many stories of the Stowe
      family life in the 1850's and after.

1912 A BOOKS - NONE

1912 B SHORTER WRITINGS

  1   ANON. "Most Harmful Book: Uncle Tom's Cabin," <u>Literary</u>
      <u>Digest</u>, XLV (December 28), pp. 1225-26.
        Comments on a speech by Hopkinson Smith which claimed
      that <u>Uncle Tom's Cabin</u> had done much harm, with remarks
      on the talk from the Boston <u>Journal</u> and the Philadelphia
      <u>Inquirer</u>.

  2   ERSKINE, JOHN and W. P. TRENT. "Harriet Beecher Stowe," <u>Great</u>
      <u>American Writers</u>. New York: Henry Holt and Company,
      pp. 197-211.

Harriet Beecher Stowe embodied the Puritan temper in her
energetic and practical scorn of evil. In <u>Uncle Tom's
Cabin</u>, she struck at the abuses resulting from the power of
sale, without being blind to the "pecularities of the negro
temperament." <u>Dred</u>, discussed here at length, is in many
respects a richer book. The New England stories served as
a model for later regional writing.

3   HILLIS, N. D. <u>The Battle of Principles</u>. New York: Fleming H.
Revell Co., pp. 136-48.
A comment on the widespread impact of <u>Uncle Tom's Cabin</u>.
In it, Harriet Beecher Stowe tried to prove that the slave
system distorted "the loftiest natures" and debased even
more the lesser men. It was a book perfectly adapted to
its end.

4   LIEBERMAN, ELIAS. <u>The American Short Story. A Study of
Locality in its Development</u>. Ridgewood, N. J.: The
Editor Company, pp. 32-35. (Reprinted by The Folcroft
Press, 1970.)
Brief treatment of Harriet Beecher Stowe as a writer of
the pre-modern era in New England. Includes excerpts from
the shorter works.

5   PAGE, JOHN T., S., W. B. and WILLOUGHBY MAYCOCK. "The
Original 'Uncle Tom,'" <u>Notes and Queries</u>, XI, s. vi,
pp. 367, 436, 393.
References to the death of Thomas Magruder, a supposed
source for the character of Tom; a note on Josiah Henson.

6   TRENT, WILLIAM P. <u>A History of American Literature, 1607-1865</u>.
New York & London: D. Appleton and Company, pp. 500-509.
Biographical sketch. Early life seen as preparation for
<u>Uncle Tom's Cabin</u>. Novel compared to Mrs. Aphra Behn's
<u>Oroonoko</u>. The later books are not great in any respect,
but some of them demand re-reading.

1913 A BOOKS

1   CROWE, MARTHA FOOTE. <u>Harriet Beecher Stowe: A Biography for
Girls</u>. New York and London: D. Appleton and Company.
Popular biography with chronology of the life of Harriet
Beecher Stowe and a list of published books. Describes
<u>Uncle Tom's Cabin</u> as flawed, but powerful. Does not deal
with later works.

1913

1913 B SHORTER WRITINGS

1   ABBOT, WILLIS J.   "The Little Woman Who Caused a Big War,"
      Women of History.   Philadelphia: The John C. Winston Co.
         Harriet Beecher Stowe first achieved success in middle
      age. A brief biographical sketch and description of the
      impact and influence of Uncle Tom's Cabin.

2   ADAMS, E. C. and W. D. FOSTER.   "Harriet Beecher Stowe,"
      Heroines of Modern Progress.   New York: Sturgis & Walton
      Company, pp. 89-119.
         Biographical sketch.

3   JAMES, HENRY.   A Small Boy and Others.   London: Macmillan &
      Company Ltd., pp. 167-68 (Reprinted by Criterion Books,
      1956).
         A frequently quoted passage describing James's early
      impressions of Uncle Tom's Cabin, book and play: it was
      "...for an immense number of people, much less a book than
      a state of vision."

4   LONG, WILLIAM J.   American Literature.   Boston: Athenaeum
      Press, pp. 409-412.
         Uncle Tom's Cabin is faulty, but it deals with "elemental
      human nature."   Later books are superior from a literary
      standpoint.

5   TOLSTOI, LEO.   "What is Art?" Works, XX, New York: Charles
      Scribner's Sons, p. 145.
         Uncle Tom's Cabin is cited as an example of the "highest
      order of art."

1914 A BOOKS - NONE

1914 B SHORTER WRITINGS

1   ANON.   "New Life of Harriet Beecher Stowe," Review of Reviews,
      XLIX (January), p. 48.
         A review of the Crowe biography--"an absorbing story"--
      with brief summary of the life of Harriet Beecher Stowe.

2   BAILEY, THOMAS PEARCE.   "'Uncle Tom's Cabin' Sixty Years
      After," Race Orthodoxy in the South.   New York: The Neale
      Publishing Company, pp. 170-205.
         An analysis of the treatment of the Negro character and
      prospects in Uncle Tom's Cabin, with an application of its
      principles to conditions existing in the South of the early

twentieth century. "One mistake made by Mrs. Stowe," the author notes, is "confounding racial with social relation- ships," thus unconsciously offending the racial sensibility of those who would have otherwise been sympathetic to her ideas.

3   WHITCOMB, SELDEN. "Harriet Beecher Stowe," Chronological Out- lines of American Literature. New York: The Macmillan Company, pp. 276-77.
      A list of the published works of Harriet Beecher Stowe.

1915 A BOOKS - NONE

1915 B SHORTER WRITINGS

1   KELLNER, LEON. American Literature. Translated from the German by Julia Franklin. Garden City, N. Y.: Doubleday, Page & Company, pp. 235-45.
      In Uncle Tom's Cabin, Harriet Beecher Stowe's talent is "essentially artistic," free from didactic unction and cant. Stowe's Negro characters are childish, semi-animal. The mulatto, George Harris, is the "centre of interest of the whole story," a forerunner of W. E. B. DuBois.

2   KOCH, FELIX J. "Where Did Eliza Cross the Ohio?" Ohio Archae- logical and Historical Publications, XXIV, pp. 588-90.
      Points out that although the crossing episode is claimed for Cincinnati, the scene fits Ripley, Ohio.

3   MAYCOCK, WILLOUGHBY. "Prefaces to Uncle Tom's Cabin," Notes and Queries, II, s. xii (July 17), p. 58.
      Identifies the authors of various early prefaces to Uncle Tom's Cabin.

1916 A BOOKS - NONE

1916 B SHORTER WRITINGS

1   ANON. "Memorial to Harriet Beecher Stowe," Outlook, CXIII (May 10), pp. 56-57.
      Report that a Tiffany glass window has been installed in the Church of Our Savior in Mandarin, Florida, in memory of Harriet Beecher Stowe.

1918 A BOOKS - NONE

1918

1918 B SHORTER WRITINGS

  1   BRADFORD, GAMALIEL. "Harriet Beecher Stowe," Atlantic
          Monthly, CXXII (July), pp. 84-94.
             Character sketch of Harriet Beecher Stowe, describing her
          personal magnetism, her lack of aesthetic and scholarly
          curiosity, the morbid religious intensity of her child-
          hood, and her reforming impulse. Notes her importance as
          a local color writer.

1919 A BOOKS - NONE

1919 B SHORTER WRITINGS

  1   BRADFORD, GAMALIEL. "Harriet Beecher Stowe," Portraits of
          American Women. Boston and New York: Houghton, Mifflin
          and Company. Reprinted from Atlantic Monthly, CXXII
          (July), 1918. (See 1918.B1.)

  2   HOWE, MARK DeWOLFE. The Atlantic Monthly and its Makers.
          Boston: The Atlantic Monthly Press, Inc., pp. 20-24, 49-50.
             Relates an anecdote from T. W. Higginson about Harriet
          Beecher Stowe at an Atlantic Club dinner, and reports the
          disastrous effect of the Byron article on the magazine's
          circulation.

  3   HUMPHREY, GRACE. "Harriet Beecher Stowe," Women in American
          History. Indianapolis: The Bobbs-Merrill Company,
          pp. 132-153.
             Simple biographical sketch, probably for children.

  4   MACY, JESSE. The Anti-Slavery Crusade. New Haven: Yale Uni-
          versity Press, pp. 131-37.
             Brief discussion of Uncle Tom's Cabin. The book was an
          attack on Northern prejudice as well as on slavery. Its
          practical political effect was primarily on the adolescents
          who were to vote in 1860.

1920 A BOOKS - NONE

1920 B SHORTER WRITINGS

  1   ALDRICH, LILIAN (Mrs. THOMAS B.) Crowding Memories. Boston:
          Houghton, Mifflin & Company, pp. 120-126.
             Story of an awkward visit made by Harriet Beecher Stowe
          to the author, during which the novelist unwittingly became
          intoxicated and fell asleep.

2 BOK, EDWARD. The Americanization of Edward Bok. New York:
   Charles Scribner's Sons, pp. 139-40.
       Two anecdotes about Harriet Beecher Stowe in her later
   years reported by a publisher of the era.

3 MURPHY, MABEL ANSLEY. "Harriet Beecher Stowe," Greathearted
   Women. Philadelphia: The Union Press, pp. 35-40.
       Brief and superficial biographical sketch.

1921 A BOOKS - NONE

1921 B SHORTER WRITINGS

1 ANON. "List of References relating to Harriet Beecher Stowe
   (exclusive of periodical articles)." Washington, D. C.:
   Library of Congress.
       Brief typewritten bibliography.

2 VAN DOREN, CARL. The American Novel. New York: The Macmillan
   Company, pp. 109-13.
       Uncle Tom's Cabin, "for all its defects of taste, style,
   and construction, still has surprising power." Praises the
   stories of New England life.

3 _____. "Mrs. Stowe," The Cambridge History of American Literature, III. New York: The Macmillan Company, pp. 69-73.
       Uncle Tom's Cabin is in the tradition of the pious in-
   structional narrative; if one leaves out the "merely domestic elements" of the book, little remains. The local
   color books are good, despite their weak structure and
   sentimentality.

1922 A BOOKS

1 MacARTHUR, RUTH A. The Story of Harriet Beecher Stowe. New
   York: Barse & Hopkins.
       Juvenile biography of Harriet Beecher Stowe.

1922 B SHORTER WORKS

1 TANDY, JEANETTE R. "Pro-Slavery Propaganda in American Fiction
   of the Fifties," South Atlantic Quarterly, XXI (January,
   April), pp. 41-50, 170-78.
       Review of responses to Uncle Tom's Cabin; little on the
   novel itself or on Harriet Beecher Stowe.

1923

1   HANEY, JOHN LOUIS. The Story of Our Literature. New York:
        Charles Scribner's Sons, pp. 98-100.
           A brief description of Harriet Beecher Stowe and of the
        effect on Uncle Tom's Cabin in the 1850's.

1   CHEW, SAMUEL C. Byron in England: His Fame and After-Fame.
        New York: Russell & Russell, pp. 275-83.
           A list of articles which may have inspired Harriet
        Beecher Stowe's Byron essay, and of the many responses to
        it.

2   GAINES, FRANCIS P. The Southern Plantation Novel. New York:
        Columbia University Press. (Reprinted by Peter Smith,
        1962), passim.
           Places Uncle Tom's Cabin in the tradition of the "plan-
        tation novel."

3   PAINE, A. B., ed. The Autobiography of Mark Twain. New York
        and London: Harper & Brothers Publishers, pp. 242-43.
           Description of Harriet Beecher Stowe in her old age,
        wandering in and out of the Nook Farm houses.

4   PHELPS, WILSON. "Uncle Tom's Cabin," Howells, James, Bryant,
        and other Essays. New York: The Macmillan Company,
        pp. 181-206.
           Historical and critical essay on Uncle Tom's Cabin and
        Harriet Beecher Stowe. The success of the novel results
        from its dramatic qualities and from the passion which in-
        forms it.

5   VAN DOREN, CARL. "Mrs. Stowe," A Short History of American
        Literature. Cambridge: Cambridge University Press,
        pp. 202-06.
           Reprint of 1921.B2.

1925 B SHORTER WRITINGS

1 ADAMS, EPHRAIM D. Great Britain and the American Civil War.
   New York: Longmans, Green & Company, pp. i, 181, ii, 33
   and note.
      Suggests that the English popularity of Uncle Tom's
   Cabin arose from wide-spread anti-American sentiments.
   Notes the 1861 Saturday Review article (1861.B1) attacking
   Harriet Beecher Stowe's description of the Civil War as a
   war against slavery.

2 BRAITHWAITE, WILLIAM STANLEY. "The Negro in American Literature," The New Negro. Edited by Alain Locke. New York:
   A. & C. Boni, pp. 29-44.
      Briefly notes that Uncle Tom is a character with a strong
   hold on popular imagination, but that the "moral gain and
   historical effect" of the book have resulted in artistic
   loss, since the stereotypes prevented the development of
   more satisfactory characterizations of Negroes in
   literature.

3 HOWARD, JOHN R. "Harriet Beecher Stowe," Remembrance of Things
   Past. New York: Thomas Y. Crowell Company, pp. 284-95.
      Memoir of Harriet Beecher Stowe written by a close friend
   of Henry Ward Beecher. Includes some of her own comments
   on her methods of work. Derives in part from Howard's
   Outlook sketch, July 25, 1896 (1896.B19).

4 STOWE, LYMAN BEECHER. "Uncle Tom's Cabin," Saturday Review of
   Literature, XI (December 12), p. 422.
      Brief history of the writing and publishing of Uncle
   Tom's Cabin.

5 WENDELL, BARRETT. A Literary History of America. New York:
   Charles Scribner's Sons, pp. 352-56.
      Unlike most American novelists, Harriet Beecher Stowe
   had a "spark of genius," most in evidence in Oldtown Folks.
   The Negro characters in Uncle Tom's Cabin are "white at
   heart," but they are honestly created and the book is
   strong and vivid.

1926 A BOOKS - NONE

1926 B SHORTER WRITINGS

1 ANON. "Notes on Sale," Times Literary Supplement (July 8),
   p. 468.

1926

> Notes on the sale of the 1852 Cassell edition of Uncle
> Tom's Cabin and comments on the first English editions of
> the novel.

2   NELSON, JOHN HERBERT. The Negro Character in American Litera-
>   ture. Lawrence, Kansas: Department of Journalism Press,
>   University of Kansas, pp. 73-81.
>   Harriet Beecher Stowe tries to be fair in Uncle Tom's
>   Cabin, but the novel is "technically faulty, crudely
>   didactic, and anything but a true reflection of life."
>   Her characters are only embodied theories, her dialogues
>   full of inconsistencies and false notes. Dred is a more
>   powerfully written book, and the central character of that
>   novel is the most interesting of her creations.

3   PRUETTE, L. "Harriet Beecher Stowe and the Universal Back-
>   drop," Bookman, LXIV (September), pp. 18-23.
>   A critical essay, commenting on the "earnest stupidity,"
>   self-dramatization, and masochism of the author of a book
>   "compounded...of pious reflections, gushing apostrophes
>   to the helpless reader, sheer brutality, immoral relations
>   between the sexes, and a happy ending."

4   ROURKE, CONSTANCE M. "Harriet Beecher Stowe; The Chronicle of
>   an Extraordinary American Woman," Woman's Home Companion,
>   LIII (February-May), pp. 22ff, 12ff, 24ff, 14ff.
>   A long and influential critical biography, sometimes
>   superficial but generally provocative, which emphasizes
>   Harriet Beecher Stowe's unconscious desire for power and
>   the complex, covert resentment of "domestic martyrdom"
>   evident in all her works. Rourke gives her highest praise
>   to Oldtown Folks, but wonders whether the author ever dis-
>   covered the "natural region of her mind." She attempts to
>   place Harriet Beecher Stowe in the context of nineteenth-
>   century feminism.

5   TURNER, LORENZO. "Anti-Slavery Sentiments in American Litera-
>   ture Prior to 1865." Ph.D. Dissertation. University of
>   Chicago. See 1929.B3.

1927 A BOOKS - NONE

1927 B SHORTER WRITINGS

1   ALDERTON, Mrs. J. P. "Mrs. Harriet Beecher Stowe," Henly
>   Congregational Church Review (Henly-on-Thames), XXV, v
>   (May), p. 178.

1928

Biographical sketch of Harriet Beecher Stowe, with notes on <u>Uncle Tom's Cabin</u>, calling for support of the League of Nations.

2   EATON, G. D.   "Harriet Beecher Stowe," <u>American Mercury</u>, X (April), pp. 449-59.
    Biographical and critical essay, generally unsympathetic, attributing "every bit of sense" in <u>Uncle Tom's Cabin</u> to Harriet Beecher Stowe's early theological training. Suggests that the motive for the Byron book was avarice; no mention of later novels.

3   HIBBEN, PAXTON.   <u>Henry Ward Beecher: An American Portrait</u>. New York: George H. Doran Company.
    Brief, not very informative, references to Harriet Beecher Stowe are scattered throughout this biography of her brother.

4   PARRINGTON, VERNON.   <u>Main Currents in American Thought</u>, II, III.   New York: Harcourt Brace & Co., pp. 371-78, 62-64.
    Places great importance on <u>Oldtown Folks</u> and <u>Poganuc People</u> as evidence of Harriet Beecher Stowe's continuing moral concern. <u>The Minister's Wooing</u>, which stands between these and the abolition novels, reveals the tender conscience beneath the "crabbed exterior of the old Calvinism." <u>Dred</u> is a better social study than <u>Uncle Tom's Cabin</u> but a weaker story. "The creative instinct was strong in (Harriet Beecher Stowe) but the critical was wholly lacking." Parrington links Harriet Beecher Stowe with Jewett and Freeman as a chronicler of decaying New England.

5   ROURKE, CONSTANCE M.   "Harriet Beecher Stowe," <u>Trumpets of Jubilee</u>.   New York: Harcourt, Brace & Co., pp. 89-148.
    Same as <u>Woman's Home Companion</u>, LIII (February-May), 1926.   (1926.B4)

6   WINTER, A. A.   "Little Woman Who Made a Great War," <u>Ladies Home Journal</u>, XLIV (December), p. 27.
    Standard biographical sketch and discussion of <u>Uncle Tom's Cabin</u>.

1928 A BOOKS - NONE

1928 B SHORTER WRITINGS

1   HOWELLS, M., ed.   <u>The Life in Letters of William Dean Howells</u>. Garden City, N. Y.: Doubleday, pp. 149-50.

1928

> Letter to James Fields (1869) defends the Byron article,
> but complains of the mistakes in it and of Harriet Beecher
> Stowe's refusal to read the proofs.

1929 A BOOKS - NONE

1929 B SHORTER WRITINGS

1   BRAYBROOKE, PATRICK. "Uncle Tom's Cabin," Great Children in
    Literature. London: Alston Rivers, pp. 161-76.
        An appreciation of little Eva--a type of humanitarian we
    still need.

2   MAXFIELD, E. K. "'Goody-goody' Literature and Mrs. Stowe."
    American Speech, IV (February), pp. 189-202.
        Uncle Tom's Cabin is a glorified Sunday School tract of
    a type familiar in the nineteenth century about a good
    child who went to heaven.

3   TURNER, LORENZO DOW. Anti-Slavery Sentiment in American
    Literature Prior to 1865. Washington, D. C.: Association
    for the Study of Negro Life and History. (Reprinted by
    Kennikat Press, 1966), p. 136.
        Mentions Uncle Tom's Cabin as a product of the "second
    stage" of abolitionism (1850-61), notes its relationship
    to the Fugitive Slave law, and discusses its success in
    converting uncommitted readers to the anti-slavery cause.
    Dissertation: University of Chicago, 1926. (See 1926.B5)

4   WINTERICH, JOHN T. Books and the Man. New York: Greenberg,
    pp. 79-101.
        Brief biographical sketch of Harriet Beecher Stowe and
    description of early editions of Uncle Tom's Cabin in
    England and America. Quotes Harriet Beecher Stowe's
    preface to the Riverside edition and Mrs. Eastman's criti-
    cisms from Aunt Phillis's Cabin (1852.B40).

1930 A BOOKS

1   LUCAS, E. La littérature Anti-Esclavagiste au Dix-Neuvième
    Siècle. Étude sur Madame Beecher Stowe et son Influence
    en France. Paris: E. deBoccard.
        This work traces "le courant nègre" in French literature
    and in translations of English and American books in order
    to give an idea of French attitudes toward slavery in the
    United States and in the French colonies in the nineteenth

century. It also examines and attempts to analyze the popularity of Uncle Tom's Cabin in France. Detailed bibliography of translations, juvenile editions, critical essays, etc.

1930 B SHORTER WRITINGS

1 ANON. "Mrs. Harriet Beecher Stowe," The Abbot Academy Bulletin, VII (April), pp. 20-26.
    Article on Harriet Beecher Stowe's years in Andover, with notes on the town's reaction to her, and descriptions of her house and person.

2 ANON. "Mrs. Harriet Beecher Stowe," The Abbot Academy Bulletin, VIII (November).
    Continues the story begun in the April number (1930.B1) about Harriet Beecher Stowe's help in raising money to furnish an Academy hall in 1854.

3 CAIRNS, WILLIAM B. A History of American Literature. Revised edition. New York: Oxford University Press.
    Standard biographical sketch; later books seem likely to appeal primarily to literary critics, but Uncle Tom's Cabin is a "sympathetic presentation of life."

4 FORD, C. WORTHINGTON, ed. The Letters of Henry Adams, I. Boston and New York: Houghton, Mifflin and Company.
    Adams notes that "Mrs. Stowe's scenes with Topsy...are about as good as anything she has done--always excepting her Byron."

1931 A BOOKS - NONE

1931 B SHORTER WRITINGS

1 BLANKENSHIP, RUSSELL. American Literature as an Expression of the National Mind. New York: Henry Holt, pp. 330-33.
    Uncle Tom's Cabin is an excessively sentimental book, its characters are types, not individuals, but its faults "assisted in its successful appeal." The later books prove Harriet Beecher Stowe a "competent American novelist."

2 LOGGINS, VERNON. The Negro Author; His Development in America. New York: Columbia University Press, pp. 213-19.
    Discusses Bibb, Clarke, and Henson as possible sources for characters in Uncle Tom's Cabin.

1931

3 MATTHIESSEN, F. O. "New England Stories," <u>American Writers on</u>
<u>American Literature</u>. Edited by John Macy. New York:
H. Liveright, Inc., pp. 400-05.
Contrasts Stowe to Jewett and Wilkins, citing her preface
to <u>Oldtown Folks</u> and noting that Harriet Beecher Stowe's
attention to conscience and evil are characteristic of her
generation.

4 MAURICE, A. B. "Literary Magazines," <u>American Writers on</u>
<u>American Literature</u>. Edited by John Macy. New York:
H. Liveright, Inc., pp. 43, 472.
Anecdotes describing Harriet Beecher Stowe's relations
with the <u>Atlantic Monthly</u>.

5 McDOWELL, TREMAINE. "The Use of Negro Dialect by Harriet
Beecher Stowe," <u>American Speech</u>, VI (June), pp. 322-26.
The foundation of the Black dialect in <u>Uncle Tom's Cabin</u>
is the common body of American folk speech, marred, however, by generalization and inconsistency. A marked im-
provement in the use of dialect can be seen in <u>The Minis-</u>
<u>ter's Wooing</u>. In general, Harriet Beecher Stowe was less
effective than many of her predecessors in recording Negro
speech.

1932 A BOOKS - NONE

1932 B SHORTER WRITINGS

1 HARVESON, MAE ELIZABETH. <u>Catharine Esther Beecher</u>. Philadelphia: The Science Press Printing Company.
This biography of Harriet Beecher Stowe's elder sister
contains many references to Harriet Beecher Stowe throughout, but most are quotations from earlier biographies or
published letters.

2 HOWE, MARK DeWOLFE, ed. <u>New Letters of James Russell Lowell</u>.
New York: Harper & Brothers, pp. 146-47.
Letter to Edmund Quincy (1869) suggests that Harriet
Beecher Stowe "understood incest where it was not meant"
in the Byron episode and was too eager to proclaim
intimacy with Lady Byron.

3 JOHNSON, MERLE. "American First Editions: Harriet (Elizabeth)
Beecher Stowe, 1811-1896," <u>Publisher's Weekly</u>, CXX
(April 16), pp. 1738-39.
List of the first editions of published works.

4   PIERSON, RALPH. "A Few Literary Highlights of 1850-52."
    <u>American Book Collector</u>, II (August-September), pp. 156-60.
        Describes the early history of <u>Uncle Tom's Cabin</u>, and
    lists many books inspired by or relating to it which
    appeared during its first year in print.

5   RAMMELKAMP, C. H., ed. "Harriet Beecher Stowe's Reply,"
    <u>Mississippi Valley Historical Review</u>, XIX, p. 261.
        Reprint of an 1887 letter from Harriet Beecher Stowe,
    denying that she ever took back any of her anti-slavery
    statements in <u>Uncle Tom's Cabin</u>, and asserting that
    Southern Negroes were, "considering their advantages, <u>far</u>
    better than many white people."

<u>1933 A BOOKS - NONE</u>

<u>1933 B SHORTER WRITINGS</u>

*1   ANON. "Part of a Letter, dated March 1870, to Edward Everett
     Hale," <u>Autograph Album</u>, I (December), p. 104.
         Cited in Leary.

2   ANON. "Power of 'Uncle Tom's Cabin' Won Author World Renown."
     <u>America's Twelve Great Women Leaders during the Past Hun-</u>
     <u>dred Years as Chosen by the Women of America</u>. Compiled
     from <u>The Ladies Home Journal</u> and <u>The Christian Science</u>
     <u>Monitor</u>. Chicago: Associated Authors' Service.
         Brief biographical sketch. <u>Uncle Tom's Cabin</u> "wasn't
     a very good book, from a literary standpoint, but it was
     a powerful polemic."

3   BROWN, STERLING. "Negro Character as Seen by White Authors,"
     <u>Journal of Negro Education</u>, II (April), 179-203.
         Although the article is primarily a discussion of stereo-
     types in Reconstruction and early modern American fiction,
     Brown notes the pro-slavery novels written in reaction to
     <u>Uncle Tom's Cabin</u> and makes many passing references to
     Harriet Beecher Stowe and the character of Uncle Tom.

4   GREGG, WILLIAM R. <u>The African in North America; Their Welfare</u>
     <u>after Freedom as Effected and Influenced by the Life of</u>
     <u>William King</u>. <u>Facts Regarding the Characters portrayed</u>
     <u>by Mrs. Stowe in Uncle Tom's Cabin</u>. Reprinted from an
     article in the Toronto <u>World</u>, July 6, 1924. Ashtabula,
     Ohio: Brooks Print Shop.
         A biography of King, whose actions in the manumitting
     and educating of slaves were cited by Harriet Beecher Stowe
     in <u>Dred</u>. Also includes comments on Josiah Henson.

1933

5   SABIN, JOSEPH W. E. and R. W. G. VAIL. "Harriet Beecher
    Stowe," Bibliotheca Americana, XXIV. New York: Biblio-
    graphical Society of America, pp. 33-73.
        Annotated and descriptive list of editions, adaptations,
    dramatizations, translations and other works related to
    the writings of Harriet Beecher Stowe published before
    1860, which have "especial American interest."

6   TALBOT, WILLIAM. "Uncle Tom's Cabin: First English Editions,"
    American Book Collector, III (May, June), pp. 292-97.
        Talbot describes the 1856 article by N. W. Senior noting
    the first English editions of Uncle Tom's Cabin, then gives
    additional facts about these early editions and their sales,
    as well as information on the publication of A Key to Uncle
    Tom's Cabin.

7   YOUNG, STARK. "Uncle Tom's Measure," New Republic, LXXVI
    (October 4), pp. 212-213.
        "As literary effort Uncle Tom's Cabin is mere period
    trash," effective only because it touches on the powerful
    themes of family break-up and the dependence of slaves on
    the kindness of the master.

1934 A BOOKS - NONE

1934 B SHORTER WRITINGS

1   COLE, ARTHUR C. The Irrepressible Conflict, 1850-1865. New
    York: The Macmillan Company, pp. 270-71.
        Brief comments on the impact of Uncle Tom's Cabin and
    its influence on masters and slaves.

2   MILLER, JAMES M. "Harriet Beecher Stowe," An Outline of Ameri-
    can Literature. New York: Farrar & Rinehart, Inc.,
    pp. 110-111.
        A list of the published writings of Harriet Beecher
    Stowe and of some biographies.

3   STOWE, LYMAN BEECHER. "Harriet Beecher Stowe," Saints, Sinners
    and Beechers. Indianapolis: The Bobbs-Merrill Company,
    pp. 154-235.
        Essay on Harriet Beecher Stowe in book on Beecher family.
    The information is drawn mostly from already published
    material, but Stowe does include some family anecdotes and
    many portraits.

4   WHITCOMB, IDA PRENTICE. "Harriet Beecher Stowe," Young
     People's Story of American Literature. New York: Dodd,
     Mead and Company, pp. 144-46.
         Standard brief biography of Harriet Beecher Stowe.

1935 A BOOKS - NONE

1935 B SHORTER WRITINGS

*1   BRADY, KATHLEEN. "The Sources, Reputation, and Influence of
     Uncle Tom's Cabin." Unpublished MA dissertation. Uni-
     versity of Minnesota.

2   CUMMINGS, E. E. Tom. Santa Fe: Rydal Press.
         A ballet based on Uncle Tom's Cabin, depicting the life,
     death, and transfiguration of the hero.

3   EMRYS-JONES, J. "The Woman Who Made the World Weep," Sunday
     Dispatch, London (March 3).
         Review of Saints, Sinners and Beechers, primarily about
     Harriet Beecher Stowe. Biographical sketch.

4   PATTEE, FRED L. The First Century of American Literature,
     1770-1870. New York: D. Appleton-Century Company,
     pp. 570-75.
         Uncle Tom's Cabin was essentially a war document, "a
     stone from a sling." Pattee comments on the later works
     but sees Harriet Beecher Stowe as "author of but a single
     book."

5   QUINN, ARTHUR H. "Saints, Sinners, and Beechers," American
     Literature, VI (January), p. 478.
         Review. Praises Lyman Stowe for "declining to use the
     methods of psychoanalysis on his forebears," but notes
     that our knowledge of Harriet Beecher Stowe will not be
     much enlarged by this book.

1936 A BOOKS - NONE

1936 B SHORTER WRITINGS

1   ANTHONY, KATHARINE. "Harriet Beecher Stowe," Dictionary of
     American Biography, XVIII. Edited by Dumas Malone. New
     York: Charles Scribner's Sons, pp. 115-120.
         Biographical sketch with familiar anecdotes and brief
     bibliography.

1936

2   BOYNTON, PERCY H.   Literature and American Life.   Boston:
         The Athenaeum Press.
         Brief description of the popular effect of Uncle Tom's
     Cabin in a discussion of the interaction of books and
     culture.

3   BROOKS, VAN WYCK.   The Flowering of New England.   New York:
         Random House, pp. 417-21.
         Brief biography of Harriet Beecher Stowe, whose passions,
     humor, and feeling for justice were all large and who
     created in Uncle Tom's Cabin, the Southern novel, producing
     "a great folk-picture of an age and a nation."

4   QUINN, ARTHUR H.   American Fiction: An Historical and Critical
         Survey.   New York: Appleton-Century-Crofts, Inc., pp. 159-
         63.
         Describes Harriet Beecher Stowe's works as representa-
     tive of the transition to realism in American fiction.
     Sees the author as a great social and moral force of her
     time, but not a great artist. Bibliography.

5   TAYLOR, WALTER FULLER.   "Harriet Beecher Stowe (1811-1896),"
         A History of American Letters.   Boston and New York:
         American Book Company, pp. 185-87.
         Compares Harriet Beecher Stowe and Whittier: the former
     had the larger nature and "the power to make people see."
     She was the most richly endowed of all our ante-bellum
     novelists. Bibliography.

1937 A BOOKS

1   GILBERTSON, CATHERINE.   Harriet Beecher Stowe.   New York: D.
         Appleton-Century Company, Inc. (Reprinted by Kennikat
         Press, 1968).
         Full-length biography, written, according to the
     preface, to correct the contrasting excesses and inaccu-
     racies of the Rourke and Stowe books. Discusses the
     sources of many characters and settings, and the probable
     and possible early reading of the author. Attempts to
     place Harriet Beecher Stowe within the context of genteel
     aspiration and mid-nineteenth-century religious turmoil.
     The early years are seen as filled with conflicts between
     self-discipline and romantic escapism. Uncle Tom's Cabin
     is a projection of the author's domestic and emotional
     suffering, but is marked by "good sense." The New England
     novels are given high praise.

1937 B SHORTER WRITINGS

1 ANON. "The Sixth Beecher," Christian Science Monitor Weekly
     Magazine (July 28), p. 11.
          Review of Gilbertson biography. This book adds little
     to our store of facts about Harriet Beecher Stowe, but the
     author of it has "orientated" Mrs. Stowe to her time and
     integrated her life into that of the communities in which
     she lived.

2 BLAIR, WALTER. Native American Humor. American Book Company,
     pp. 136-37, 140-43.
          Ranks Harriet Beecher Stowe as an important local
     colorist, noting her success in the New England tales,
     where the traditional framework--contrasting the language
     of the writer with that of the story-teller--is effectively
     used.

3 BROWN, STERLING. The Negro in American Fiction. Washington,
     D. C.: Associates in Negro Folk Education. (Reprinted by
     Kennikat Press, 1968).
          Harriet Beecher Stowe faced the problem of whether to
     show Negroes as brutalized by slavery or as idealized
     heroes; in Uncle Tom she does the latter, but the other
     characters of the novel do show the negative effects of
     the system. Despite its sentimentality and melodrama,
     Uncle Tom's Cabin contains "essential truth." In Dred,
     Harriet Beecher Stowe adds a new character to her reper-
     toire, but she was not very successful with him, and the
     book is marred by polemic.

4 BUCK, PAUL H. The Road to Reunion, 1865-1900. Boston: Little,
     Brown and Company, pp. 209-210.
          Historian points out the ironic similarity between
     descriptions of slaves in Uncle Tom's Cabin and descrip-
     tions of them in the various works which attacked the
     novel.

5 DAYKIN, WALTER L. "Negro Types in American White Fiction,"
     Sociology and Research, XXII (September-October), pp. 45-
     52.
          Uncle Tom's Cabin possesses little literary merit and
     presents a biased view of Negro life and personality; it
     was received favorably only because it appeared at the
     correct psychological moment.

6 FLORY, CLAUDE R. Economic Criticism in American Fiction, 1792-
     1900. Philadelphia: University of Pennsylvania Press,

1937

        pp. 45–50. (Reprinted by Russell & Russell, 1969).
The economic arguments behind Uncle Tom's Cabin and Dred
are best understood by inference from other economic
writings of the time. In Dred, "there is an attempt to
substitute some economic argument for the more general
humanitarian appeal of the earlier novel." "Mrs. Stowe
holds that slavery is a wasteful system and that
Southerners must abolish it for their own future economic
good."

7   MUSSEY, J. BARROWS, ed. We Were New England, or, Yankee Life
      by Those who Lived It. New York: Stackpole Sons Publishers,
      pp. 29–32, 110–11.
      A portion of an Harriet Beecher Stowe memoir which gives
an account of her childhood, and a dialogue between Lyman
Beecher and "Uncle Lot" (a character in an early Harriet
Beecher Stowe story).

8   RANDALL, JAMES. Civil War and Reconstruction. Boston: D. C.
      Heath & Company, pp. 169–70.
      Harriet Beecher Stowe set up a Christian martyr in a
black skin, and dramatized for the nation the existing
sectional conflict. Her facts are chiefly from Weld's
book.

1938 A BOOKS – NONE

1938 B SHORTER WRITINGS

1   BERNBAUM, E. "Harriet Beecher Stowe," American Literature, IX
      (November), p. 385.
      Review of Gilbertson biography. This work is a fair-
minded study of the life of Harriet Beecher Stowe and her
works, "the composition of a scholarly mind and temper."

2   KLINGBERG, F. J. "Uncle Tom in England," American Historical
      Review, XLIII (April), pp. 542–52.
      Uncle Tom's Cabin was seized upon as an argument for the
emancipation of white workers in England. A summary of
the comments of the contemporary British press, with an
extensive list of early English reviews of Uncle Tom's
Cabin, A Key to Uncle Tom's Cabin, and Dred. Documents
also the extraordinary reception given to Harriet Beecher
Stowe on her first visit to England.

3   KUNITZ, STANLEY and HOWARD HAYCRAFT. "Harriet Beecher Stowe,"
      American Authors, 1600–1900. New York: The H. W. Wilson

Company, pp. 722-24.
  A biographical sketch and brief list of published works
by Harriet Beecher Stowe.

4 PURCELL, J. M. "Mrs. Stowe's Vocabulary," <u>American Speech</u>,
      XIII (October), pp. 230-31.
      Cites and defines a number of unusual or infrequently
  used words found in <u>Uncle Tom's Cabin</u>.

5 TINKER, EDWARD L. "Uncle Tom's Cabin," <u>New York Times Book
      Review</u> (January 16).
      Review of the limited edition of <u>Uncle Tom's Cabin</u>
  (1938.B6), highly critical of the illustrations.

6 WEAVER, RAYMOND. "Introduction," <u>Uncle Tom's Cabin</u>. New York:
      The Limited Editions Club, pp. iii-xv.
      Weaver contrasts the instant success of <u>Uncle Tom's
  Cabin</u> with the failure of <u>Moby Dick</u>, written the same year.
  His background sketch recounts the various stories told by
  Harriet Beecher Stowe about the origin and composition of
  her first novel.

<u>1939 A BOOKS - NONE</u>

<u>1939 B SHORTER WRITINGS</u>

1 ADAMS, JOHN R. "The Literary Achievements of Harriet Beecher
      Stowe." Ph.D. dissertation. University of Southern
      California. <u>See</u> 1963.A1.

2 BROWN, STERLING. "The American Race Problem as Reflected in
      American Literature," <u>Journal of Negro Education</u>, VIII
      (July), pp. 275-90.
       In <u>Uncle Tom's Cabin</u>, Harriet Beecher Stowe seems "per-
  plexed about the future of the free Negro," as is evidenced
  by her treatment of the colonization issue, but she seems
  to believe that the African race is generally of a "higher
  moral character" than the Anglo-Saxon.

3 HERRON, IMA HONAKER. <u>The Small Town in American Literature</u>.
      Raleigh: Duke University Press, pp. 76-79. (Reprinted by
      Pageant Books, 1959).
      Although sentimental and weak in plot construction,
  Harriet Beecher Stowe is "significant for her varied
  records of a rapidly obsolescent village life" in the New
  England novels.

1939

4   MALONE, DUMAS. "Some Women Saints," <u>Saints in Action</u>. New
        York: The Abingdon Press, pp. 92-94.
            Brief biographical comment. Harriet Beecher Stowe was
        "far more warm hearted than the great body of the Aboli-
        tionists," and "inveterate in reforming tendencies," but
        she had been liberated and humanized by her years in the
        West.

5   McILWAINE, SHIELDS. <u>The Southern Poor-White from Lubberland
        to Tobacco Road</u>. Norman, Oklahoma: University of Oklahoma
        Press, pp. 34-36.
            Brief comments on the "poor-white" types in <u>Uncle Tom's
        Cabin</u> and <u>Dred</u>, and on the distorted view of their numbers
        held by Harriet Beecher Stowe and others.

1940 A BOOKS - NONE

1940 B SHORTER WRITINGS

1   BOYNTON, PERCY H. "The Novel of Puritan Decay from Mrs. Stowe
        to John Marquand," <u>New England Quarterly</u>, XIII (December),
        pp. 626-37.
            Harriet Beecher Stowe's New England novels are valuable
        for the veracity of the background material and the
        "critical soundness" of their observation. In contrast
        to later writers, she sees the New England virtues as the
        "seedbed" of American values. Reprinted in Boynton,
        <u>America in Contemporary Fiction</u>. Chicago: University of
        Chicago Press, pp. 35-52.

2   BROWN, HERBERT ROSS. "Uncle Tom's and Other Cabins," <u>The
        Sentimental Novel in America, 1789-1860</u>. Chapel Hill:
        Duke University Press, pp. 241-280. (Reprinted by Books
        for Libraries Press, 1970).
            Numerous references to Harriet Beecher Stowe and her use
        of the sentimental conventions can be found throughout the
        book. Her works are placed in the tradition of the senti-
        mental novel and compared to pro- and anti-slavery versions
        of the familiar story. <u>Uncle Tom's Cabin</u> is more than a
        sentimental novel because the social problem resisted
        resolution within the usual literary framework.

3   EATON, CLEMENT. <u>Freedom of Thought in the Old South</u>.
        Durham, N. C.: Duke University Press, pp. 36-37.
            Notes the Southern sensitivity to criticism, citing a
        letter from John R. Thompson to George Frederick Holmes
        which asked for a highly critical review of <u>Uncle Tom's
        Cabin</u> for the <u>Southern Literary Messenger</u>.

4   HADLEY, B.   "Uncle Tom's Cabin in Brazil," Inter-America, II
       (October), pp. 26-27.
          Discusses briefly the influence of Uncle Tom's Cabin,
       book and play, in Brazil.

5   HOOVER, KENNETH WARD.   "A Stowe Memorial," Florida Historical
       Society, XVIII (January).
          A description of the stained glass memorial window in
       Mandarin, and of Harriet Beecher Stowe's Southern life.

6   MYERS, A. J. W.   "Harriet Beecher Stowe," Women Leaders.
       Edited by P. H. Lotz.   New York: Association Press,
       pp. 109-117.
          Short biographical sketch with questions for discussion.

7   NELSON, J. H.   "A Note on the Genesis of Mrs. Stowe's Dred,"
       Studies in English in honor of Raphael Dorman O'Leary and
       Selden Lincoln Whitcomb by the members of the English
       Department, University of Kansas.   Lawrence, Kansas:
       University of Kansas Press, pp. 59-65.
          Dred owed more to the author's reading than did Uncle
       Tom's Cabin.   Sources for many of the characters and inci-
       dents can be found in the documents of the Key.

8   PATTEE, FRED L.   The Feminine Fifties.   New York: D. Appleton-
       Century Company, pp. 130-145.   (Reprinted by Kennikat
       Press, 1966).
          General discussion of the impact of Uncle Tom's Cabin,
       novel and play, with quotations from some of the book's
       contemporary critics.

9   RANDALL, D. A. and J. T. WINTERICH.   "One Hundred Good Novels:
       Stowe, Harriet Beecher: Uncle Tom's Cabin," Publishers'
       Weekly, CXXXVII (May 18), pp. 1931-32.
          Brief bibliographical notes and comment on Harriet Beecher
       Stowe and Uncle Tom's Cabin.

10 SCHRIFTGIESSER, KARL.   "God's Family: The Beechers," Families.
       New York: Howell, Soskin, pp. 55f.
          A popular history of the Beechers.   Pages 81-86 and 92-
       95 deal specifically with Harriet, especially noting her
       "hunger for love" and her morbidity.

11 WARD, AILEEN.   "In Memory of 'Uncle Tom!'" Dalhousie Review,
       XX (October), pp. 335-38.
          Sketch of the life and death of Josiah Henson, one of
       the models for Uncle Tom.

1941

1941 A BOOKS

1   WILSON, R[OBERT] FORREST. <u>Crusader in Crinoline</u>. Philadel-
     phia, London, New York: J. B. Lippincott Company.
       The longest and most detailed biography to date. Wilson
     draws on previous biographies, on letters hitherto un-
     published, on reminiscences of literary personalities, and
     on newspaper files from many parts of the country to pro-
     duce a readable life of the author and her family. He
     points out the many contradictions in Harriet Beecher
     Stowe's comments on her career and in her personality.
     Relatively little attention is paid to the style and con-
     tent of her works, although some interpretation is im-
     plicit. No footnotes are included, but there is a long
     bibliographical summary for each chapter and a comprehen-
     sive index.

1941 B SHORTER WORKS

1   ALBERT, SARAH TRUAX. "An Entertaining Biography," <u>Argus</u>
     (March 22), p. 2.
       Generally favorable review of the Wilson biography.

2   ANON. "Uncle Tom's Mammy," <u>Time</u>, XXXVII (March 10), p. 90.
       Review of Wilson biography. The book "shares the flaw
     of all...Stowe biographies," that is, everything in the
     life of Harriet Beecher Stowe before and after <u>Uncle Tom's
     Cabin</u> "looks like filler." Notes the immense popularity
     of the novel.

3   ANTHONY, KATHARINE. "Christian Soldier," <u>New Republic</u>, CV
     (September 19), p. 348.
       Review of the Wilson biography. An exception to the
     full and generally convincing portrait provided by this
     book is the overestimation of the impact of the Byron
     scandal on Harriet Beecher Stowe's career.

4   BROWNE, MARGARET A. "Southern Reactions to 'Uncle Tom's
     Cabin.'" Unpublished MA dissertation. Duke University.
       Browne discusses the effect of <u>Uncle Tom's Cabin</u> on
     Southern slaveholders and reception of the novel in the
     South, the North, and abroad.

5   BUCKMASTER, HENRIETTA. <u>Let My People Go</u>. Boston: Beacon
     Press, pp. 221-224.
       A brief discussion of the impact of <u>Uncle Tom's Cabin</u>
     in a general history of the American anti-slavery movement.

6   COMMAGER, H. S. "She Conquered a Crown," <u>Saturday Review of</u>
     <u>Literature</u>, XXIII (March 15), p. 6.
         Review of the Wilson biography: an interpretation of the
     life of Harriet Beecher Stowe which is "not profound, but
     intelligent and reflective." Wilson, however, has not
     done justice to the religious aspects of Harriet Beecher
     Stowe's life and writing nor to her local color novels.

7   COWIE, ALEXANDER. "Crusader in Crinoline," <u>American Litera-</u>
     <u>ture</u>, XIII (May), pp. 171-73.
         Review of Wilson biography. Wilson's book is for the
     scholar as well as the general reader; it is a brilliant
     and valuable work, although the author is less at home
     critically and historically than biographically.

8   HART, JAMES. "Harriet Beecher Stowe," <u>Oxford Companion to</u>
     <u>American Literature</u>. New York: Oxford University Press,
     pp. 812-13.
         Biographical sketch.

9   HOGARTH, D. H. "Crusader in Crinoline," <u>Saturday Review of</u>
     <u>Literature</u>, XXIII (March 29), p. 9.
         Letter correcting the errors of fact relating to Cin-
     cinnati geography made in the Wilson book.

10   HOLDING, E. "Crusader in Crinoline," <u>Nation</u>, CLII (March 29),
     p. 384.
         Review of Wilson biography. This is a "fascinating and
     balanced" history of the life of Harriet Beecher Stowe,
     despite the bias of the author in favor of his subject.
     A brief summary of Harriet Beecher Stowe's life included.

11   KIRK, CLARA MARBURG. "Saints, Sinners and Beechers," <u>Survey</u>
     <u>Graphic</u>, XXX (May), pp. 309-10.
         Review of Wilson biography. This life of Harriet Beecher
     Stowe is an "enthralling and detailed" narrative. Brief
     biographical sketch included.

12   PARSONS, ALICE BEAL. "Harriet Beecher Stowe, a 'Natural
     Force,'" <u>New York Herald Tribune</u> (March 9), IX, p. 3.
         Review of Wilson biography. Criticizes Wilson's handling
     of the Byron scandal.

13   WILSON, R. FORREST. "The Book that Brewed a War: Uncle Tom's
     Cabin," <u>Reader's Digest</u>, XXXVIII (May), pp. 103-07.
         A biographical sketch of Harriet Beecher Stowe, con-
     densed from parts of <u>Crusader in Crinoline</u>.

1941

14   WILSON, R. FORREST. "Crusader in Crinoline--Reply," <u>Saturday
        Review of Literature</u>, XXIII (April 12), p. 13.
           An answer to letter of March 29 (1941.B9), commenting on
        Harriet Beecher Stowe's penchant for romanticizing her
        past.

1942 A BOOKS - NONE

1942 B SHORTER WRITINGS

1   ANON. "Crusader in Crinoline," <u>Times Literary Supplement</u>
        (May 2), p. 235.
           Review of the Wilson biography and biographical sketch
        of Harriet Beecher Stowe. Reviewer feels that Wilson
        underestimates Calvin Stowe.

2   BEETON, M. M. "Mr. Beeton and 'Uncle Tom,'" <u>Times Literary
        Supplement</u> (July 4), p. 331.
           Report of an 1853 letter to correspondent's father from
        Harriet Beecher Stowe, noting her failure to resent the
        English piracy of <u>Uncle Tom's Cabin</u>.

3   GARWOOD, H. P. "Mr. Beeton and 'Uncle Tom,'" <u>Times Literary
        Supplement</u> (May 16), p. 250.
           A letter noting that Harriet Beecher Stowe had received
        some money for one English edition of <u>Uncle Tom's Cabin</u>
        from the publisher, Beeton.

4   MALONE, TED [FRANK A. RUSSELL]. <u>American Pilgrimage</u>. New
        York: Dodd, Mead & Co., pp. 82-98. (Reprinted by Books
        for Libraries Press, 1972).
           A very informal short biography of Harriet Beecher Stowe.

1943 A BOOKS - NONE

1943 B SHORTER WRITINGS

1   BELLOWS, STEVEN BUSH. "Paging Sam Lawson," <u>Christian Science
        Monitor</u>, XXXV (August 11), p. 8.
           "In Sam Lawson's Fireside Stories, Harriet Beecher Stowe
        captured...the essence of an era, a locality, and a
        people."

2   BORLAND, H. "Little Lady Who Made a Great War," <u>New York
        Times Magazine</u> (February 14), pp. 16-17.

Photo story, summary, and comment on the Ryerson play,
Harriet. (See Appendix II).

3 FLEMING, BEATRICE JACKSON. "Harriet Beecher Stowe, Militant
   Dreamer," The Negro History Bulletin, VI (June), pp. 195-
   96.
      Sketch of the life of Harriet Beecher Stowe, culminating
   in the publication of Uncle Tom's Cabin and brief discussion
   of that novel.

4 GILDER, ROSAMUND. "Actors in their Stride: Helen Hayes as
   Harriet," Theatre Arts, XXVII (May), pp. 265-66.
      Review of Fyerson play (Appendix II). Summarizes the
   life of Harriet Beecher Stowe and discusses the difficulty
   of encompassing historical issues on stage.

5 GASSNER, J. "Harriet Beecher Stowe on the Stage," Current
   History, n.s. IV (April), pp. 156-58.
      Review of Ryerson play (Appendix II) with additional
   information about Harriet Beecher Stowe's preparation for
   writing Uncle Tom's Cabin and her career after its publication.

6 REYNOLDS, R. "The Business of Being a Beecher," Sunday News
   Magazine (May 2), p. 62ff.
      Informal biographies of the members of the Beecher
   family, including Harriet, inspired by the Ryerson play.

7 WYATT, E. V. R. "Harriet," Catholic World, CLVII (April),
   pp. 77-78.
      A review of the Ryerson play (Appendix II). Critic
   regrets that no mention was made in the play of the
   religious aspects of Harriet Beecher Stowe's life.

8 YOUNG, STARK. "Gentle Mrs. Stowe," New Republic, CVIII
   (March 22), p. 381.
      A review of the Ryerson play (Appendix II), calling
   Uncle Tom's Cabin dated, bombastic, turgid and lurid, and
   noting that the Byron article had been "nauseous,"
   "meddlesome," and filled with resentment.

1944 A BOOKS - NONE

1944 B SHORTER WRITINGS

1 GOHDES, CLARENCE. American Literature in Nineteenth Century
   England. New York: Columbia University Press, pp. 29-31.

1944

>Summarizes the history of the first English printing of Uncle Tom's Cabin and discusses the initial impact of the book. Includes a list of articles about Harriet Beecher Stowe in nineteenth-century periodicals.

2   LAMPREY, L. "Eduring Errors; Big, Savage Bloodhounds Chasing Eliza," American Mercury, LVIII (January), pp. 49-50.
>Notes that there are no hounds chasing Eliza in Uncle Tom's Cabin--the error derives from the popular play.

3   SCUDDER, H. H. "Mrs. Trollope and Slavery in America," Notes and Queries, CLXXXVII (July 29), pp. 46-48.
>Points out the parallels between Uncle Tom's Cabin and Jonathan Jefferson Whitlaw (1836) by Frances Trollope.

1945 A BOOKS - NONE

1945 B SHORTER WRITINGS

1   BROWN, JOHN MASON. "Topsy-turvy: Uncle Tom's Cabin Barred in Bridgeport and New Haven," Saturday Review of Literature, XXVIII (October 6), pp. 24-25.
>Comment on the barring of a production of Uncle Tom's Cabin in two Connecticut cities, noting the irony and condemning censorship.

2   WAYNE, J. L. "The History of Uncle Tom's Cabin," Hobbies, L (August), pp. 106-07.
>Comment on the early editions of Uncle Tom's Cabin.

1946 A BOOKS - NONE

1946 B SHORTER WRITINGS

1   ANON. "Words That Shook the World; Uncle Tom's Cabin," Scholastic, XLIX (November 4), p. 22.
>A description of the writing and impact of Uncle Tom's Cabin.

2   BULLARD, F. LAURISTON. "Abraham Lincoln and Harriet Beecher Stowe," Lincoln Herald, XLVIII (June), pp. 11-14.
>A discussion of the Stowe-Lincoln meeting in 1862, the Emancipation proclamation, Harriet Beecher Stowe's Reply to the Women of England, and her biographical essay on Lincoln in Men of Our Time (1868).

3   BURNS, WAYNE and EMERSON GRANT SUTCLIFFE. "Uncle Tom's Cabin
        and Charles Reade," American Literature, XVII (January),
        pp. 334-47.
        Uncle Tom's Cabin and A Key to Uncle Tom's Cabin may
        have furnished ideas for the social propaganda in It Is
        Never Too Late to Mend and aided Reade's development as a
        documentary realist in fiction.

4   CAYTON, HORACE. See 1946.B12 below.

5   CLARK, THOMAS D. "An Appraisal of Uncle Tom's Cabin," Lincoln
        Herald, XLVIII (June), pp. 25-29.
        The novel is a tawdry book, filled with amateurish
        writing, and a "strong undertone of propaganda for the
        saving grace of the Methodist denomination." Clark notes
        that Shelby and Legree were names of prominent Southern
        families, and comments on Harriet Beecher Stowe's approach
        to the problem of miscegenation, to Ohio politics, etc.
        In A Key to Uncle Tom's Cabin, Harriet Beecher Stowe is "a
        historical charlatan."

6   COLEMAN, J. WINSTON, JR. "Mrs. Stowe, Kentucky, and Uncle
        Tom's Cabin," Lincoln Herald, XLVIII (June), pp. 2-9.
        Standard biographical sketch with discussion of the
        sources of incidents, places, etc. in Uncle Tom's Cabin,
        a book which contains "a grossly exaggerated picture of
        the horrors of slavery." Writer quotes Lewis Clarke as
        saying that the novel was commissioned by Gamaliel Bailey.

7   DAY, KATHERINE SEYMOUR. "Harriet Beecher Stowe," Lincoln
        Herald, XLVIII (June), pp. 15-18.
        A short biography of Harriet Beecher Stowe by a member
        of the family.

8   DORSON, RICHARD M. Jonathan Draws the Long Bow. Cambridge,
        Mass.: Harvard University Press, pp. 218-21.
        A discussion of Harriet Beecher Stowe's literary and
        oral transmission of folk tales in the Oldtown and Orr's
        Island books.

9   DRUMMOND, ANDREW L. "New England Puritanism in Fiction,"
        London Quarterly and Holborn Review, CLXXI (January),
        pp. 19-33.
        Pages 21-29 deal with Harriet Beecher Stowe, primarily
        the New England novels, which are discussed in terms of
        the theological controversies they present. They are
        "accurate in portrayal" of New England life and "free
        from excessive sentimentality."

1946

10   FORSTER, T. HENRY. "America's Most Famous Book," Book
        Collector's Packet, IV (no. v), pp. 5-7.
            Describes the author's collection of Stowiana, including
        various early editions of Uncle Tom's Cabin and related
        works.

11   GYSIN, BYRON. To Master--A Long Good Night: The Story of
        Uncle Tom, a Historical Narrative. New York: Creative
        Age Press.
            A biography of Josiah Henson and a discussion of the
        development and meaning of Uncle Tom as an American symbol.

12   LEE, WALLACE, et al. "Is Uncle Tom's Cabin Anti-Negro?"
        Negro Digest, IV (January), pp. 68-72.
            Presents the results of a survey showing that Uncle Tom's
        Cabin is generally felt to be anti-Negro by Negroes, pro-
        Negro by whites. A condensation of John Mason Brown's de-
        fense of the novel and play (1945.B1) is included and an
        essay by Horace Cayton commenting on the inadequacy of the
        racial stereotype. No clear distinction is made between
        Harriet Beecher Stowe's novel and the play.

13   McMURTY, R. GERALD. "The Influence of the Stowe Book on the
        Popular Music of the Civil War Period," Lincoln Herald,
        XLVIII (June), pp. 38-39.
            Lists seven songs derived from Uncle Tom's Cabin, all
        laments for Eva. Lyrics included.

14   NEWMAN, RALPH G. "Uncle Tom's Cabin," Lincoln Herald, XLVIII
        (June), pp. 23-25.
            List of the early editions of Uncle Tom's Cabin and
        related bibliographical data.

1947 A BOOKS - NONE

1947 B SHORTER WRITINGS

1   BIRDOFF, HARRY. The World's Greatest Hit--Uncle Tom's Cabin.
        New York: S. F. Vanni.
            An informal history of the "Tom" plays in America.
        Chapter I contains a short biographical sketch of Harriet
        Beecher Stowe and a discussion of the novel and its back-
        ground.

2   BULLARD, F. L. "Scenes from Uncle Tom's Cabin; Enlightening
        Comments on Abraham Lincoln and Harriet Beecher Stowe,"
        Hobbies, LI (February), pp. 97-99.

Description of an old glass depicting scenes from <u>Uncle Tom's Cabin</u> is followed by discussion of Harriet Beecher Stowe's tenure as a columnist for the <u>Independent</u> and her relationship with Lincoln. <u>See</u> 1946.B2.

3 BUSHWELL, G. H. "Soiled Brown Paper," <u>From Papyrus to Print</u>. London: Grafton & Co., pp. 185-89.
Biographical sketch of Harriet Beecher Stowe and description of the writing and popularity of <u>Uncle Tom's Cabin</u> by a British bibliographer.

4 MOTT, FRANK LUTHER. <u>Golden Multitudes: The Story of Best Sellers in the United States</u>. New York: The Macmillan Company, pp. 114-122.
The book opens with the "God wrote it" anecdote about Harriet Beecher Stowe. Mott later describes the writing, first publication, and early success of <u>Uncle Tom's Cabin</u>.

5 NEVINS, ALLAN. <u>The Ordeal of the Union</u>, I. New York: Charles Scribner's Sons, pp. 404-11.
A full discussion of <u>Uncle Tom's Cabin</u> and its "almost miraculous" success. Its moral qualities allowed it to be read where fiction was ordinarily forbidden. Its chief fault was idealization of the Negro character, which led to false expectations and subsequent disappointments in the Reconstruction period.

<u>1948 A BOOKS</u>

1 JACKSON, PHYLLIS WYNNE. <u>The Story of Harriet Beecher Stowe, Victorian Cinderella</u>. New York: Holiday House.
Juvenile biography of Harriet Beecher Stowe.

<u>1948 B SHORTER WRITINGS</u>

1 ANON. "Just Growed Again: Uncle Tom's Cabin," <u>Newsweek</u>, XXXI (June 14), p. 98.
A comment inspired by the Modern Library edition: the tale is as dramatic today as it was ninety-seven years ago.

2 ANON. "Uncle Tom's Effect on a Contemporary Reader," <u>Illinois State History Journal</u>, XLI (Summer), p. 305.
A paragraph quoted from the Alton, Illinois <u>Presbytery Reporter</u>, III (September 1, 1852), p. 20. "It would take fifty fugitive slave bills to counteract the influence" of this work.

1948

3   BAKER, CARLOS. Literary History of the United States, I.
      Edited by Robert Spiller, et al. New York: The Macmillan
      Company, pp. 843-44.
         Discusses Harriet Beecher Stowe's success as a local
      color novelist whose weaknesses were also those of the
      tradition. Reprinted in later editions.

4   COWIE, ALEXANDER. "Harriet Beecher Stowe," The Rise of the
      American Novel. New York: American Book Company, pp. 447-
      463.
         A discussion of each of the major and several of the
      lesser novels and a critical summary of Harriet Beecher
      Stowe's literary virtues and faults. Her best writing
      contains the energy of her New England past, but her craft
      and command of structure are weak. The later works are
      placed in the context of popular fiction of the period.

5   _____. "Victorian Cinderella," American Literature, XX (No-
      vember), pp. 348-50.
         Review of the Jackson biography (1948.A1). The book in
      question is not designed for scholars, but is a "human
      document" of particular interest to teenagers.

6   FOSTER, C. H. "The Genesis of Harriet Beecher Stowe's The
      Minister's Wooing," New England Quarterly, XXI (December),
      pp. 493-517.
         Traces Harriet Beecher Stowe's disillusionment with
      Calvinism back at least to the time of her English tour
      and her first sight of the ruins left by Cromwell. Dis-
      cusses the impact upon Harriet Beecher Stowe of Catharine
      Beecher's religious development and suggests other bio-
      graphical sources for the 1859 novel. (See 1954.A1).

7   HARROD, HAZEL. "Correspondence of Harriet Beecher Stowe and
      Elizabeth Barrett Browning," Texas University Studies in
      English, XXVII (June), pp. 28-34.
         A letter from Harriet Beecher Stowe to the English poet,
      discussing spiritualism, reported communications between a
      friend and Harriet's dead son, Henry; contains also a
      religious poem by Harriet Beecher Stowe.

8   JOHNSON, THOMAS H. "Harriet Beecher Stowe," Literary History
      of the United States, III. Edited by Robert Spiller, et
      al. New York: The Macmillan Company, pp. 736-38.
         Bibliography of writings by and about Harriet Beecher
      Stowe. Revised and updated in later editions.

9   WHICHER, GEORGE. Literary History of the United States, I.
         Edited by Robert Spiller, et al. New York: The Macmillan
         Company, pp. 581-86.
            A generally unsympathetic biographical and critical
         comment. The Minister's Wooing is useful for its "masterly
         revelation of the springs of Puritan character," and Old-
         town Folks merits attention, but Uncle Tom's Cabin is im-
         portant for its social effects rather than its artistic
         qualities and Dred is a failure.

10   WILSON, EDMUND. "'No! No! No! My Soul Ain't Yours, Mas'r!'"
         New Yorker, XXIV (November 27), pp. 134ff.
            Uncle Tom's Cabin is a national, not a sectional book,
         containing generous emotion and a grasp of a complex
         social situation "not unworthy to be compared" with that
         of Shaw or E. M. Forster. Ideas developed at greater
         length in 1955.B8 and 1962.B5.

1949 A BOOKS

1   WIDDEMER, MABEL CLELAND. Harriet Beecher Stowe--Connecticut
         Girl. Indianapolis & New York: Bobbs-Merrill, Co., Inc.
            A story of Harriet Beecher Stowe's childhood, told for
         young children.

1949 B SHORTER WRITINGS

1   BALDWIN, JAMES. "Everybody's Protest Novel," Partisan Review,
         XVI (June), pp. 578-85.
            A widely discussed and quoted article. Uncle Tom's
         Cabin, "a very bad novel," is activated by the terror of
         damnation, with its source in medieval morality. Harriet
         Beecher Stowe could embrace blacks only by purifying them,
         casting out humanity and sex. Baldwin links the book with
         all "protest novels," including Native Son, which inevi-
         tably fail because they elevate category over individuality
         and reject life.

2   SEILER, GRACE. "Harriet Beecher Stowe," College English, XI
         (December), pp. 127-37.
            Standard biographical sketch.

3   WILLIAMS, BEN AMES, ed. A Diary from Dixie by Mary B. Chesnut.
         Boston: Houghton, Mifflin & Company, Passim.
            Mrs. Chesnut's diary, written in 1862, contains numerous
         references to Harriet Beecher Stowe and Uncle Tom, none

clearly opposed to or approving of the novel. She notes
especially the sexual consequences of the system and connects them with Harriet Beecher Stowe's observations:
"Mrs. Stowe did not hit the sorest spot. She makes Legree
a bachelor." (A heavily abridged version of the diary was
published in 1905 and later reprinted. It contains fewer
references to Harriet Beecher Stowe.)

1950 A BOOKS - NONE

1950 B SHORTER WRITINGS

1   ANDREWS, KENNETH R. Nook Farm--Mark Twain's Hartford Circle.
        Cambridge, Mass.: Harvard University Press.
          The organization, growth, and dissolution of the Hartford
        literary community, 1851-1918. Much attention is paid to
        Harriet Beecher Stowe throughout, with separate sections
        on her character, her religious convictions, her attitude
        toward feminism and contemporary society, her literary
        achievements, and her family relationships during this
        period. Andrews feels that the novels of the Hartford
        period are filled with a nostalgia that turns them into
        myth.

2   HART, JAMES D. The Popular Book: A History of America's
        Literary Taste. New York: Oxford University Press,
        pp. 110-112.
          Cites evidence of the immense contemporary popularity of
        Uncle Tom's Cabin.

3   IGLESIAS, A. "Classic Blend in Literature," Saturday Review
        of Literature, XXXIII (January 14), p. 6.
          Uncle Tom's Cabin is an example of the propaganda novel
        that arose spontaneously from the author's religious
        nature and human sympathies.

4   NYE, RUSSEL B. "Eliza Crossing the Ice: A Reappraisal of
        Sources," Bulletin of the Historical and Philosophical
        Society of Ohio (April), pp. 105-112.
          Suggests that the source of the ice-crossing incident
        was an item from the Salem, Ohio Bugle, reprinted in A
        Friend of Youth, edited by Margaret Bailey; questions
        Forrest Wilson's attribution of the story to Rankin.

1951 A BOOKS - NONE

1951 B SHORTER WRITINGS

1   ANGLE, PAUL M. "<u>Uncle Tom's Cabin</u> 100th Anniversary Exhibit,"
       <u>Chicago History</u>, II (Summer), pp. 353-64.
            Brief description of the contents of the <u>Uncle Tom's</u>
       <u>Cabin</u> centenary exhibit: music, theater programs, early
       editions, etc.

2   DEMPSEY, DAVID. "Uncle Tom, Centenarian," <u>New York Times</u>
       <u>Magazine</u> (June 3), pp. 55-56.
            General history of the writing and popular impact of
       <u>Uncle Tom's Cabin</u>.

3   QUINN, ARTHUR HOBSON. <u>The Literature of the American People</u>.
       New York: Appleton-Century-Crofts, pp. 460-61, 640-41.
            For <u>Uncle Tom's Cabin</u>, Harriet Beecher Stowe "chose
       exceptionally high examples of the Negro race and unusually
       low specimens of the white race." <u>Dred</u> has been completely
       forgotten, and <u>Oldtown Folks</u>, "slow-paced, episodical" is
       an example of the "Dorfgeschicte of an age of sentiment--
       now outmoded."

4   WESTBROOK, PERCY D. <u>Acres of Flint: Writers of Rural New</u>
       <u>England, 1870-1900</u>. Washington, D. C.: Scarecrow Press,
       pp. 21-26.
            Discussion of the New England novels which, despite their
       "excrescence of trashiness and endless arguments on theo-
       logical subjects" are built on a solid basis of realism.
       The influence of Scott is noted, as well as Harriet
       Beecher Stowe's success in catching the rhythms and
       Biblical allusions of Down-East speech.

5   WOODWARD, WILLIAM E. <u>Years of Madness</u>. New York: G. P. Put-
       nam's Sons, pp. 13-14.
            Comment on the popularity of <u>Uncle Tom's Cabin</u> in the
       pre-war period.

1952 A BOOKS

1   JORGENSON, CHESTER E. <u>Uncle Tom's Cabin as Book and Legend</u>:
       <u>A Guide to an Exhibition</u>. Detroit: The Friends of the
       Detroit Public Library, Inc.
            Contains a chronology of Harriet Beecher Stowe's life
       and a descriptive bibliography of some editions of <u>Uncle</u>
       <u>Tom's Cabin</u>, gathered for the centennial exhibit; lists
       letters and documents having to do with slavery and
       "Uncle Tomism," early responses to the novel and reviews

of it, a selection of Harriet Beecher Stowe letters, miscellaneous items (cartoons, posters, etc.) mentioning the book, and includes a checklist of scholarship on the work. In his foreword, Jorgenson defends <u>Uncle Tom's Cabin</u> as "America's prime narrative of an inner war that could be resolved only on fields of death," and calls Harriet Beecher Stowe "the only American woman who made a Myth." "Like Emerson and Thoreau her sense of art was the organic."

1952 B SHORTER WRITINGS

1   HUGHES, LANGSTON. "Introduction," <u>Uncle Tom's Cabin</u>. New York: Dodd, Mead & Company.
      Three page essay notes the book's power and its place as "the most cussed and discussed book of its time." Hughes also wrote informative captions for the sixteen illustrations reproduced from previous editions of the novel.

2   LANDON, FRED. "When <u>Uncle Tom's Cabin</u> Came to Canada," <u>Ontario History</u>, XLIV (January), pp. 1-5.
      Early sales and publishing information on <u>Uncle Tom's Cabin</u>. Publication of the book coincided with the formation of the anti-slavery society in Ontario and with the widespread immigration of Negroes following passage of the Fugitive Slave law; it thus affected Canadian sentiments toward the Northern cause before and during the war.

3   MELCHER, F. G. "America's Number One Best Seller Reaches a Centenary: Uncle Tom's Cabin," <u>Publisher's Weekly</u>, CLXI (March 15), p. 1290.
      A centenary note on the commercial success of <u>Uncle Tom's Cabin</u>.

4   SHERMAN, DAVID E. and ROSEMARIE REDLICH. <u>Literary America: A Chronicle of American Writers from 1607-1952 with 173 Photographs of the American Scenes that Inspired Them</u>. New York: Dodd, Mead, & Company, pp. 56-57.
      A brief text describing the work of Harriet Beecher Stowe, with several pictures of locales similar to those mentioned in her stories.

5   WAGENKNECHT, EDWARD. <u>Cavalcade of the American Novel</u>. New York: Henry Holt & Company, pp. 91-102.
      A discussion of the novels of Harriet Beecher Stowe, including <u>The Minister's Wooing</u>, <u>My Wife and I</u>, and <u>Agnes of</u>

Sorrento. In her books, the author touched on universal problems. She "lived in a world of confusion, fatigue, and cloudy abstraction....But she had the root of the matter in her, as a writer and as a woman." A useful bibliography is included, pp. 515-16.

6   WYMAN, MARGARET. "Harriet Beecher Stowe's Topical Novel on Woman Suffrage," New England Quarterly, XXV (Summer), pp. 383-90.
     Despite Harriet Beecher Stowe's early sympathy for suffrage, My Wife and I contains satirical portraits of suffrage leaders, probably because of the public emergence of Victoria Woodhull, who belied the moral advantages of enfranchising women.

1953 A BOOKS - NONE

1953 B SHORTER WRITINGS

1   AUSTIN, JAMES C. "Harriet Beecher Stowe," Fields of the Atlantic Monthly: Letters to An Editor, 1861-1870. San Marino, California: Huntington Library, pp. 266-99.
     A detailed discussion of Harriet Beecher Stowe's relationship with Fields and the Atlantic in the 1860's, with many letters printed in full. Harriet Beecher Stowe was the "least dignified" and most demanding of the early contributors: her work was full of errors of grammar and fact; she made salary demands and failed to produce copy on time. Nonetheless, she was, next to Longfellow, the most popular writer on the magazine.

2   BROWN, KARL. The Cup of Trembling. New York: Duell, Sloan & Pearce. Boston: Little, Brown and Company.
     Novel based on the life of Fred Stowe, with much discussion of Harriet Beecher Stowe, her immediate family, and her relations with Henry Ward Beecher. Fred's disappearance is attributed in part to his growing suspicion that his late brother Henry had been the child of his uncle.

3   GRAFF, MARY B. Mandarin on the St. John. Gainesville: University of Florida Press, pp. 44-79.
     Description of the life of the Stowe's in their Mandarin home (1867-84) and the effect of their residence on the Florida town.

1953

4   JACKSON, F. H.   "Uncle Tom's Cabin in Italy," _Symposium_, VII
     (November), pp. 232-32.
        The _Risorgimento_ provided a responsive environment for
     Uncle Tom's Cabin, as can be seen by the large number of
     contemporary translations, public debate over the issues,
     and the impact of the play on the Italian theater.   Adverse
     reactions came mainly from the Catholic press.   Biblio-
     graphical footnotes list articles in Italian, translations,
     etc.

5   JAFFE, ADRIAN.   "Uncle Tom in the Penal Colony: Heine's View
     of _Uncle Tom's Cabin_," _American German Review_, XIX
     (February), pp. 5-6.
        Heine responded to the "intuitive" religion of Tom ac-
     cording to his own needs, rather than to the social or
     literary aspects of the novel.   Jaffe compares Heine's
     comments on Tom's final state with Kafka's "In the Penal
     Colony."

6   NICHOLAS, H. G.   "Uncle Tom's Cabin, 1852-1952," _American
     Heritage_, IV (Winter), pp. 20-23, 72.
        A short summary of the writing of _Uncle Tom's Cabin_ and
     its popular and political impact, suggesting that, while
     not directly affecting legislation, "it filled the vacuum
     of idealism created by the Compromise of 1850."

7   SHEPPERSON, GEORGE.   "Harriet Beecher Stowe and Scotland,
     1852-53," _Scottish Historical Review_, XXXII (April),
     pp. 40-46.
        Discusses the background and effect of Harriet Beecher
     Stowe's first visit to Scotland, and her position on the
     eviction issue.   Her visit to Scotland and her near-
     recognition by the Queen made the anti-slavery cause
     respectable abroad and in America.

8   STOVALL, FLOYD.   "The Decline of Romantic Idealism, 1855-1871,"
     Transitions in American Literary History.   Edited by
     H. H. Clark.   Durham: Duke University Press, pp. 348-49.
        Author praises Harriet Beecher Stowe's local color works
     and compares them to the writings of George Eliot.

9   SUCKOW, RUTH.   "An Almost Lost American Classic," _College
     English_, XIV (March), pp. 314-25.
        Urges re-evaluation of _Oldtown Folks_, a "seminal novel
     of American life," and examines the characters in it as
     embodiments of continuing cultural dilemmas.

10   TROUGHTON, M.   "Eminent Victorians," <u>Contemporary Review</u>,
      CLXXXIII (February), pp. 97-101.
      A very brief comment on Harriet Beecher Stowe.

11   WEISERT, J. J.   "Lewis N. Dembitz and Onkel Toms Hütte,"
      <u>American German Review</u>, XIX (February), pp. 7-8.
      Identifies Dembitz as the translator of the first of
      three German-American versions of <u>Uncle Tom's Cabin</u>.

12   WINTERICH, J. T.   "Bookmarks: Centennial of Uncle Tom's
      Cabin," <u>Saturday Review of Literature</u>, XXXVI (February 28),
      p. 23.
      Comments on some of the centenary observations across
      the country.

1954 A BOOKS

1   FOSTER, CHARLES H.   <u>The Rungless Ladder: Harriet Beecher Stowe
     and New England Puritanism</u>.   Durham, N. C.: Duke University
     Press.
     A critical study of the novels of Harriet Beecher Stowe
     and their relationship to the author's religious heritage.
     Harriet Beecher Stowe was an "Edwardsean Calvinist" whose
     books represent symbolic equivalents of her theological
     struggles. The Oldtown books are her best works; they
     embody, as do all her novels, "New England doubleness,"
     i.e., a regional mixture of Puritan seriousness and Yankee
     humor. Foster sees Harriet Beecher Stowe as more within
     the New England tradition than Hawthorne. She speaks in
     the voice of the nineteenth-century romantics and gives
     an accurate sense of the complex past. <u>Dred</u> and <u>Uncle
     Tom's Cabin</u> are also placed within this religious-regional
     context. <u>See</u> 1948.B6 for chapter on <u>The Minister's Wooing</u>.

1954 B SHORTER WRITINGS

1   CUNLIFFE, MARCUS.   <u>The Literature of the United States</u>.   Balti-
     more: Penguin Books, pp. 176-77.
     <u>Uncle Tom's Cabin</u> is a highly effective novel; in the
     later books, Harriet Beecher Stowe's knowledge of the
     Puritan heritage rivals that of Hawthorne. The local
     color stories are strong in description and analysis.

2   HUBBELL, JAY B.   <u>The South in American Literature</u>.   Durham,
     N. C.: Duke University Press, pp. 385-93, 962.
     Description of Harriet Beecher Stowe's background and of

1954

the writing of <u>Uncle Tom's Cabin</u>. A short critical evalua-
tion of the novel--"melodrama, seasoned with romance and
propaganda"--is followed by a summary of critical reactions
in Southern periodicals and brief comments on subsequent
literary influence. Bibliography included.

3   LEARY, LEWIS. <u>Articles in American Literature</u>. Durham, N. C.:
Duke University Press, pp. 282-83.
Articles about Harriet Beecher Stowe.

4   NICHOLAS, H. G. "Uncle Tom's Cabin, 1852-1952," <u>Georgia
Review</u>, VIII (Summer), pp. 140-48.
Reprint of 1953.B6.

5   NOEL, MARY. <u>Villains Galore; the Hey-day of the Popular Story
Weekly</u>. New York: Macmillan & Company, pp. 302-03.
Notes the outraged reaction of the lurid "story-papers"
to the Stowe-Byron scandal in 1869, citing especially the
opinions of the <u>Ledger</u> and the <u>New York Weekly</u>.

6   ROPPOLO, J. P. "Uncle Tom in New Orleans: Three Lost Plays,"
<u>New England Quarterly</u>, XXVII (June), pp. 213-26.
Describes three plays which used the Uncle Tom character
to attack Harriet Beecher Stowe and suggests that their
failure resulted from missing the point of the novel.

<u>1955 A BOOKS - NONE</u>

<u>1955 B SHORTER WRITINGS</u>

1   BANNING, M. C. "<u>Uncle Tom's Cabin</u> by Harriet Beecher Stowe,"
<u>Georgia Review</u>, IX (Winter), pp. 461-65.
Critic attributes the success of <u>Uncle Tom's Cabin</u>,
still a powerful story, to its "unembarrassed intensity of
purpose" and notes its "astonishingly modern" portrayal of
characters and situation.

2   BLOTNER, JOSEPH L. "Harriet Beecher Stowe and the Civil War,"
<u>The Political Novel</u>. Garden City, N. Y.: Doubleday &
Company, Inc.
Though "artistically" the novel is very bad, with pages
peopled by cardboard figures, <u>Uncle Tom's Cabin</u> is "a
prime example of the novel as political instrument."

3   DAVIS, R. B. "The Rungless Ladder," <u>American Literature</u>,
XXVII (May), pp. 280-82.
Review of Foster book. The work makes stimulating

reading, but Davis feels that Foster rides too hard his
thesis that New England Puritanism accounts for everything
significant in the work of Harriet Beecher Stowe.

4   GEBO, DORA R. "Uncle Tom's Cabin and Biblical Ideas of Free-
     dom and Slavery," Negro History Bulletin, XIX (October),
     19ff.
         Discusses Harriet Beecher Stowe's use of scriptural
     passages to support the narrative of Uncle Tom's Cabin.
     Brief bibliography.

5   LEARY, LEWIS. "The Rungless Ladder," Saturday Review of
     Literature, XXXVIII (March 26), p. 19.
         A short review of the Foster study. Although we read
     the regional novels now out of literary curiosity rather
     than taste, Foster does convince us to consider Harriet
     Beecher Stowe as a representative of changing New England
     values.

6   MOODY, RICHARD. "Uncle Tom, the Theatre, and Mrs. Stowe,"
     American Heritage, VI (October), pp. 29-33, 102-03.
         A brief illustrated history of some nineteenth-century
     theatrical versions of Uncle Tom's Cabin, including an
     excerpt from an Harriet Beecher Stowe letter refusing Asa
     Hutchinson permission to dramatize the book, and the story
     of her alleged visit to a production of the play in 1854.

7   SILLEN, SAMUEL. Women Against Slavery. New York: Masses &
     Mainstream, Inc., pp. 76-82.
         Short biographical sketch of Harriet Beecher Stowe and
     comments on the success of Uncle Tom's Cabin as aboli-
     tionist literature.

8   WILSON, EDMUND. "Books: Harriet Beecher Stowe," New Yorker,
     XXXI (September 10), pp. 137ff.
         A review of the Foster book. Wilson laments the lack of
     a critical biography of this "complex personality" and
     "considerable writer." He emphasizes the importance of
     Harriet Beecher Stowe as a chronicler of religious history
     who dramatized the nineteenth-century crisis in Calvinist
     thought and points out her weaknesses as a creator of
     fiction as well as her mimetic gifts. Briefly discussed
     also are the Burr figure in her fiction, the "brilliant
     book on the Byrons," and Poganuc People, the best novel
     after Uncle Tom's Cabin. Many of the same points are made
     by Wilson in Patriotic Gore (1962.B5).

1956

<u>1956 A BOOKS</u>

  1   FURNAS, J. C. <u>Goodbye to Uncle Tom</u>. New York: William Sloane
        Associates.
          A discussion of the "illiberal" assumptions about race
        underlying <u>Uncle Tom's Cabin</u> and pervading American cul-
        ture. By effectively voicing the popular racist propa-
        ganda of her time, Harriet Beecher Stowe instilled stereo-
        types and prejudices into the minds of several generations
        of readers and is thus in large part responsible for
        America's failure to solve "the Negro problem." Furnas
        analyzes Harriet Beecher Stowe's assumptions and tests
        them against informed nineteenth- and twentieth-century
        opinion. Pages 1-64 are devoted to a discussion of
        Harriet Beecher Stowe (irresponsible, lazy-minded, possessed
        of a minor degree of intelligence), <u>Uncle Tom's Cabin</u>, and
        <u>Dred</u>, but references to the author and her works fill the
        book.

  2   BOREHAM, F. W. <u>The Gospel of Uncle Tom's Cabin</u>. London:
        Epworth Press.
          A series of sermons, explicating for the mid-twentieth
        century layman, the spiritual example set by Uncle Tom and
        illustrated by his behavior.

<u>1956 B SHORTER WRITINGS</u>

  1   BROOKS, VAN WYCK and OTTO L. BETTMANN. "Harriet Beecher Stowe,"
        <u>Our Literary Heritage; A Pictorial History of the Writer in</u>
        <u>America</u>. New York: E. P. Dutton & Company, Inc., pp. 88-
        89.
          An illustrated biographical sketch.

  2   BUTCHER, MARGARET JUST. <u>The Negro in American Culture</u>. New
        York: Alfred A. Knopf, pp. 152-55.
          <u>Uncle Tom's Cabin</u> had a "human authenticity" which could
        not be offset by any single piece of Southern propaganda.
        In its sharp contrasts, it exemplifies the problems of
        writing about the Negro; a more balanced picture is pro-
        vided in the artistically superior <u>Dred</u>.

  3   CADY, EDWIN H. <u>The Road to Realism: The Early Years of</u>
        <u>William Dean Howells, 1837-1885</u>. Syracues: Syracuse Uni-
        versity Press, pp. 136-37.
          Describes Howells's role in and apparent feelings about
        the publication of the Byron article in the <u>Atlantic</u>
        <u>Monthly</u>.

4   CHASE, RICHARD. "Adam Fallen and Unfallen," Commentary, XXI
     (March), p. 283.
        A review of The Rungless Ladder and The American Adam,
     by R. W. B. Lewis. Chase finds the "dialectical view of
     literary history" represented by the two books conservative
     and conventional. The Foster book is competent, but it
     fails to offer a general view of Harriet Beecher Stowe's
     relation to American literature.

5   DOWNS, ROBERT. "Harriet Beecher Stowe: Crusader for the
     Lowly," Books That Changed the World. Chicago: American
     Library Association, pp. 76-85.
        A description of the background and popular success of
     Uncle Tom's Cabin.

6   FURNAS, J. C. "Goodbye to Uncle Tom," Saturday Review of
     Literature, XXXIX (May 26), pp. 12-13, 28-30.
        Excerpt from Furnas's book (1956.A1).

7   _____. Reply with rejoinder by P. Pickrel to review of Good-
     bye to Uncle Tom. Harper's, CCXIII (September), pp. 6, 10.
        Furnas defends his book and Pickrel defends his review
     (1956.B10), the latter pointing out that Furnas has still
     failed to come to terms with the question of moral respon-
     sibility and where it lies.

8   GANNETT, LEWIS. "Goodbye to Uncle Tom," New York Herald
     Tribune (June 21).
        Review. Furnas's book is "rambling, rambunctious, and
     sometimes enlightening."

9   PAPASHVILY, HELEN W. All the Happy Endings: A Study of the
     Domestic Novel in America, the Women who Wrote It, the
     Women wo Read It, in the Nineteenth-Century. New York:
     Harper & Row, pp. 64-74. (Reprinted by Kennikat Press,
     1972).
        Papashvily describes the domestic conditions behind
     Harriet Beecher Stowe's writing of Uncle Tom's Cabin, and
     sees the book as a domestic novel with an "especial"
     message to women, an important segment of the "lowly."
     The book "sounded the death knell of the master."
     Responses of other nineteenth-century women writers are
     noted.

10   PICKREL, P. "Goodbye to Uncle Tom," Harper's, CCXXXI (July),
     p. 88.
        Review of Furnas's book. "Furnas' condescension [to
     Harriet Beecher Stowe] is quite misplaced," and he

1956

"manhandles quotations from her work." His framework re-
grettably weakens a possibly valuable book.

1957 A BOOKS - NONE

1957 B SHORTER WRITINGS

1   KNIGHT, G. WILSON. Lord Byron's Marriage: The Evidence of
     Asterisks. London: Routledge and Kegan Paul, pp. 113-115.
     The contents of the Harriet Beecher Stowe articles on
     Byron generally agree with the known views of Lady Byron.
     Knight suggests that the publication of the pornographic
     "Don Leon" poems in 1865-66 may have indirectly prompted
     Harriet Beecher Stowe's defense.

2   ROPPOLO, J. P. "Harriet Beecher Stowe and New Orleans: A
     Study in Hate," New England Quarterly, XXX (Summer),
     pp. 346-62.
     The published attacks on Harriet Beecher Stowe in New
     Orleans in the 1850's are unequaled in bitterness and
     vituperation. Roppolo traces the growth of this sentiment
     from 1852 to its disappearance in the 1950's.

3   SMITH, H. "Feminism and the Household Novel," Saturday Review
     of Literature, XL (March 30), p. 22.
     Notes that Harriet Beecher Stowe is the only one of the
     many female writers of the 1850's and 1860's widely read
     in the mid-twentieth century.

4   STONE, HARRY. "Charles Dickens and Harriet Beecher Stowe,"
     Nineteenth Century Fiction, XII (December), pp. 198-202.
     Dickens's growing dissatisfaction with Harriet Beecher
     Stowe and her work is traced from his initial reserved
     praise of Uncle Tom's Cabin in 1852 (1852.B40), to his
     defensiveness in the face of Denham's scorn of his pub-
     lished review, to his final disgust with Harriet Beecher
     Stowe's revelations about Byron.

5   TROUGHTON, MARION. "Americans in Britain," Contemporary
     Review, CCIV (December), pp. 338-42.
     A brief reference to Harriet Beecher Stowe's comments on
     England and Scotland in Sunny Memories of Foreign Lands.

6   WEISERT, J. J. "Mrs. Stowe First Writes of Kentucky for Ken-
     tuckians," Papers of the Bibliographical Society of America,
     LI (IV Quarter), pp. 340-41.

Description of an early Harriet Beecher Stowe story, published in Lexington, Kentucky in 1839, but omitted from The Mayflower.

1958 A BOOKS - NONE

1958 B SHORTER WRITINGS

1   DUVALL, SEVERN. "W. G. Simms' Review of Mrs. Stowe," American Literature, XXX (March), pp. 107-17.
        Duvall suggests that the unsigned review of A Key to Uncle Tom's Cabin in the Southern Quarterly Review (1853.B29) is by Simms, on the grounds that it is based on Simms's previously articulated theories of literature, that it is similar in its anti-feminism to his attack on Harriet Martineau, and that it often echoes his essay "The Morals of Slavery."

2   HALE, NANCY. "What God Was Writing," Texas Quarterly, I (Spring), pp. 35-40.
        Uncle Tom's Cabin is about Harriet Beecher Stowe's inner life; it is a record of the deliverance of enslaved emotions into consciousness. This "psychological" reading of the novel identifies Topsy as the shadow or id, Miss Ophelia as the "white principle of consciousness," and Tom as God.

3   HEWELL-THAYER, HARVERY W. American Literature as Viewed in Germany, 1818-1861. Chapel Hill: University of North Carolina Press, pp. 57-58.
        Summarizes the German critical reaction to Uncle Tom's Cabin, Dred, and The Minister's Wooing.

4   JACKSON, F. H. "An Italian Uncle Tom's Cabin," Italica, XXXV (March), pp. 38-42.
        Description of a play by Giovanni Sabbatini, "Gli Spazzacamini della Valle d'Aosta," apparently inspired by Uncle Tom's Cabin.

5   KRAMER, MAURICE I. "The Fable of Endurance: A Study of the American Novel between Hawthorne and Howells." Ph.D. dissertation. Harvard University, pp. 100-130.
        Part of a chapter is devoted to close examination of Harriet Beecher Stowe's novels, including the New England books, the society stories, and Agnes of Sorrento. In her works she favors "allegorical techniques of characterization" and often in the later ones divorces idealism from

1958

intellect. Her New York novels exhibit sentimentality
turned to satire, and "mark a step toward realism" in
their "recognition of the serious fictional possibilities
of the commonplace."

6   NICHOLS, CHARLES. "The Origins of Uncle Tom's Cabin," Phylon,
     XIX (Fall), pp. 328-34.
          Uncle Tom's Cabin is primarily a "derivative piece of
     hack work," which nevertheless served to awaken the public.
     Harriet Beecher Stowe deals in stereotypes, but there is
     in this a "curious ambivalence" which suggests awe. Some
     sources of the novel are discussed. Dred paved the way for
     later novels of Southern life.

7   PEASE, WILLIAM H. and JANE H. "Uncle Tom and Clayton: Fact,
     Fiction, and Mystery," Ontario History, L (Spring),
     pp. 61-73.
          Recounts and discusses the histories of Josiah Henson
     and William King, the latter an acknowledged source of the
     Edward Clayton figure in Dred.

8   VAN WHY, JOSEPH S. "A Brief Description of the Stowe-Beecher-
     Hooker-Seymour-Day Foundation," Trinity College Library
     Gazette (December), pp. 25ff.
          A description of the manuscripts, portraits, and first
     editions owned by the Foundation, pointing out incidentally
     that the New England novels of Harriet Beecher Stowe are
     works meriting the attention of the student of American
     literature.

9   _____. "Index of A.L.S.'s by Harriet Beecher Stowe Which
     Belong to the Stowe...Day Foundation," Bulletin of the
     Stowe...Day Foundation, I (May), pp. 4-15.
          A list of seventy-nine Harriet Beecher Stowe letters,
     most unpublished and hitherto unexamined by Harriet
     Beecher Stowe biographers.

1959 A BOOKS - NONE

1959 B SHORTER WRITINGS

1   BAENDER, PAUL. "Mark Twain and the Byron Scandal," American
     Literature, XXX (January), pp. 467-85.
          Baender contends that six unsigned editorials in the
     Buffalo Express defending the Stowe article were written
     by Mark Twain, who was at the same time publishing jokes
     and writing a burlesque letter (never published) about the
     situation.

2   BEATTY, LILLIAN. "The Natural Man versus the Puritan," The
Personalist, XL (Winter), pp. 22-30.
      Compares The Minister's Wooing to The Last Puritan, the
central theme of both books being "the inadequacy of
Puritanism as a moral ideal."

3   LUDWIG, RICHARD M. "Harriet Beecher Stowe," Literary History
of the United States, Bibliography Supplement, I. New
York: The Macmillan Company, pp. 195-96.
      Writings about Harriet Beecher Stowe, 1948-1958.

4   LYNN, KENNETH. Mark Twain and Southwestern Humor. Boston:
Little, Brown & Company, pp. 107-11, 123-26, 240-41 and
passim.
      The fiction of Harriet Beecher Stowe is "an anatomy of
religious doubt that tells us much about the mind of American Protestantism in the nineteenth century." Uncle Tom,
the Black Christ figure, continued to provide a moral commentary on white America. In Uncle Tom's Cabin, the author
acutely diagnosed the moral paralysis of the South. Lynn
sees a connection between the Tom-Eva and Huck-Jim relationships, and also notes similarities between Cassy and
Roxy (Pudd'nhead Wilson).

5   NICHOLS, CHARLES. "Who Read the Slave Narratives?" Phylon,
XX (Summer), pp. 149-62.
      Little material specifically on Harriet Beecher Stowe,
but author notes that the slave narratives whetted the
appetite for and prepared readers to respond to Uncle
Tom's Cabin.

6   ROSSI, JOSEPH. "Uncle Tom's Cabin and Protestantism in Italy,"
American Quarterly, XI (Fall), pp. 416-24.
      Examines the hostility to Uncle Tom's Cabin from the
Catholic press, which distrusted the novel's Protestant
bias, and notes some responses to the attack. Includes a
list of early Italian reviews designed to supplement those
in Jackson's article (1953.B4).

1960 A BOOKS - NONE

1960 B SHORTER WRITINGS

1   BODE, CARL. The Anatomy of American Popular Culture, 1840-
1961. Berkeley and Los Angeles: University of California
Press, pp. 183-87.
      Uncle Tom's Cabin would never have achieved success

1960

without the presence of the archetypal figures of the
child and the wise old man; the timeliness of the topic
was also essential.

2   DEVANEY, SALLY G. "The Poem That Wouldn't Die," The Courant
    Magazine (September 4).
       Reports the discovery of a previously unpublished poem
    by Harriet Beecher Stowe, "Who Shall Not Fear Thee, Oh
    Lord?"

3   FIEDLER, LESLIE A. Love and Death in the American Novel.
    Cleveland: World Publishing Company, pp. 261-67.
       Uncle Tom's Cabin is "an astonishingly various and com-
    plex book" of which we remember only the characters of
    archetypal stature--Tom, Topsy, Eva. The chief pleasures
    of the book are rooted "not in the moral indignation of
    the reformer but in the more devious titillations of the
    sadist." Eva represents the substitution of sexless child
    for seductive girl as love object in Victorian literature.

4   _____. No, In Thunder. Boston: Beacon Press, pp. 9, 258,
    and passim.
       The death of the immaculate child (Eva) illustrates a
    recurrent theme of period fiction. Topsy is the "Really
    Bad Girl." Fiedler calls Uncle Tom's Cabin an "easy No,"
    but notes its influence on him in childhood.

5   MAYE, ERNEST J. "Mark Twain Meets a Lady from Finland," Mark
    Twain Journal, XI (ii), pp. 9-10, 25.
       Reports an anecdote told by Twain about the worldwide
    popularity of Harriet Beecher Stowe.

6   MURRAY, A. L. "Harriet Beecher Stowe on Racial Segregation
    in the Schools," American Quarterly, XII (Winter), pp. 518-
    19.
       A note on Harriet Beecher Stowe's attempt to start a
    "semi-segregated" school at Mandarin, Florida, in 1869,
    where black and white children could be educated in the
    same school, but at separate times or in separate rooms.

*7 POSIN, JACK A. "A Sportsman's Sketches by Turgenev versus
    Uncle Tom's Cabin by Beecher Stowe: A Study in Understate-
    ment," Comparative Literature, IX (II), pp. 455-62.
       Unlocatable. Cited in MLA, 1960, p. 356.

8   RIDGELY, J. V. "Woodcraft: Simms' First Answer to Uncle Tom's
    Cabin," American Literature, XXXI (January), pp. 421-33.
       Modifies Duvall's case (1958.B1) that Simms did not

review Uncle Tom's Cabin directly by suggesting that he
answered the book in Woodcraft, where he presents a vision
of an ordered Southern society, responsible masters and
devoted slaves.

9   VAN WHY, JOSEPH S., ed. "Letters of Harriet Beecher Stowe,"
        Bulletin of the Stowe...Day Foundation, I, ii (May).
            Various letters from Harriet Beecher Stowe, 1852-1875,
        with explanatory introductions.

1961 A BOOKS - NONE

1961 A SHORTER WRITINGS

1   BROOKS, VAN WYCK. "Introduction," Uncle Tom's Cabin, Every-
        man's Library. London: J. M. Dent & Sons Ltd. New York:
        E. P. Dutton, pp. v-viii.
            A short comment on the popularity of the novel and a
        sketch of the life of Harriet Beecher Stowe. The author
        "foresaw the Africa of our day"; the book remains "readable
        and even exciting."

2   GERSTENBERGER, DONNA and GEORGE HENDRICK. The American Novel,
        1789-1958: A Checklist of Twentieth Century Criticism.
        Denver: Alan Swallow, pp. 231-32.
            Articles about Harriet Beecher Stowe.

3   HAMBLEN, ABIGAIL ANN. "Uncle Tom and 'Nigger Jim': A Study in
        Contrasts and Similarities," Mark Twain Journal, XI (iii),
        pp. 13-17.
            Uncle Tom is the stock symbol of an oppressed race, Jim
        the colored "funny man," but both are depicted as believable
        persons in these novels and inspire devotion from the
        characters around them. Mark Twain and Harriet Beecher
        Stowe differ more in personality than in attitude.

4   JOBES, KATHERINE TAYLOR. "The Resolution of Solitude: A Study
        of Four Writers of the New England Decline." Ph.D.
        Dissertation, Yale University, pp. 6-65.
            The thematic movement of Harriet Beecher Stowe's best
        writing is toward resolving the tension between the indi-
        vidualism fostered by Puritan theology and the need for
        Christian fellowship. Harriet Beecher Stowe's power comes
        from a clear intellectual perspective and deep emotional
        involvement in theological matters. She renders psycho-
        logical states well through exposition and imagery, but
        weakens her perceptions by surrounding them with awkward

plots and conventions. Jobes writes mainly of the New
England novels and of the religious aspects of Harriet
Beecher Stowe's work.

5   LADER, LAWRENCE. The Bold Brahmins: New England's War Against
      Slavery: 1831-1863. New York: E. P. Dutton, pp. 169-73.
          A brief discussion of the origin and impact of Uncle
      Tom's Cabin. Harriet Beecher Stowe's prime accomplishment
      was convincing the great mass of people in the free states
      that God was on the side of the North.

6   LIEDEL, DONALD E. "The Anti-Slavery Novel, 1836-1861." Ph.D.
      Dissertation, University of Michigan.
          Uncle Tom's Cabin was not the first anti-slavery novel;
      it released a score of others, most of them emphasizing
      brutality and miscegenation. Dred is also discussed.

7   MANIERRE, W. R. "A Southern Response to Mrs. Stowe: Two
      Letters of John R. Thompson." Virginia Magazine of History
      and Biography, LXIX (January), pp. 83-92.
          Two letters from Thompson to G. F. Holmes expressing
      Thompson's eagerness to publish a review of Uncle Tom's
      Cabin "as hot as hell-fire, blacking and searing the repu-
      tation of the vile wretch in petticoats who could write
      such a volume." Manierre summarizes the Thompson review
      and the response to it in the Key, and notes the reviewer's
      comments on the role of women and the nature of fiction.
      The two documents contain most of the arguments splitting
      the country at the time.

8   STONE, ALBERT E. ᴊ. The Innocent Eye: Childhood in Mark
      Twain's Imagination. New Haven: Yale University Press,
      pp. 9-10.
          Harriet Beecher Stowe's comments on infant damnation in
      Oldtown Folks are cited as an example of the attitude
      toward children prevalent in Nook Farm in the 1870's.

9   TAYLOR, W. R. "Whistling in the Dark," Cavalier and Yankee.
      New York: George Braziller, pp. 299-313.
          Harriet Beecher Stowe used the conventions of the plan-
      tation novel--e.g. the traditional opposition to business
      --but she used them to attack, not defend, the Southern
      system. Legree's house is the home-become-factory, a
      parody of the old homestead. "Since she had made it clear
      from the beginning that she was examining the moral logic
      of slavery rather than its sociology, there really was no
      answer to what she had written...."

10   VAN WHY, JOSEPH. "Letters of Harriet Beecher Stowe," <u>Bulletin</u>
     <u>of the Stowe...Day Foundation</u>, I, iii (Summer), pp. 2-14.
         Some letters from Harriet Beecher Stowe to Martha and
     Rebecca Wetherill published and described. They "provide
     a key to her revolt against Calvinism and a clear statement
     of her religious beliefs."

<u>1962 A BOOKS - NONE</u>

<u>1962 B SHORTER WRITINGS</u>

1   JACOBSON, DAN. "Down the River," <u>New Statesman</u>, LXIV
     (October 12), pp. 490-91.
         Jacobson notes the power of <u>Uncle Tom's Cabin</u> and the
     author's exhilarating confidence in the flexibility of the
     novel form. The book is difficult for liberals to read,
     since they persist in hoping for easier ways to solve the
     problems raised by the novel than the ones suggested by
     Harriet Beecher Stowe.

2   LYNN, KENNETH S. "Introduction," <u>Uncle Tom's Cabin</u>. Cambridge,
     Mass.: Belknap Press of the Harvard University Press,
     pp. vii-xxviii.
         The force of this novel comes from the unification of
     sentimental convention and real issues. Harriet Beecher
     Stowe's characterizations are of "Balzacian variousness,"
     her Negroes "an amazing achievement." Her realism origi-
     nated in her rejection of Calvinism, since Romanticism,
     like Byronism, is a product of this theology. The book is
     suffused with the religion of love and the affirmation of
     feminine values. A chronology of the life of Harriet
     Beecher Stowe and a history of the text are included.

3   PACKARD, ROSALIE. "The Age for Little Eva," <u>The Spectator</u>, I
     (June 8), p. 761.
         Discussion of <u>Uncle Tom's Cabin</u> as children's literature:
     it is "well-written and never boring" with live characters;
     it should be kept out of the hands of children, however,
     because of the cruelty and pain evoked by the picture of
     racial prejudice.

4   VAN WHY, JOSEPH S. "Nook Farm," <u>Bulletin of the Stowe...Day</u>
     <u>Foundation</u>, I, iv (Summer), pp. 4-14.
         A description of Nook Farm, its inhabitants in the late
     nineteenth century, and their backgrounds, including a
     biographical sketch of Harriet Beecher Stowe.

1962

5   WILSON, EDMUND. "Harriet Beecher Stowe," <u>Patriotic Gore</u>.
     New York: Oxford University Press, pp. 3-58.
          Chapter on <u>Uncle Tom's Cabin</u> and Harriet Beecher Stowe,
     with a biographical sketch and long quotations from
     letters. The "obscure personal anguish" of Harriet Beecher
     Stowe's early married life "energized" <u>Uncle Tom's Cabin</u>,
     a book which has vital characters and "eruptive force"
     despite the author's lack of warmth and of real interest
     in literature. The New England books are verbose but in-
     telligent. The characterizations of Burr, Byron, and
     other villains derive from Harriet Beecher Stowe's con-
     tinuing struggle to reject Calvinist theology. The next
     chapter deals in part with Calvin Stowe (pp. 59-70);
     references to Harriet Beecher Stowe are found throughout.
     <u>See</u> 1948.B10, 1955.B8.

1963 A BOOKS

1   ADAMS, JOHN R. <u>Harriet Beecher Stowe</u>. TUSAS XLII. New York:
     Twayne Publishing Co.
          A critical biography with close readings of all of
     Harriet Beecher Stowe's literary work. <u>Uncle Tom's Cabin</u>,
     a work of emotional power, is an "hysterical, apocalyptic
     vision," an interruption of the predictable development of
     her talent. Her work lacks the "verbal magic and com-
     plexity of images" necessary to keep it alive, but has
     much documentary value. <u>Oldtown Folks</u> is her best book,
     the most realistic and, "in the persuasiveness of its il-
     lusions, the most imaginative." A chronology, extensive
     footnotes, and a useful bibliography are included. <u>See</u>
     1939.B1.

2   JOHNSTON, JOHANNA. <u>Runaway to Heaven: The Story of Harriet
     Beecher Stowe</u>. Garden City, N. Y.: Doubleday & Company.
          A readable popular biography of Harriet Beecher Stowe,
     deriving mainly from secondary sources. The author
     attempts to explain the contradictions of Harriet Beecher
     Stowe's character, "to present her against the background
     of her century and to trace her history in terms of the
     history of her time."

1963 B SHORTER WRITINGS

1   ABEL, DARREL. "Harriet Beecher Stowe," <u>American Literature</u>,
     <u>II: Literature of the Atlantic Culture</u>. Woodbury, N. Y.:
     Barron's Educational Series, Inc., pp. 231-47.

114

Biographical sketch of Harriet Beecher Stowe and plot summary of Uncle Tom's Cabin. The book is a series of melodramatic confrontations and repetitious debates about slavery. It has glaring faults but is a great work of popular literature. The New England stories are better.

2 ABER, M. E. "Rankin House; Stop on the Underground Railroad," Negro History Bulletin, XXVI (May), p. 253.
Description of the house in Ripley, Ohio supposedly used as the site of an incident in Uncle Tom's Cabin.

3 ALTICK, ROBERT. The Art of Literary Research. New York: W. W. Norton and Company, Inc., pp. 42-43.
A comment on Forrest Wilson's use of sources to discover that Harriet Beecher Stowe could not have been influenced by the July, 1869 Blackwood's article in the writing of her own Byron piece.

4 ANON. "God Was Her Co-Author," Newsweek, LXI (April 8), p. 96.
Review of the Johnston biography: a "painstaking and occasionally overwrought" book.

5 ANON. "Uncle Tom's Message: The Book of War and Freedom." Times Literary Supplement, IV (October), pp. 777-78.
Review of the Harvard edition of Uncle Tom's Cabin. Biographical and critical essay on Harriet Beecher Stowe, noting the general tendency to underestimate the novel and suggesting that many of the book's difficulties for modern readers arise from the intensity of Harriet Beecher Stowe's evangelical religion.

6 AXELRAD, ARTHUR. "Harriet Beecher Stowe as a New England Local-Colorist," Utah Academy Proceedings, XI (Spring), pp. 34-44.
Harriet Beecher Stowe's local color works enable us to re-create the New England character and the appearances and circumstance of New England life, all natural out-growth of the Puritan tradition.

7 DUVALL, SEVERN. "Uncle Tom's Cabin: The Sinister Side of the Patriarchy," New England Quarterly, XXXVI (March), pp. 3-22.
In Uncle Tom's Cabin and Dred, Harriet Beecher Stowe dramatizes the essential tension between patriarchal de-fenses of slavery and its legal definition through de-piction of domestic separation and miscegenation. Southern answers to the novel were legalistic, missed the point, and

1963

betrayed a persistent and fearful anti-feminism. Responses
to the problems first exposed by Harriet Beecher Stowe are
still appearing.

8   EMIG, JANET A. "The Flower in the Cleft: The Writings of
     Harriet Beecher Stowe," Bulletin of the Historical and
     Philosophical Society of Ohio, XXI (October), pp. 223-38.
        A single theme unites the fictional and non-fictional
     works of Harriet Beecher Stowe: her effort to reproduce
     the family and images of her childhood, as they are
     described in her vaious memoirs. The charming sprite,
     the dark and fair brothers, the wife-mother-goddess figure
     all recur in the books, and betray her unconscious concerns.

9   HUDSON, BENJAMIN F. "Another View of 'Uncle Tom,'" Phylon,
     XXIV (I quarter), pp. 79-87.
        Discussion of a review by Jules Janin in Journal des
     Debats, January 24, 1854, of a French play based on Uncle
     Tom's Cabin, where Uncle Tom's philosophy is praised and
     compared to the stoicism of Epictetus.

10   KAZIN, ALFRED. "The First and the Last: New England in the
     Novelist's Imagination," Saturday Review, XLVI (February 2),
     p. 12ff.
        Uncle Tom's Cabin is "one of the greatest representations
     of the New England mind in our fiction." All the author's
     works are marked by "prophetic intensity."

11   LYNN, KENNETH S. "Mrs. Stowe and the American Imagination,"
     New Republic, CXLVIII (June 29), pp. 20-21.
        Review of Runaway to Heaven. This biography is dis-
     appointing, but Uncle Tom's Cabin should be re-read for
     its literary and social merits. Lynn emphasizes the suc-
     cess of Harriet Beecher Stowe and Henry Ward Beecher in
     releasing the sometimes illicit emotions of their contempo-
     raries by encapsulating common nightmares in moral outrage.

12   MOERS, ELLEN. "The Angry Young Women," Harper's, CCXXVII
     (December), pp. 88-95.
        Mentions Harriet Beecher Stowe with George Eliot and
     others as women novelists of a scope and power that have
     disappeared in recent years. Uncle Tom's Cabin is espe-
     cially interesting as a woman's book because of its
     critique of the sex and its appeal to the female conscience.

13   TAYLOR, HUGH ALFRED. A reply to Kenneth Lynn's "Mrs. Stowe
     and the American Imagination," New Republic, CXLIX
     (July 13), p. 31.

Letter claiming that in Uncle Tom's Cabin Harriet Beecher Stowe unwittingly encouraged Northern indifference to the problems that would arise in Reconstruction and reinforced popular stereotypes.

1964 A BOOKS - NONE

1964 B SHORTER WRITINGS

1   CHAPAT, DONALD. "Uncle Tom and Predestination," Negro History Bulletin, XXVII (March), p. 143.
    Harriet Beecher Stowe did a great disservice to the American Negro by placing her Calvinist philosophy in the mouth of Uncle Tom, thus suggesting that all Negroes are and ought to be passive and helpless.

2   COOPER, ALICE A. "Harriet Beecher Stowe: A Critical Study." Ph.D. Dissertation, Harvard University.
    The slavery novels succeed as documents; the New England works are historical rather than regional; the social novels often show "originality of conception and mastery of execution," anticipating in some techniques the works of Howells and James; the Byron episode is the product of nineteenth-century religious doubt. Cooper summarizes the existing literature on Harriet Beecher Stowe and deals with the author's use of rhetoric and imagery, her alternation between the didactic and sentimental modes. Five chapters and a bibliography.

3   FLORY, CLAUDE R. "Huck, Sam and the Small-Pox," Mark Twain Journal, XII (Winter), pp. 1-2, 8.
    Notes Walter Blair's suggestion of a likeness between Sam Lawson, as direct narrator, and Huck, as well as the friendship between Twain and Harriet Beecher Stowe. Both defended the rejected wives of English poets. Points out the antecedents of the small-pox ruse reported in Sam Lawson's Oldtown Fireside Stories.

4   HALEY, ALEX. "In 'Uncle Tom' Are Our Guilt and Hope," New York Times Magazine (March 1), pp. 23, 90.
    A discussion of the origin and evolution of the epithet "Uncle Tom," and its significance in the 1960's.

5   OAKS, HAROLD RASMUS. "An Interpretative Study of the Effects of Some Upper Mid-West Productions of Uncle Tom's Cabin as Reflected in Local Newspapers Between 1852 and 1860." Ph.D. Dissertation, University of Minnesota.

1964

        Oaks tests the hypothesis that productions of "Uncle
Tom" plays influenced the growth of the abolitionist
movement, and concludes that they probably did not. Some
discussion of the novel and its impact are included in the
first chapter.

6   STERN, PHILIP VAN DOREN. "Introduction" and "Notes," The
      Annotated Uncle Tom's Cabin. New York: Paul S. Eriksson,
      Inc., pp. 7-37.
        Harriet Beecher Stowe, through her use of stereotypes,
did much to harm post-bellum race relations, but this
"poorly written novel" is nonetheless essential reading.
Biographical sketch notes that Harriet Beecher Stowe "let
herself go" in her old age, and wrote a very poor pastiche
of Lincoln's Second Inaugural Address for her introduction
to the 1878 edition of Uncle Tom's Cabin, having been
"spoiled not by failure but by success." Endnotes explain
some archaic terms to the modern reader, but mostly give
information supplied by A Key to Uncle Tom's Cabin and
standard biographies of Harriet Beecher Stowe.

7   TIMPE, EUGENE. American Literature in Germany, 1861-1872.
      Chapel Hill: University of North Carolina Press, pp. 35-38.
        Describes the impact of Uncle Tom's Cabin and later
Stowe works on the German reading public, claiming for
Harriet Beecher Stowe "tremendous influence" upon German
interest in American literature in the 1850's.

1965 A BOOKS

1   WAGENKNECHT, EDWARD. Harriet Beecher Stowe: The Known and
      the Unknown. New York: Oxford University.
        Not a biography, but a "psychography" or character study,
based in part on unpublished letters. Wagenknecht
describes Harriet Beecher Stowe in separate chapters as
mother, sister, reader, artist, reformer, etc., giving
primacy to her family relationships. Her literary affini-
ties are with Twain and Cable rather than the sentimental
novelists. Extensive useful footnotes and bibliography
included.

2   WISE, WINIFRED E. Harriet Beecher Stowe: Woman With a Cause.
      Lives to Remember Series. New York: G. P. Putnam's Sons.
        A popular, rather than a scholarly biography, covering
Harriet Beecher Stowe's life prior to the publication of
Uncle Tom's Cabin. Later years are only briefly sketched
in.

1965 B SHORTER WRITINGS

1   BLANCK, JACOB, ed. <u>Merle Johnson's American First Editions</u>,
    4th edition. Revised and enlarged. Waltham, Mass.: Mark
    Press, pp. 481-84.
       A list of the first editions of the works of Harriet
    Beecher Stowe. <u>See also</u> 1932.B3.

2   HILL, HERBERT. "'Uncle Tom,' an Enduring American Myth."
    <u>Crisis</u>, LXXII (May), pp. 289-95.
       A short biography of Josiah Henson, highly critical of
    the assumptions made by Harriet Beecher Stowe of white
    superiority and Negro docility, and of the stereotypes
    promulgated by <u>Uncle Tom's Cabin</u> and the play.

3   KASPIN, ALBERT. "<u>Uncle Tom's Cabin</u> and Uncle Akim's Inn: More
    on Harriet Beecher Stowe and Turgenev." <u>Slavic and East
    European Journal</u>, IX, pp. 47-55.
       Notes similarities and differences between <u>Uncle Tom's
    Cabin</u> and Turgenev story published the same year. Alike
    in that both authors hated bondage yet upheld the virtues
    of resignation, the books differ in sophistication, in the
    use made of historical convention, and in character devel-
    opment. The place, time, and possibility of a meeting
    between the authors is discussed.

4   OLIVER, EGBERT S. "The Little Cabin of Uncle Tom" <u>College
    English</u>, XXVI (February), pp. 355-61.
       The cabin metaphor, standing for the values of the
    family, gives form and meaning to <u>Uncle Tom's Cabin</u>.
    Various houses and homes in the novel are described and
    examined.

5   WOODS, JOHN A. "Introduction," <u>Uncle Tom's Cabin</u>. London:
    Oxford University Press.
       The popularity of this book was due in part to timing,
    but the artist, despite her lack of traditional literary
    discipline, has told a compelling story and created
    effective characters. Harriet Beecher Stowe was the
    founder of the modern Southern novel, and her other books
    are worth reading.

6   WRIGHT, LYLE H. <u>American Fiction, 1851-1865: A Contribution
    toward a Bibliography</u>. San Marino: Huntington Library,
    pp. 319-321.
       Published works of Harriet Beecher Stowe.

1965

7   WRIGHT, NATHALIA. "Harriet Beecher Stowe," <u>American Novelists</u>
     <u>in Italy</u>. Philadelphia: University of Pennsylvania Press,
     pp. 86-103.
          Describes Harriet Beecher Stowe's several trips to Italy,
     which resulted in <u>Agnes of Sorrento</u>, an historical novel
     characteristically American in its realism, nationalism,
     and use of symbols. Some parallels may be drawn between
     it, <u>The Minister's Wooing</u>, and Hawthorne's <u>The Marble Faun</u>.

<u>1966 A BOOKS - NONE</u>

<u>1966 B SHORTER WRITINGS</u>

1   BURGESS, ANTHONY. "Making de White Boss Frown," <u>Encounter</u>,
     XXVII (July), pp. 54-58.
          <u>Uncle Tom's Cabin</u> provides the background of the litera-
     ture of the modern South and of the novel of protest.
     Burgess laments the style of the work, but praises its
     characterization and structure as well as the prophetic
     vision of Harriet Beecher Stowe.

2   DUVALL, SEVERN. "'Uncle Tom's Cabin': The Sinister Side of
     the Patriarchy." <u>Images of the Negro in American Litera-</u>
     <u>ture</u>. Edited by Seymor Gross and John Hardy. Chicago &
     London: University of Chicago Press.
          Reprinted from <u>New England Quarterly</u>. <u>See</u> 1963.B7.

3   HARRIS, NEIL. <u>The Artist in American Society: The Formative</u>
     <u>Years, 1790-1860</u>. New York: George Braziller, pp. 135-6,
     139-41, passim.
          Discusses briefly Harriet Beecher Stowe's reactions to
     European art, as they appeared in <u>Sunny Memories of Foreign</u>
     <u>Lands</u>.

4   LARGE, ARLEN J. "Uncle Tom, Agitator," <u>Wall Street</u> Journal
     (November 25).
          Suggests that contemporary usage maligns Uncle Tom, and
     describes the original character.

5   LENTRICCHIA, FRANK, JR. "Harriet Beecher Stowe and the Byron
     Whirlwind," <u>Bulletin of the New York Public Library</u>, LXX
     (April), pp. 218-28.
          Harriet Beecher Stowe's article and subsequent book
     "generated a new public interest in Byron" while causing
     the author's reputation to plummet. Includes a summary of
     American newspaper and magazine reactions to the piece.

6   MAY, HENRY F. "Introduction," <u>Oldtown Folks</u>. Cambridge, Mass.:
     The Belknap Press of Harvard University Press, pp. 3-43.
          <u>Oldtown Folks</u> is a record of the "intense and painful"
     attempt of a gifted woman "to find her way through the
     difficult issues of her day." May discusses the place of
     Edwardsian theology in Harriet Beecher Stowe's development
     and fiction. Of her three styles in this novel--conven-
     tional, prophetic, and dialect--the latter is admirable
     and innovative and bears comparison with the work of Mark
     Twain.

7   NELSON, TRUMAN, ed. "Uncle Tom and an Anti-Tom Convention,"
     <u>Documents of Upheaval: Selections from William Lloyd</u>
     <u>Garrison's 'The Liberator,' 1831-1865</u>. New York: Hill and
     Wang, pp. 239-40.
          Several paragraphs from Garrison's review of <u>Uncle Tom's</u>
     <u>Cabin</u> are included and discussed. Nelson notes that Garri-
     son felt popular enthusiasm for the book was racist, but
     that his review reveals a contradiction in his position
     on non-violence.

8   PRICE, LAWRENCE MARSDEN. <u>The Reception of United States</u>
     <u>Literature in Germany</u>. Chapel Hill: University of North
     Carolina Press, pp. 100-01.
          Description of the impact of <u>Uncle Tom's Cabin</u> in Germany
     and discussion of its possible influence on German
     novelists.

9   WARD, JOHN W. "Uncle Tom's Cabin, as a Matter of Historical
     Fact," <u>Columbia University Forum</u>, IX (Winter), pp. 42-47.
          <u>Uncle Tom's Cabin</u> is a radical novel, since in it
     slavery is shown as the manifestation of a sick society.
     Confusion arises in the book, however, from the contrast
     of two Protestant themes: the emphasis on feeling right
     as a source of salvation and the bleak view of a sinful
     world that can be saved only by a miracle.

10   ZANGER, JULES. "The 'Tragic Octoroon' in Pre-Civil War
     Fiction," <u>American Quarterly</u>, XVIII (March), pp. 63-70.
          The 'octoroon' figure in the sentimental novels of the
     mid-nineteenth century, among them <u>Uncle Tom's Cabin</u>, was
     more than a manifestation of racial prejudice; instead, it
     inspired complex responses, helping to arouse Northerners
     against slavery. Some discussion of Legree.

<u>1967 A BOOKS - NONE</u>

1967

1967 B SHORTER WRITINGS

1   ANON. "Note: Collected Poems of Harriet Beecher Stowe,"
      American Literary Realism, p. 163.
           Criticizes severely Moran's editing of the Stowe poems
      (1967.B5), claiming that Moran attributes to Stowe the
      work of another author, prints lines of prose as poetry,
      omits stanzas, and includes poems of dubious authorship.
      "There probably are other errors, but these should suffice
      to indicate the poor quality of the enterprise."

2   DAVIS, RICHARD BEALE. "Mrs. Stowe's Characters in Situations
      and a Southern Literary Tradition," Essays on American
      Literature in Honor of Jay B. Hubbell. Edited by Clarence
      Gohdes. Durham, N. C.: Duke University Press, pp. 108-125.
           The tradition of moral seriousness in the modern Southern
      novel begins with Uncle Tom's Cabin and Dred. After
      describing the major characters and problems presented in
      these two books, Davis points out their recurrence and
      traces their development in the works of Cable, Twain,
      Warren, Faulkner, and others.

3   EDWARDS, HERBERT. "Harriet Beecher Stowe at Brunswick,"
      Down East, XIV (August).
           A short description of the Maine years of Harriet Beecher
      Stowe and the writing of Uncle Tom's Cabin.

4   MARTIN, JAY. Harvests of Change: American Literature 1865-
      1914. Englewood Cliffs, N. J.: Prentice-Hall, pp. 137-39.
           Harriet Beecher Stowe's New England stories, like those
      of Cooke and Jewett, are "far from an objective mirroring
      of the New England past," but instead reflect a desire to
      re-create an innocent era where rigorous Puritanism is
      modified. In her art, "myth and fiction are virtually
      one."

5   MORAN, JOHN M., ed. "The Collected Poems of Harriet Beecher
      Stowe," Emerson Society Quarterly, XLIX (IV quarter),
      pp. 1-100.
           A collection of Harriet Beecher Stowe's poetry, with
      notes and illustrations.

6   SEE, FRED G. "Metaphoric and Metonymic Imagery in Nineteenth
      Century American Fiction: Harriet Beecher Stowe, Richard
      Harding Davis, and Harold Frederic." Ph.D. Dissertation,
      University of California at Berkeley.
           A study and analysis of the kinds of imagery identified
      by Roman Jakobson as they appeared in the works of Harriet

Beecher Stowe and others; the shift from romanticism to
literary realism may be observed in the changes of style
that occur.

7   WOODRESS, JAMES. "Uncle Tom's Cabin in Italy," Essays in
American Literature in Honor of Jay B. Hubbell. Edited
by Clarence Gohdes. Durham, N. C.: Duke University Press,
pp. 126-40.
    Summarizes the reception of Uncle Tom's Cabin in Italy
from 1852 until the present, noting that periods of maxi-
mum popularity have coincided with major political crises
there. A bibliography of sixty-seven Italian editions of
the novel is appended.

1968 A BOOKS - NONE

1968 B SHORTER WRITINGS

1   ANON. "Lady Byron Vindicated," Literary Sketches, VIII
(March).
    A brief comment on the Byron article and its effect on
the circulation of the Atlantic Monthly.

2   COHEN, HENNIG. "American Literature and American Folklore,"
Our Living Traditions. Edited by Tristan Coffin, III.
New York: Basic Books, pp. 238-47.
    Oldtown Fireside Stories mentioned and discussed briefly
as an example of the literary use of folk tradition.

3   HAYNE, BARRIE. "Yankee in the Patriarchy: T. B. Thorpe's Reply
to Uncle Tom's Cabin," American Quarterly, XX (Summer),
pp. 180-195.
    Analysis of the sixteen major fictional rebuttals of
Uncle Tom's Cabin (See Appendix I), distinguishing between
Northern and Southern, national and sectional replies,
with particular attention given to Thrope's The Master's
House.

4   LOMBARD, CHARLES M. "Harriet Beecher Stowe's Attitude toward
French Romanticism," College Language Association Journal,
XI (March), pp. 236-40.
    Harriet Beecher Stowe was attracted to Mme. de Staël,
Chateaubriand, George Sand, and other French romantics,
despite her later criticism of French novels, because of
their "ideality" and emphasis on intuition and emotion.

1968

5   MERIDETH, ROBERT. The Politics of the Universe: Edward
      Beecher, Abolition and Orthodoxy. Nashville: Vanderbilt
      University Press, pp. 178-200 and passim.
         The pages cited discuss the relationship between Edward
      Beecher's theology--especially the concept of organic sin--
      and the meaning of Uncle Tom's Cabin and Dred. Harriet
      Beecher Stowe ended with a conviction that the individual
      was powerless. The Alton riots are seen as central to
      Dred, and the Parker lawsuit is explained by Harriet
      Beecher Stowe's closeness to Edward.

6   RUSSELL, ROBERT L. "The Background of the New England Local
      Color Movement." Ph.D. Dissertation, University of North
      Carolina.
         Discusses Harriet Beecher Stowe as a pioneer of and sub-
      stantial contributor to the New England local color move-
      ment.

7   STROUT, CUSHING. "Uncle Tom's Cabin and the Portent of
      Millenium," Yale Review, LVII (Spring), pp. 375-85.
         An answer to Baldwin's 1948 condemnation of Uncle Tom's
      Cabin (1948.B1), which is "half right for all the wrong
      reasons." The novel is a primary source for understanding
      the millenial expectations of nineteenth-century revivalist
      theology, "the encounter of the American Protestant imagi-
      nation with history." Calvinism is replaced in it by the
      faith of Tom and the popular cults of home, love, and
      "instant salvation," while colonization and romantic
      racism betray the evasion inherent in American race re-
      lations.

8   VEACH, CARSTON. "Harriet Beecher Stowe: A Critical Study of
      Her Early Novels." Ph.D. Dissertation, University of
      Indiana.
         An analysis of Uncle Tom's Cabin, Dred, and The Minister's
      Wooing, novels which represent the author's best work. The
      focus is on Harriet Beecher Stowe's attempt to fuse re-
      ligious issues and the problem of slavery, with Calvinism
      emerging as "the steadfast influence in her art."

9   WAGER, WILLIS. American Literature: A World View. New York:
      New York University Press.
         Uncle Tom's Cabin did not create the Civil War but
      "brought to a focus much that had been rather diffused."
      It had an international appeal in a period when human
      rights were being re-evaluated all over the world.

Harriet Beecher Stowe: A Reference Guide

1969 A BOOKS

1   CROZIER, ALICE. <u>The Novels of Harriet Beecher Stowe</u>. New
York: Oxford University Press.
The major writings of Harriet Beecher Stowe are seen in
the context of "providential history"; in them, the religion of love, motherhood, and home replaces the Calvinism
of the early nineteenth-century, but the moral fervor remains. The structure and conventions of the slavery and
New England novels show the influence of Scott and the
historical novel, while the society works crudely antici-
pate the concerns of Howells and James. One chapter is
devoted to the artistic techniques of the novels, another
to the influence of Byron in nineteenth-century America.
Bibliography appended.

1969 B SHORTER WRITINGS

1   ADAMS, JOHN R. "Harriet Beecher Stowe," <u>American Literary
Realism</u>, II (Summer), pp. 160-64.
A review of the major biographical and critical studies
of Harriet Beecher Stowe, with an indication of areas
still to be explored.

2   BROWN, DOROTHY S. "Thesis and Theme in Uncle Tom's Cabin,"
<u>English Journal</u>, LVIII (December), pp. 133-34, 72.
The thesis of <u>Uncle Tom's Cabin</u> is the evil of slavery;
its theme, the power of love. The former is more universal
and timeless, but Brown discusses the development of the
latter in the various locales of the action, emphasizing
Tom's function as a Christ figure.

3   KIRKHAM, E. BRUCE. "Harriet Beecher Stowe and the Genesis,
Composition and Revision of Uncle Tom's Cabin." Ph.D.
Dissertation, University of North Carolina.
A comparison of the extant manuscript pages, the
<u>National Era</u> text, and the revisions made prior to book
publication reveals that Harriet Beecher Stowe was a more
careful literary craftsman than critics have generally
allowed. Biographical and literary sources, especially
the sentimental novels, are also cited as important forma-
tive influences.

4   PICKENS, DONALD K. "Uncle Tom Becomes Nat Turner: A Commentary
on Two American Heroes," <u>Negro American Literary Forum</u>,
III (Summer), pp. 45-48.
Both Uncle Tom and Nat Turner are products of the American

tradition of the "hero in space," caught between nature
and society. Uncle Tom's Cabin exhibits nineteenth-century
racism; it is a novel about the sociology of slavery, and
the weakness of the male characters suggests that it is
actually a covert feminist tract. Tom's submissiveness is
part of the Christian heritage, but he is also "the nineteenth-century woman's ideal of the perfect mate," who
can reform society through love.

5   REXROTH, KENNETH. "Uncle Tom's Cabin," Saturday Review, LII
     (January 11), p. 71.
         Defends the novel and the character of Tom. Harriet
     Beecher Stowe was the only major novelist of her time to
     face the importance of slavery; because she was a "more
     emancipated and radical person" than Dickens, her charac-
     ters lack the "subtle lewdness" that marks his little
     girls. Her gift was "secular, evangelical humanism," and
     she insists on the integrity of the individual, slave and
     master. Both Faulkner and Tennessee Williams show her
     influence.

6   TAYLOR, GORDON O. The Passages of Thought: Psychological
     Representation in the American Novel, 1870-1900. New
     York: Oxford University Press, pp. 7-10, 18-27.
         Harriet Beecher Stowe's work is representative of the
     conventional fictive psychology of the nineteenth-century.
     Taylor examines in detail several passages from Uncle
     Tom's Cabin as part of his discussion of changes in the
     method of depicting mental process in the novel during the
     latter part of the century.

7   WARD, JOHN WILLIAM. "The Meaning of History in Uncle Tom's
     Cabin," Red, White, and Blue: Men, Books, and Ideas in
     American Culture. New York: Oxford University Press.
         An analysis of the success of Uncle Tom's Cabin from the
     viewpoint of the social historian. Slavery in the book
     represents the sickness of society, the absence or in-
     effectiveness of love. The ending of the novel presents
     contradictory solutions to the problem: reliance on
     Christian brotherhood on the one hand, and millenial
     judgments on the Anglo-Saxon ruling class on the other.
     Printed as "Afterword," Uncle Tom's Cabin. New York: New
     American Library. Similar to, but not identical with
     "Uncle Tom's Cabin as a Matter of Historical Fact,"
     Columbia University Forum, IX (Winter, 1966) (1966.B9).

1970 A BOOKS - NONE

1970 B SHORTER WRITINGS

1   ALLEN, PETER R.   "Lord Macauley's Gift to Harriet Beecher
       Stowe," Notes and Queries, n.s. XVII (January), pp. 23-24.
          An obscure reference to giving someone the devil suggests
       that Macauley and his circle did not think highly of
       Harriet Beecher Stowe.

2   BRUMM, URSULA.   American Thought and Religious Typology.
       Translated from the German by John Hoaglund.   New Bruns-
       wick: Rutgers University Press, pp. 200-203.
          The Minister's Wooing embodies Harriet Beecher Stowe's
       revolt against the severity of the Calvinist doctrines of
       predestination and damnation of the unregenerate.

3   COYNE, Sister MARY REGAN.   "New England Regionalism in the
       Context of Historical Change."   Ph.D. Dissertation, Case
       Western Reserve University.
          Harriet Beecher Stowe, with other regional writers,
       displays in her New England novels an ambivalence toward
       past and present visible also in James, Adams, Twain, etc.
       The real significance of these writers has been in their
       efforts to "preserve the greatness of the past in order to
       enrich their contemporary world."

4   GRIMSTED, DAVID.   "Uncle Tom from Page to Stage: Limitations
       of Nineteenth Century Drama," Quarterly Journal of Speech,
       LVI (October), pp. 235-44.
          Compares the same story in two genres to suggest reasons
       for the weakness of nineteenth-century drama: the compro-
       mises of conventional dramatic form caused a loss of
       strength and breadth.

5   HOVET, THEODORE RICHARD.   "Harriet Beecher Stowe: Holiness
       Crusade Against Slavery."   Ph.D. Dissertation, University
       of Kansas.
          Harriet Beecher Stowe's moral response to slavery was
       shaped by the liberal doctrines of the evangelical move-
       ment; her views on the ideas of Christian perfection (the
       "holiness movement") may be seen in her Evangelist and
       Independent articles, 1845-61.   In Dred, these views were
       abandoned for a revolutionary Christianity which helped
       anti-slavery people to develop a theology to explain "the
       metaphysical significance" of the Civil War.

6   LEARY, LEWIS.   Articles in American Literature, 1950-1967.
       Durham, N. C.: Duke University Press, pp. 593-95.
          Articles about Harriet Beecher Stowe.

1970

7   LEVY, DAVID. "Racial Stereotypes in Antislavery Fiction,"
      Phylon, XXXIV (Fall), pp. 265-279.
        An analysis of the Negro characters in Uncle Tom's Cabin
      and other books, pointing out that the author consistently
      used the same stereotypes as her pro-slavery opponents.

8   LYCETTE, RONALD. "Diminishing Circumferences: Feminine
      Responses in Fiction to the New England Decline." Ph.D.
      Dissertation, Purdue University.
        Harriet Beecher Stowe's New England fiction established
      the tradition of the New England decline in its conflicts
      of head and heart, ritualism and revolt, Calvinism and
      romanticism. Her grotesque characters are prototypes for
      those of later works, and "her moral idealism reduces
      identity to self-denial."

9   MILLER, ELEANOR AILEEN. "The Christian Philosophy in the New
      England Novels of Harriet Beecher Stowe." Ph.D. Disserta-
      tion, University of Nevada at Reno.
        A discussion of the doctrines of New England Puritanism
      and Harriet Beecher Stowe's responses to them in Uncle
      Tom's Cabin and the four New England novels. Guidance is
      offered her tormented characters in the form of an evangel,
      who leads others by example toward the love of God and
      away from the harsh tenets of Edwards and like theologians.

10 MOERS, ELLEN. "Nat Turner and Dred," New York Review of Books,
      XV (November 19), p. 52.
        Reply to the Styron letter (1970.B12), defending the
      Crozier review (1970.B10), and commenting that Harriet
      Beecher Stowe's widest departure from the historical
      record was her refusal to show her hero engaged in acts
      of violence.

11   _____. "Mrs. Stowe's Vengeance," New York Review of Books,
      XV (September 3), pp. 25-32.
        Review of Crozier book (1969.A1) and discussion of Dred.
      Crozier, by overemphasixing Puritanism and underemphasizing
      slavery, fails to place Harriet Beecher Stowe in context
      as a member of the "radical wing of Victorian women writers."
      Dred is an undeservedly ignored work, although a chaotic
      one; it shows the influence of Scott. Harriet Beecher
      Stowe's ability to arouse a moral revulsion at slavery is
      a literary accomplishment, her awareness of the profit
      motive in the system percipient: "When maternal imagination,
      Christian spirit, and Yankee sense of the value of a
      dollar come together to bear on the black experience in
      Harriet Beecher Stowe's fiction, her finest work as a
      novelist results."

12   NILON, CHARLES H. "Harriet Beecher Stowe," Bibliography of
      Bibliographies in American Literature. New York & London:
      R. R. Bowker, pp. 148-49.

13   STYRON, WILLIAM. "Nat Turner and Dred." Letter to New York
      Review of Books, XV (November 19), p. 52.
         Discussion of Styron's use of the Confessions of Nat
      Turner and Harriet Beecher Stowe's use of them, asking
      that both writers be granted the right to historical
      license. See 1970.B10 and 1970.B11.

1971 A BOOKS - NONE

1971 B SHORTER WRITINGS

1   ANON. "Uncle Tom: That Enduring Old Image," American Heritage,
      XXIII (December), pp. 50-57.
         A collection of political cartoons using stereotyped
      figures borrowed from Uncle Tom's Cabin.

2   BIRDOFF, HARRY. "The Voice of Harriet Beecher Stowe," Hobbies,
      LXXVI (July), pp. 35-36.
         Reports efforts to determine the authenticity of a
      cylinder recording of a voice purported to be that of
      Harriet Beecher Stowe; also lists recordings of Stowe
      works by various actors and actresses.

3   CROSS, BARBARA. "Harriet Beecher Stowe," Notable American
      Women. Cambridge, Mass.: The Belknap Press of the Harvard
      University Press, pp. 393-402.
         Biographical and critical essay. In Uncle Tom's Cabin,
      Harriet Beecher Stowe placed slavery and human cruelty
      "within God's providence" by using the framework of the
      drama of judgment, with the home and the "communion of
      the powerless" as instruments of redemption. Dred and A
      Key to Uncle Tom's Cabin offer no similar promise of sal-
      vation, but the New England novels successfully set idyllic
      childhood against the serious and often grim comedy of the
      adult world.

4   DOUGLAS, ANN. See Wood, Ann Douglas (1971.B15).

5   EICHELBERGER, CLAYTON. A Guide to Critical Reviews of United
      States Fiction, 1870-1910. Metuchen, N. J.: Scarecrow
      Press, Inc., pp. 290-291.
         A list of some reviews of Harriet Beecher Stowe's later
      works.

1971

6   FOSTER, CHARLES H.   "The Novels of Harriet Beecher Stowe by
     Alice Crozier," American Literature, XLII (January),
     p. 575.
        Review. Foster finds the book "dull and haphazard,"
     showing little familiarity with extant work. Two inter-
     esting observations made by Crozier, however, are Harriet
     Beecher Stowe's failure to refer to the work of Bushnell
     and the influence of Byron on her writing.

7   FREDERICKSON, G. W.   The Black Image in the White Mind. New
     York: Harper & Row, pp. 110-121.
        Harriet Beecher Stowe, possibly influenced by Kinmont's
     lectures on race, views the Negro as a "natural Christian."
     Her novels illustrate the war of instinct against doubting
     intellect. Dred is a kind of black Byron, warped by soli-
     tude to near-insanity. Mary has the black role in The
     Minister's Wooing. For Harriet Beecher Stowe, women and
     Negroes are "almost interchangeable when it comes to their
     natural virtues."

8   GLAZIER, LYLE.   "Pointing Upward," Hacettepe Bulletin of Social
     Sciences and Humanities, III (no. 1), pp. 34-39.
        Attacks the "double standard" underlying Uncle Tom's
     Cabin which subordinates earthly suffering to heavenly
     rewards. Tom protects only his individual virtue, not
     justice or right, and though he will not be an instrument
     of violence, he will remain passive when violence is in-
     flicted. St. Clare is a brilliant character, but Harriet
     Beecher Stowe has "no solid grasp of the social and eco-
     nomic principles" behind his anti-capitalist arguments and
     finally sends him to heaven like the rest.

9   JONES, MICHAEL.   "Ye Must Contrive Allers to Keep Jest the
     Happy Medium Between Truth and Falsehood: Folklore and the
     Folk in Mrs. Stowe's Fiction," New York Folklore Quarterly,
     XXVII (December), pp. 357-69.
        Examines Harriet Beecher Stowe's connection with the oral
     story-telling tradition and her use of folk-lore as local
     color, and as substance and style in The Pearl of Orr's
     Island, Oldtown Folks and, particularly, in Oldtown Fire-
     side Stories. The author is most effective in fiction
     when she relies most heavily on tradition.

10   KIRKHAM, E. BRUCE.   "The First Editions of Uncle Tom's Cabin:
     A Bibliographical Study," Papers of the Bibliographical
     Society of America, LXV (IV quarter), pp. 365-82.
        A description of the early editions of Uncle Tom's Cabin,
     including a discussion of the textual variations and a
     list of 288 of the earliest copies and their locations.

130

11   LEVIN, DAVID. "American Fiction as Historical Evidence: Re-
     flections on Uncle Tom's Cabin," Negro American Literary
     Forum, V (Winter), pp. 132-36, 154.
          A reading of Uncle Tom's Cabin both as historical evi-
     dence and as complex novel of manners, embodying a valuable
     perception of American social patterns and contradictions.
     Tom's place in the slave hierarchy and his command over
     his actions, for example, are carefully described, as are
     Sam and Andy's use of their stereotyped image to trick
     Legree. Harriet Beecher Stowe's emphasis on feeling is a
     comment on the misuse of reason in her society. Levin
     notes also the moral development of women in the book and
     the economic value of the Christian slave.

12   OPPERMAN, HARRY. "Two Ghost Editions of Uncle Tom's Cabin,"
     Papers of the Bibliographical Society of America, LXV,
     pp. 295-96.
          Notes a possible source for a mistake in Sabin, Biblio-
     theca Americana. (1933.B5).

13   REED, KENNETH T. "Thoreauvian Echo in Uncle Tom's Cabin?"
     American Transcendental Quarterly, XI (Summer), pp. 37-38.
          Points out the similarity between comments in "Civil
     Disobedience" and the discussion between Senator Bird and
     his wife in Chapter IX of Uncle Tom's Cabin.

14   STARKE, CATHERINE JUANITA. Black Portraiture in American
     Fiction. New York & London: Basic Books, Inc., pp. 107-11.
          Uncle Tom is a "classic archetypal figure" of the sacri-
     fice symbol, drawn on an heroic scale to evoke sympathy.
     He is also "an emotionally attached father-daddy accommo-
     dationist." Starke discusses the evolution of this stereo-
     type and the use of the black Christ figure in Faulkner's
     "The Bear." Other well-known figures from the novel--
     Topsy, George Harris, Eva's Mammy--are mentioned through-
     out.

15   WOOD, ANN DOUGLAS. "'The Scribbling Women' and Fanny Fern:
     Why Women Wrote," American Quarterly, XXIII (Spring),
     pp. 3-24.
          Harriet Beecher Stowe was behaving conventionally when
     she said of Uncle Tom's Cabin, "God wrote it," and refused
     to acknowledge that for women writing was a way out of the
     home.

1972 A BOOKS - NONE

1972

1972 B SHORTER WRITINGS

1   ADAMS, JOHN R.   "Introduction" and Bibliographical Notes,
       Regional Sketches: New England and Florida, by Harriet
       Beecher Stowe.   Edited for the modern reader by J. R.
       Adams.   New Haven: College and University Press, pp. 7-28.
          Adams traces the development of Harriet Beecher Stowe
       as a regionalist from her first publication to the Florida
       stories, calling Sam Lawson's Oldtown Fireside Stories her
       best short fiction.   This collection of pieces is "chrono-
       logical by groups," and several stories are published for
       the first time since their original appearance.   The bib-
       liographical notes comment on works about Harriet Beecher
       Stowe and explain the choice of each text.

2   DOUGLAS, ANN.   See Wood, Ann Douglas.   (1972.B9).

3   KERR, HOWARD.   Mediums, and Spirit-Rappers, and Roaring Radi-
       cals: Spiritualism in American Literature, 1850-1900.
       Urbana: University of Illinois Press.
          Harriet Beecher Stowe's involvement with spiritualism
       and her relationship with her sister Isabella in Hartford
       are described and discussed.

4   LUDWIG, RICHARD M.   "Harriet Beecher Stowe," Literary History
       of the United States, Bibliography Supplement II.   New
       York: The Macmillan Company, pp. 260-62.
          Writings about Harriet Beecher Stowe, 1958-1970.

5   OPPERMAN, HARRY E., III.   "A Bibliography and Stemma Codicum
       for British Editions of Uncle Tom's Cabin, 1852-53."
       Ph.D. Dissertation, Kansas State University.
          Description of early English editions of Uncle Tom's
       Cabin, many of which were censored, abridged, revised,
       or otherwise corrupted.

6   PARKER, GAIL THAIN.   The Oven Birds: American Women on Women-
       hood.   Garden City: Anchor Books.
          Includes four essays from Household Papers and Stories.
       Comments on Harriet Beecher Stowe in the introductory essay
       emphasize her effort to infuse everyday actions with
       "higher meaning" while simultaneously denigrating romantic
       dreams.

7   STEELE, THOMAS J., S.J.   "Tom and Eva: Mrs. Stowe's Two Dying
       Christs," Negro American Literary Forum, VI (Fall),
       pp. 85-90.
          Eva is modeled on the "Christ of the Last Discourse of

St. John's gospel," Tom on the "suffering Servant of the
synoptic tradition." The emphasis of the former is on
Christian love, the latter on the fulfillment of destiny
through death. The reversal of the north-south movement
patterns and the merging of gender further illustrates
Harriet Beecher Stowe's use of and variations upon tradi-
tional motifs.

8   VAN WHY, JOSEPH S. and E. BRUCE KIRKHAM. "A Note on Two Pages
     of the Manuscript of Uncle Tom's Cabin," Papers of the
     Bibliographical Society of America, LXVI, pp. 433-34.
        A note that both pages which have recently been identi-
     fied are "versions of the text earlier than that which
     appeared in the National Era."

9   WOOD, ANN DOUGLAS. "The Literature of Impoverishment: The
     Women Local Colorists in America, 1865-1914," Women's
     Studies, I, pp. 3-45.
        A detailed study of two generations of American women
     writers; Harriet Beecher Stowe is discussed as a member
     of the earlier, apparently sentimental but covertly
     aggressive and feminist group which was predominantly
     middle-class, mobile, married, and convinced of the ulti-
     mate superiority of the female. Many informative foot-
     notes and two appendices are included.

10   YELLIN, JEAN FAGAN. "Harriet Beecher Stowe," The Intricate
     Knot: Black Figures in American Literature, New York: New
     York University Press, pp. 121-53.
        Describes the abolitionism in Harriet Beecher Stowe's
     background and compares Uncle Tom's Cabin and Dred to
     their sources in slave narrative. The novels are "Chris-
     tianized, sentimentalized, sensationalized versions" of
     the narratives; they deal in stereotypes, fail to challenge
     white racism, and are essentially religious in thrust.
     Notes the criticisms of Uncle Tom's Cabin made by Garrison
     and other anti-slavery spokesmen.

1973 A BOOKS - NONE

1973 B SHORTER WRITINGS

1   ANON. "Mrs. Stowe, Painter," American Heritage, XXIV
     (August), pp. 6-7.
        The first reproductions of paintings by Harriet Beecher
     Stowe owned by the Stowe-Day Foundation.

1973

2 CASSARA, ERNEST. "The Rehabilitation of Uncle Tom: Significant Themes in Mrs. Stowe's Antislavery Novel," College
Language Association Journal, XVII (December), pp. 230-40.
Harriet Beecher Stowe was a "hard-headed" author who, in
her efforts to awaken the individual consciences of
Christian America, depicted the brutalizing effects of
slavery and created in Tom a black Christ.

3 DAVIDSON, MARSHALL B. and the EDITORS OF AMERICAN HERITAGE.
The American Heritage History of The Writer's America.
New York: American Heritage Publishing Company, Inc.
Conventional comment on Harriet Beecher Stowe's career,
with a double page illustration entitled "Uncle Tom in
Art and Theatre."

4 GRAHAM, THOMAS. "Harriet Beecher Stowe and the Question of
Race," New England Quarterly, XLVI (December), pp. 614-622.
An answer to Furnas's 1956 book (1956.A1), pointing out
that Harriet Beecher Stowe, while she shared some of the
racist preconceptions of her time, rose above them in many
instances by emphasizing the role of social and environ-
mental factors in the formation of the Negro character.

5 HENRY, STUART. Unvanquished Puritan: Lyman Beecher. Grand
Rapids: William B. Eerdman Publishing Company.
This study of Lyman pays little specific attention to
Harriet Beecher Stowe other than noting (page 109) that
she peopled her novels with various versions of family
members, but discusses in detail the ways in which the
father's character and opinions shaped and otherwise
affected his children.

6 KIRKHAM, E. BRUCE. "Andover, Gettysburg, and Beyond: The
Military Career of Frederick W. Stowe," Essex Institute
Historical Collections, CIX (January), pp. 87-96.
Kirkham draws on letters and military sources to describe
Fred Stowe's army career (1861-65), in an attempt to cor-
rect the mistaken assumptions of Harriet Beecher Stowe's
biographers; he concludes that Fred joined and fought to
show himself and his father that "he could become a man."

7 LYNN, KENNETH. "Uncle Tom's Cabin," Visions of America.
Westport, Conn.: Greenwood Press, Inc., pp. 27-48.
Reprinted from Uncle Tom's Cabin, Harvard University
Press, 1962.

8 McCULLOUGH, DAVID. "Unexpected Mrs. Stowe," American Heritage,
XXIV (August), pp. 4-9, 76-80.
An illustrated biographical sketch of the life of Harriet
Beecher Stowe.

9 MOERS, ELLEN. "Money, the Job, and Little Women," Commentary, LV (January), pp. 57-65.
   Compares Harriet Beecher Stowe to Jane Austen in her precision about money matters, a characteristic and distinguishing trait of female writing. "The brilliance of Stowe's attack on slavery was her success in associating it with the cash nexus of mid-century American society."

10 NDU, POL. "From 'Jegar Sahadutha' to Gary, Indiana: Uncle Tomism and the Black Literary Revolution," Ufahamu, IV (Spring), pp. 119-133.
   Uncle Tom and Dred are exemplars of Melville's "chronometrical" perfection in a materialistic world. A psychological barrier exists between these men, "visible symbols of courage and resolution," and their creator. "The literature of Uncle Tomism might yet be reassessed in the course of the Black socio-literary revolution."

11 SKLAR, KATHRYN KISH. Catharine Beecher: A Study in American Domesticity. New Haven & London: Yale University Press.
   This biography of Catharine Beecher refers throughout to Harriet Beecher Stowe. Sklar discusses at some length The Minister's Wooing and the view of Calvinism as a "social rather than a religious system" which the sisters shared.

12 SMYLIE, JAMES H. "Uncle Tom's Cabin Revisited: The Bible, the Romantic Imagination, and the Sympathies of Christ," Interpretation, XXVII (i), pp. 67-85.
   Harriet Beecher Stowe illustrated for a believing generation "the sympathies of Christ" through the actions of her black and white characters. She shifted attention from the master-slave images of the Old Testament to the New Testament passages on the oppressed, the outcast, and the poor. Smylie notes that Tom's sorrow is not a substitute for Christ's, but that Christ's sorrow gives him power.

13 TRAUTMANN, FREDRICK. "Harriet Beecher Stowe: Public Readings in the Central States," Central States Speech Journal, XXV (Spring), p. 21ff.
   Harriet Beecher Stowe's readings in the midwest in 1873 were generally well-attended and favorably received. She chose her passages wisely and turned her natural gift for telling a story to good account.

14 VAN HOY, MILTON S. "Two Allusions to Hungary in Uncle Tom's Cabin," Phylon, XXXIV (Winter), pp. 433-35.
   Harriet Beecher Stowe used references to the Hungarian Revolution of 1848 to gain sympathy for slaves by comparing

1973

them to figures white Americans admired, but her analogies
bear little connection to the facts.

1974 A BOOKS - NONE

1974 B SHORTER WRITINGS

1   LEBEDUN, JEAN. "Harriet Beecher Stowe's Interest in Sojourner
     Truth, Black Feminist," American Literature, XLVI (Novem-
     ber), pp. 359-63.
        Describes a meeting of Harriet Beecher Stowe and Sojourner
     Truth. Harriet Beecher Stowe, as a result, wrote an intro-
     duction to a new edition of Sojourner Truth's autobiography
     and talked about her to W. W. Story. Lebedun sees echoes
     of her in Candace (The Minister's Wooing); she notes other
     pro-feminist positions in Harriet Beecher Stowe's work.

2   MAROTTA, KENNY RALPH. "The Literary Relationship of George
     Eliot and Harriet Beecher Stowe." Ph.D. Dissertation,
     Johns Hopkins University.
        The common ground of the novels of these two writers is
     a "transfigured realism" involving "typology," i.e., "the
     application of Biblical types to the interpretation of
     daily life." Both authors believe that "the basis of re-
     ligion is a faith that significantly resembles the faith
     we give to fiction." Various novels of the two are con-
     sidered in conjunction as they exemplify this thesis:
     Adam Bede and The Minister's Wooing, Romola and Agnes of
     Sorrento, Middlemarch and Oldtown Folks, etc.

3   TRAUTMANN, FREDRICK. "Harriet Beecher Stowe's Public
     Readings in New England," New England Quarterly, XLVII
     (June), pp. 279-289.
        In 1872, Harriet Beecher Stowe undertook a series of
     readings. Her performances were generally well-received,
     despite a few negative reviews and some awkward situations.
     Trautmann notes that Garrison's introduction of her in
     Boston was mildly critical.

Appendix I: Fictional Responses to *Uncle Tom's Cabin*, 1852-1861

1852

ANON. Uncle Tom in England; or, A Proof that Black's White. New York: A. D. Failing.

CRISWELL, ROBERT. "Uncle Tom's Cabin" contrasted with Buckingham Hall, a Planter's Home: or, A Fair View of Both Sides of the Slavery Question. New York: D. Fanshaw.

EASTMAN, MARY H. Aunt Phillis's Cabin; or, Southern Life as It Is. Philadelphia: Lippincott, Grambo and Co. (See 1852.B40).

HALE, SARAH J. Northwood (new edition, with anti-slavery material added). New York: H. Long & Brother.

HALL, BAYARD R. Frank Freeman's Barber Shop: A Tale. Rochester, New York. Charles Scribner.

RANDOLPH, J. THORNTON [pseud.] CHARLES JACOBS PETERSON. The Cabin and Parlor: or, Slaves and Masters. Philadelphia: T. B. Peterson.

RUSH, CAROLINE. The North and South: or, Slavery and its Contrasts. Philadelphia: Crissy & Markley.

SMITH, WILLIAM L. G. Life at the South: or, "Uncle Tom's Cabin" As It Is. Being Narratives, Scenes, and Incidents in the Real "Life of the Lowly." Buffalo: Geo. H. Derby & Co.

1853

BUTT, MARTHA HAINES. Antifanaticism. Philadelphia: Lippincott Grambo & Co.

HALE, SARAH J. ("edited by"). Liberia: or Mr. Peyton's Experiments. New York: Harper & Bros.

HERNDON, MARY E. Louise Elton: or, Things Seen and Heard. Philadelphia: Lippincott, Grambo & Co.

McINTOSH, MARIA J. The Lofty and the Lowly: or, Good in All and None
All-Good. 2 volumes. New York: D. Appleton.

PAGE, JOHN W. Uncle Tobin in his Cabin in Virginia, and Tom Without
One in Boston. Richmond: J. W. Randolph.

SIMMS, WILLIAM F. Woodcraft. Philadelphia: Lippincott, Grambo & Co.
(See 1960.B8). New edition, 1854.

VIDI [pseud.] Mr. Frank, The Underground Mail-Agent. Philadelphia:
Lippincott, Grambo & Co.

1854

CHASE, LUCIEN B. English Serfdom and American Slavery; or, Ourselves
as Others See us. New York: H. Long & Brother.

HENTZ, CAROLINE LEE. The Planter's Northern Bride: A Novel.
2 volumes. Philadelphia: A. Hart.

1861

ADAMS, NEHEMIAH. The Sable Cloud: A Southern Tale. Boston: Ticknor &
Fields. (See Browne, 1941.B4).

SCHOOLCRAFT, Mrs. HENRY R. The Black Gauntlet: A Tale of Plantation
Life in South Carolina. Philadelphia: J. B. Lippincott.

Summaries of and comments on many of these may be found
in Tandy (1922.B1), Browne (1941.B4), and Hayne (1896.B3).

Appendix II: Plays based on the Life of Harriet Beecher Stowe

JACKSON, PHYLLIS W. Hattie Beecher (A Victorian Cinderella).
  Tucson, Arizona: P. J. Sortomme. 1838.

LEVY, MELVIN P. An American Incident. A Play in One Act. New York &
  Los Angeles: S. French. 1942.

RYERSON, FLORENCE and COLIN CLEMENTS. Harriet. A Play in Three Acts.
  New York: Charles Scribner's Sons. 1943.

JACKSON, PHYLLIS WYNN. Hattie. An Historical Comedy in One Act for
  Two Women and Four Men. Evanston, Illinois and New York: Row,
  Peterson & Company. 1944.

*HAY, IAN [pseud.]. Hattie Stowe. (Reviewed in Theatre Arts, XXXI
  [May, 1947], p. 26.)

Appendix III: *Uncle Tom's Cabin* on Stage (Selected Articles)

1897

PECK, H. T. "Uncle Tom's Cabin in Liverpool; Criticism of a production of the play," <u>Bookman</u>, VI (December), pp. 310-16.

1902

ARNETT, F. S. "Fifty Years of Uncle Tom," <u>Munsey</u>, XXVII (September), pp. 897-902.

1911

ANON. "Novel that Overruled the Supreme Court," <u>Current Literature</u>, LI (August), pp. 208-10. (<u>See</u> 1911.B5).

1926

CORBETT, E. F. "Footnote to the Drama; America's One Folk Play, Uncle Tom's Cabin." <u>Drama</u>, XVI (May), pp. 285-86.

PILCHER, VELONA. "The Variorum Stowe," <u>Theatre Arts</u>, X (April), pp. 226-39.

1929

KAYE, JOSEPH. "Famous First Nights: 'Uncle Tom's Cabin'" <u>Theatre Magazine</u> (August), pp. 26, e5.

1931

CORBETT, ELIZABETH. "Uncle Tom is Dead," <u>Theatre Guild Magazine</u>, VIII (January), p. 16.

1932

ANON. "Uncle Tom in Russia," Literary Digest, CXIV (July 2), p. 16.

1933

ANON. "Uncle Tom, Authentic Americana," Literary Digest, CXV
(June 17), p. 13.

SKINNER, OTIS. "Uncle Tom and Eva Take Another Bow," New York Times
Magazine (May 28), p. 9.

SKINNER, R. D. "Players Revive Uncle Tom," Commonweal, XVIII
(June 9), p. 160.

1940

HADLEY, B. "Uncle Tom's Cabin in Brazil," Inter-America, II
(October), pp. 26-27. (See 1940.B4).

1945

LAURIE, JOE, JR. "The Theatre's All-Time Hit," American Mercury, LXI
(October), pp. 469-72.

1946

BULLARD, F. LAURISTON. "Uncle Tom on the Stage," Lincoln Herald,
XLVIII (June), pp. 19-22.

1947

BIRDOFF, HARRY. The World's Greatest Hit--Uncle Tom's Cabin. New
York: S. F. Vanni. (See 1947.B1).

1951

HEWITT, BERNARD. "Uncle Tom and Uncle Sam: New Light from an Old
Play," Quarterly Journal of Speech, XXXVII (February), pp. 63-70.

1952

DRUMMOND, A. M. and RICHARD MOODY. "The Hit of the Century: Uncle
Tom's Cabin--1852-1952," Educational Theatre Journal, IV (December), pp. 315-22.

RAHILL, FRANK. "America's Number One Hit," Theatre Arts, XXXVI (October), pp. 18-24.

1955

MOODY, RACHARD. "Uncle Tom, the Theatre and Mrs. Stowe," American Heritage, VI (October), pp. 29-33, 102-03. (See 1955.B6).

REARDON, WILLIAM and JOHN FOXEN. "Civil War Theater: The Propaganda Play," Civil War History, I (Summer), pp. 281-93.

1956

FISHER, A. and O. RABE. "Uncle Tom's Cabin: Drama," Plays, XV (March), pp. 24-30.

MacDONALD, CORDELIA HOWARD. "Memories of the Original Little Eva," edited by George P. Howard, Educational Theatre Journal, VIII, pp. 267-82.

1957

FLETCHER, E. G. "Illustrations for Uncle Tom," Texas Quarterly, I (Spring), pp. 166-80.

1963

COLLINS, JOHN. "American Drama in Anti-Slavery Agitation, 1792-1861." Ph.D. Dissertation, State University of Iowa.

HUDSON, BENJAMIN F. "Another View of 'Uncle Tom,'" Phylon, XXIV (I quarter), pp. 79-87. (See 1963.B9).

LIPPMAN, MONROE. "Uncle Tom and his Poor Relations: American Slavery Plays," Southern Speech Journal, XXVIII (Spring), pp. 183-97.

McDOWELL, J. H. "Original Scenery and Documents for Productions of Uncle Tom's Cabin," Revue d'Histoire du Theatre, XV (January-March), pp. 71-79.

1964

OAKS, HAROLD RASMUS. "An Interpretative Study of the Effects of Some Upper Mid-West Productions of Uncle Tom's Cabin as Reflected in Local Newspapers between 1852 and 1860." Ph.D. Dissertation, University of Minnesota. (See 1946.B5).

1970

GRIMSTED, DAVID. "Uncle Tom from Page to Stage: Limitations of Nineteenth Century Drama," Quarterly Journal of Speech, LVI (October), pp. 235-44. (See 1970.B4).

WADSWORTH, FRANK W. "Webster, Horne, and Mrs. Stowe: American Performances of The Duchess of Malfi," Theatre Survey, XI, pp. 151-66.

NOTE:

At least four film versions of Uncle Tom's Cabin were made in the first quarter of the twentieth century:

Edison, 1903.

World Producing Corporation, 1914.

Famous Players - Lasky Corporation, 1918.

Universal, 1927.

My Wife and I was produced by Warner Brothers in 1925. The Edison version is supposed to be the first example of fiction on film.

Author/Title Index

Note: Items in the Appendices are not listed.

Abbott, Willis J.
  Women of History, 1913.B1
Abbott, Lyman
  Henry Ward Beecher, 1883.B1
Abel, Darrel
  American Literature, II,
    1963.B1
Aber, M. E.
  "Rankin House," 1963.B2
Adams, E. C.
  Heroines of Modern Progress,
    1913.B2
Adams, Ephraim D.
  Great Britain and the Ameri-
    can Civil War, 1925.B1
Adams, F. C.
  Uncle Tom at Home, 1853.A1
Adams, Henry, 1930.B4
Adams, John R.
  Harriet Beecher Stowe, 1963.A1
  "Harriet Beecher Stowe," ALR,
    1969.B1
  "Introduction" and biblio-
    graphical notes to
    Regional Sketches, 1972.B1
  Literary Achievements of
    Harriet Beecher Stowe
    (dissertation), 1939.B1
Albert, Sarah T.
  "An Entertaining Biography,"
    1941.B1
Alderson, J. P. (Mrs.)
  "Mrs. Harriet Beecher Stowe,"
    1927.B1
Aldrich, Lillian
  Crowding Memories, 1920.B1

Allan, Peter R.
  "Lord Macauley's Gift to
    Harriet Beecher Stowe,"
    1970.B1
Allen, Eleanor P.
  "Harriet Beecher Stowe,"
    1890.B1
Allen, James L.
  "Mrs. Stowe's 'Uncle Tom' at
    Home in Kentucky," 1887.B1
Allen, W. F.
  "The Minister's Wooing,"
    1859.B1
Alpha [Pseud.]
  "The War of the Fanatics,"
    1853.B2
Altick, Robert
  The Art of Literary Research,
    1963.B3
"American Literature and the
    Civil War," 1863.B1
"American Slavery and Emancipa-
    tion by the Free States,"
    1853.A2
"The American Woman's Home,"
    1869.B2
Anderson, Edward P.
  "Harriet Beecher Stowe,"
    1890.B2
Anderson, John Parker
  Description of Harriet Beecher
    Stowe exhibit, 1898.B1
Andrews, Kenneth R.
  Nook Farm—Mark Twain's Hart-
    ford Circle, 1950.B1

Angle, Paul M.
    "Uncle Tom's Cabin One
        Hundredth Anniversary
        Exhibit," 1951.B1
Anthony, Katharine
    "Christian Soldier," 1941.B3
    "Harriet Beecher Stowe,
        1936.B1
Anthony, Susan B.
    "Mrs. Stowe," 1896.B11
Austen, Jane, 1973.B9
Austin, James C.
    Fields of the Atlantic
        Monthly, 1953.B1
Axelrad, Arthur
    "Harriet Beecher Stowe as a
        New England Local-Color-
        ist," 1963.B6
Aytoun, W. E.
    "Sunny Memories of Foreign
        Lands," 1854.B11

Bacon, L.
    "The Literature of Slavery,"
        1852.B37
    "The Minister's Wooing,"
        1860.B3
Baender, Paul
    "Mark Twain and the Byron
        Scandal," 1959.B1
Bailey, Thomas Pearce
    Race Orthodoxy in the South,
        1914.B2
Baker, Carlos
    "Harriet Beecher Stowe,"
        1949.B3
Baldwin, James, 1968.B7
    "Everyone's Protest Novel,"
        1949.B1
Banning, M. C.
    "Uncle Tom's Cabin by Harriet
        Beecher Stowe," 1955.B1
Barnum, P. T., 1896.B22
Bartlett, D. W.
    Modern Agitators, 1856.B12
Beach, Seth C.
    Daughters of the Puritans,
        1905.B1
Beadle, J. H.
    "Harriet Beecher Stowe,"
        1889.B3

Beatty, A.
    "The Evils of Slavery,"
        1853.B21
Beatty, Lillian
    "The Natural Man Versus the
        Puritan," 1959.B2
Beecher, Catharine, 1948.B6;
    1973.B11
Beecher, Edward, 1968.B5
Beecher family, 1852.B1; 1853.B1,
    B22; 1858.B2; 1871.B1;
    1891.B3; 1898.B3; 1905.B1;
    1911.B8; 1934.B3; 1940.B10;
    1943.B6; 1973.B5
Beecher, Henry Ward, 1853.B22;
    1869.B1,B15; 1882.B5; 1883.B1;
    1888.B2,B3; 1896.B17,B21;
    1910.B1; 1927.B3; 1953.B2;
    1963.B11
Beecher, Lyman, 1973.B5
Beecher, William E. and Samuel
    Scoville
    Henry Ward Beecher, 1888.B2
"The Beechers of Today," 1871.B1
Beers, Henry A.
    An Outline Sketch of American
        Literature, 1887.B2
Beeton, M. M.
    "Mr. Beeton and 'Uncle Tom,'"
        1942.B2
Behn, Aphra
    Oroonoko, Uncle Tom's Cabin
        compared to, 1912.B6
Bellows, Stephen Bush
    "Paging Sam Lawson," 1943.B1
Bernbaum, E.
    "Harriet Beecher Stowe,"
        1938.B1
Birdoff, Harry
    "The Voice of Harriet Beecher
        Stowe," 1971.B2
    The World's Greatest Hit,
        1947.B1
Birney, William
    "Some Account of Mrs. Beecher
        Stowe and Her Family,"
        1852.B1; 1853.B1
"Blackwood's Magazine," 1853.B4
Blair, Walter
    Native American Humor, 1937.B2

Bullen, George
"Bibliography" of Uncle Tom's
Cabin, 1878.B9
Burgess, Anthony
"Making de White Boss Frown,"
1966.B1
Burnett, Frances Hodgson
The One I Knew Best of All,
1893.B1
Burney, Fanny, 1856.B11
Burns, Wayne and E. G. Sutcliffe
"Uncle Tom's Cabin and Charles
Reade," 1946.B3
Burritt, Elihu
"Introduction" to Uncle Tom's
Cabin, 1852.B38
Burton, Richard
"The Author of Uncle Tom's
Cabin," 1896.B12
"Mrs. Stowe at Eighty-Five,"
1896.B13
Bushwell, G. H.
From Papyrus to Print,
1947.B3
Butcher, Margaret Just
The Negro in American Culture,
1956.B2
"The Byron Case," 1869.B3,B4
"The Byron Controversy," 1869.B5
"The Byron Horror," 1869.B6
"The Byron Mystery," 1869.B7
"The Byron Mystery and Mrs.
Stowe," 1870.B1
Byron Painted by His Compeers,
1869.A1
"The Byron Revelations," 1869.B8
"The Byron Scandal," 1869.B9,B10
"The Byrons and Their Latest
Biographer," 1869.B11

Cable, George Washington, Harriet
Beecher Stowe compared to,
1965.A1; 1967.B2
Cady, Edwin H.
The Road to Realism, 1956.B3
Cairns, William B.
A History of American Litera-
ture, 1930.B3
"Uncle Tom's Cabin and its
Author," 1911.B7

Carlisle, The Earl of
"Introduction" to Uncle Tom's
Cabin, 1852.B39
"The Case Stated," 1869.B12
Cassara, Ernest
"The Rehabilitation of Uncle
Tom," 1973.B2
Cayton, Horace
"Uncle Tom," 1946.B12
Chadwick, J. W.
"Harriet Beecher Stowe,"
1890.B10
Chandler, P. W.
"Lady Byron Vindicated,"
1870.B6
Chapat, Donald
"Uncle Tom and Predestina-
tion," 1964.B1
Chase, Richard
"Adam Fallen and Unfallen,"
1956.B4
Chesnut, Mary B.
A Diary from Dixie, 1949.B3
Chew, Samuel C.
Byron in England, 1924.B1
Clare, Edward
The Spirit and Philosophy of
Uncle Tom's Cabin, 1853.A5
Clark, Thomas D.
"An Appraisal of Uncle Tom's
Cabin," 1946.B5
Cobbe, Frances P.
"Rejoinder to Mrs. Stowe's
Reply," 1863.B4
Cohen, Hennig
"American Literature and
American Folklore,"
1968.B2
Cole, Arthur C.
The Irrepressible Conflict,
1850-1865, 1934.B1
Coleman, J. W.
"Mrs. Stowe, Kentucky, and
Uncle Tom's Cabin,"
1946.B6
Commager, Henry Steele
"She Conquered a Crown,"
1941.B6
"Consistency, Thou Art a Jewel,"
1869.B13

Iglesias, A.
"Classic Blend in Literature,"
1950.B3
"An Interview with Harriet
Beecher Stowe," 1896.B6

Jackson, F. H.
"An Italian Uncle Tom's
Cabin," 1958.B4
"Uncle Tom's Cabin in Italy,"
1953.B4
Jackson, Phyllis Wynn
The Story of Harriet Beecher
Stowe, 1948.A1
reviewed: 1948.B5
Jacobson, Dan
"Down the River," 1962.B1
Jaffe, Adrian
"Uncle Tom in the Penal
Colony," 1953.B5
James, Henry, 1969.A1; 1970.B3
A Small Boy and Others,
1913.B3
"We and Our Neighbors,"
1875.B6
Jerrold, Walter
"The Author of 'Uncle Tom's
Cabin': Some Centenary
Notes," 1911.B10
Jewett, John P., 1883.B2
Jewett, Sarah Orne, 1911.B10
Jobes, Katherine T.
"The Resolution of Solitude"
(dissertation), 1961.B4
Johnson, Merle
"American First Editions:
Harriet Beecher Stowe,"
1932.B3; 1965.B1
Johnson, Thomas H.
"Harriet Beecher Stowe,"
1948.B8
Johnston, Reverend B.
"Lives Worth Living," 1893.B2
Johnston, Johanna
Runaway to Heaven, 1963.A2
reviewed: 1963.B4
Jones, J. H.
"Mrs. Stowe and her Critics,"
1860.B4
"Mrs. Stowe and her Critics,
II," 1861.B4

Jones, Michael
"Ye Must Contrive Allers to
Keep Jest the Happy Medium
Between Truth and False-
hood," 1971.B9
Jorgenson, Chester E.
Uncle Tom's Cabin as Book and
Legend, 1952.A1
"Just Growed Again: Uncle Tom's
Cabin," 1948.B1

Kaspin, Albert
"Uncle Tom's Cabin and Uncle
Akim's Inn," 1965.B3
Kazin, Alfred
"The First and the Last,"
1963.B10
Kellner, Leon
American Literature, 1915.B1
Ket, Leander
Slavery Consistent With
Christianity, 1853.B26
Kerr, Howard
Mediums, and Spirit-Rappers,
and Roaring Radicals,
1972.B3
Kimball, A. R.
"Hartford's Literary Corner,"
1895.B2
King, William, 1933.B4; 1958.B7
Kinney, M. B.
"Mrs. Stowe, Mrs. Somerville,
and Mrs. Browning,"
1869.B36
Kirk, Clara Marburg
"Saints, Sinners, and
Beechers," 1941.B11
Kirkham, E. Bruce
"Andover, Gettysburg, and
Beyond: The Military
Career of Frederick W.
Stowe," 1973.B6
"The First Editions of Uncle
Tom's Cabin," 1971.B10
"Harriet Beecher Stowe and
the Genesis, Composition,
and Revision of Uncle Tom's
Cabin" (dissertation),
1969.B3
Kirkland, Caroline M. (Mrs.)
"Uncle Tom's Cabin," 1852.B50

Lucas, Samuel
  Eminent Men and Popular Books,
    1859.B6
Ludwig, Richard M.
  "Harriet Beecher Stowe,"
    1959.B3; 1972.B4
Lycette, Ronald
  "Diminishing Circumferences:
    Feminine Responses in
    Fiction" (dissertation),
    1970.B8
Lynn, Kenneth S.
  "Introduction" to Uncle Tom's
    Cabin, 1962.B2
  Mark Twain and Southwestern
    Humor, 1959.B4
  "Mrs. Stowe and the American
    Imagination," 1963.B11
  Visions of America, 1973.B7

MacArthur, R. A.
  The Story of Harriet Beecher
    Stowe, 1922.A1
Macaulay, Thomas B., 1970.B1
Mackay, Charles (editor)
  Medora Leigh, 1870.A1
Mackay, Constance D.
  "The Harriet Beecher Stowe
    Centenary," 1911.B11
MacLean, Grace Edith
  Uncle Tom's Cabin in Germany,
    1910.A1
MacTavish, Newton
  "The Original Uncle Tom,"
    1907.B1
Macy, Jesse
  The Anti-Slavery Crusade,
    1919.B4
Malone, Dumas
  Saints in Action, 1939.B4
Malone, Ted (Frank A. Russell)
  American Pilgrimage, 1942.B4
Manierre, W. R.
  "A Southern Response to Mrs.
    Stowe," 1961.B7
Marotta, Kenny R.
  "The Literary Relationship of
    George Eliot and Harriet
    Beecher Stowe" (disserta-
    tion), 1974.B2

Martin, Jay
  Harvests of Change, 1967.B4
Massey, J. Barrows (editor)
  We Were New England, 1937.B7
Matthews, Brander
  "Uncle Tom's Cabin," 1891.B1
Matthiessen, F. O.
  "New England Stories," 1931.B3
Maurice, A. B.
  "Famous Novels and Their Con-
    temporary Critics," 1903.B2
  "Literary Magazines," 1931.B4
Maxfield, E. K.
  "'Goody-Goody' Literature and
    Mrs. Stowe," 1929.B2
May, Henry F.
  "Introduction" to Oldtown
    Folks, 1966.B6
Maycock, S. W., W. B. Maycock and
    Willoughby Maycock
  "The Original 'Uncle Tom,'"
    1912.B5
Maycock, Willoughby
  "Prefaces to Uncle Tom's
    Cabin," 1915.B3
Maye, Ernest J.
  "Mark Twain Meets a Lady From
    Finland," 1960.B5
McCarthy, Justin
  "Mrs. Stowe's Last Romance,"
    1869.B37
McCord, Louisa S.
  "Uncle Tom's Cabin," 1853.B27
McCray, Florine Thayer
  The Life Work of the Author of
    Uncle Tom's Cabin, 1889.A1
  "Mrs. Stowe's Biographers,"
    1889.B4
  "Uncle Tom's Cabin and Mrs.
    Stowe," 1890.B13
McCullough, David
  "Unexpected Mrs. Stowe,"
    1973.B8
McDowell, G. S.
  "Harriet Beecher Stowe at
    Cincinnati and Sources for
    Characters in Uncle Tom's
    Cabin," 1895.B3
McDowell, Tremaine
  "The Use of Negro Dialect by
    Harriet Beecher Stowe,"
    1931.B5

McIlwaine, Shields
  The Southern Poor White,
    1939.B5
M'Leod, Donald
  Donald M'Leod's Gloomy Memo-
    ries, 1857.A1
McMurtry, R. Gerald
  "The Influence of the Stowe
    Book on Popular Music of
    the Civil War Period,"
    1946.B13
Melcher, F. G.
  "America's Number One Best
    Seller Reaches a Centen-
    ary," 1952.B3
Melville, Herman, 1973.B10
  Moby Dick, 1938.B6
"Memorial to Harriet Beecher
    Stowe," 1916.B1
Merideth, Robert
  The Politics of the Universe,
    1968.B5
Merriam, George S.
  "Introduction" to excerpts
    from Uncle Tom's Cabin and
    The Minister's Wooing,
    1897.B6
Miles, George H.
  "The Atlantic Monthly: Its
    Charge Against Byron,"
    1869.B39
Mill, John Stuart, 1869.B42
Miller, Eleanor H.
  "Christian Philosophy in the
    New England Novels of
    Harriet Beecher Stowe"
    (dissertation), 1970.B9
Miller, James M.
  An Outline of American Litera-
    ture, 1934.B2
Miller, Josiah
  Singers and Songs of the
    Church, 1869.B38
Miller, Olive Thorne
  "The Life of Harriet Beecher
    Stowe," 1889.B5
Moers, Ellen
  "The Angry Young Women,"
    1963.B12
  "Money, the Job and Little
    Women," 1973.B9

"Mrs. Stowe's Vengeance,"
    1970.B11
"Nat Turner and Dred,"
    1970.B10
Moody, Richard
  "Uncle Tom, the Theatre, and
    Mrs. Stowe," 1955.B6
Moore, Rebecca
  "The Byron Scandal," 1869.B40
Moran, John M. (editor)
  "The Collected Poems of
    Harriet Beecher Stowe,"
    1967.B5
Morse, James Herbert
  "Harriet Beecher Stowe,"
    1896.B20
  (editor) The Life and Letters
    of Oliver Wendell Holmes,
    1896.B21
"Most Harmful Book: Uncle Tom's
    Cabin," 1912.B1
Mott, Frank L.
  Golden Multitudes, 1947.B4
"Moving Novel Sixty Years After:
    Uncle Tom's Cabin," 1911.B4
"Mrs. Beecher Stowe's Wounded
    Feelings," 1861.B1
"Mrs. Stowe's Birthday," 1882.B2
"Mrs. Stowe, Painter," 1973.B1
"Mrs. Stowe's Vindication,"
    1870.B4
Munroe, Kirk
  "Introduction" to Lives and
    Deeds of Our Self Made Men,
    1889.B6
Murphy, G. M.
  The Slave Among Pirates,
    1852.A6
Murphy, Mabel
  Greathearted Women, 1920.B3
Murray, A. L.
  "Harriet Beecher Stowe and
    Racial Segregation,"
    1960.B6
Myers, A. J. W.
  "Harriet Beecher Stowe,"
    1940.B6

Ndu, Pol
  "From 'Jegar Sahadutha' to
    Gary, Indiana: Uncle

157

Tomism and the Black Liter-
ary Revolution," 1973.B10
Neal, John
"Lady Byron," 1870.B10
"Negro Life in America," 1852.B4,
B5
Nelson, John Herbert
The Negro Character in Ameri-
can Literature, 1926.B2
"A Note on the Genesis of
Mrs. Stowe's Dred,"
1940.B7
Nelson, Truman (editor)
Documents of Upheaval, 1966.B7
Nevins, Allan
The Ordeal of the Union, I,
1947.B5
Newcomer, Alphonso G.
American Literature, 1901.B3
Newman, Ralph G.
"Uncle Tom's Cabin," 1946.B14
Nichol, John
American Literature, 1882.B6
Nicholas, H. G.
"Uncle Tom's Cabin, 1852-
1952," 1953.B6; 1954.B4
Nichols, Charles
"The Origins of Uncle Tom's
Cabin," 1958.B6
"Who Read the Slave Narra-
tives?" 1959.B5
Nilon, Charles H.
Bibliography of Bibliographies
in American Literature,
1970.B12
Noel, Mary
Villains Galore, 1954.B5
Northcote, J. S.
"Uncle Tom's Cabin," 1852.B51
Norton, C. E.
The Letters of James Russell
Lowell, 1894.B2
"Note: Collected Poems of Harriet
Beecher Stowe," 1967.B1
"Notes on Sales," 1926.B1
"Notes on Uncle Tom's Cabin,"
1854.B1
"The Novel that Overruled the
Supreme Court," 1911.B5
Nye, Russel B.
"Eliza Crossing the Ice,"
1950.B4

Oaks, Harold R.
"An Interpretative Study...
Some...Productions of
Uncle Tom's Cabin" (disser-
tation), 1964.B5
Oliver, Egbert S.
"The Little Cabin of Uncle
Tom," 1965.B4
Olmsted, F. L.
A Journey in the Seaboard
Slave States, 1856.B17
Opperman, Harry E., III
"A Bibliography and Stemma
Codicum for British
Editions of Uncle Tom's
Cabin, 1852-1853" (disser-
tation), 1972.B5
"Two Ghost Editions of Uncle
Tom's Cabin," 1971.B12
Outis [pseud.]
The 'True Story' of Mrs.
Stowe, 1869.A7

Packard, Rosalie
"The Age for Little Eva,"
1962.B3
Page, John T.
"The Original 'Uncle Tom,'"
1912.B5
Paget, John
"Lord Byron and His Calumnia-
tors," 1870.B11
Paine, Albert B. (editor)
The Autobiography of Mark
Twain, 1924.B3
Papashvily, Helen W.
All the Happy Endings, 1956.B9
Parker, Edward Pond
Eminent Women of the Age,
1868.B3
Parker, Gail T.
The Oven Birds, 1972.B6
Parker, Rev. Joel, 1852.B27;
1888.B2
Parrington, Vernon L.
Main Currents in American
Thought, 1927.B4
Parsons, Alice Beal
"Harriet Beecher Stowe, a
'Natural Force,'" 1941.B12

"Part of a Letter, dated March
1870, to Edward Everett Hale,"
1933.B1
Parton, James
Noted Women of Europe and
America, 1883.B4
The Patent Key to Uncle Tom's
Cabin by a Lady in New York,
1853.A7
Patmore, Coventry
"American Novels," 1853.B28
Pattee, Fred L.
The Feminine Fifties, 1940.B8
The First Century of American
Literature, 1770-1870,
1935.B4
Peabody, A. P.
"The Mayflower," 1855.B2
"Sunny Memories," 1854.B14
Pease, William H. and Jane H.
"Uncle Tom and Clayton,"
1958.B7
Perry, Thomas S.
"American Novels," 1872.B6
Phelps, Elizabeth S. (Ward)
"Reminiscences of Harriet
Beecher Stowe," 1896.B22
Phelps, F.
"Pink and White Tyranny,"
1873.B4
Phelps, Wilson
Howells, James, Bryant, and
Other Essays, 1924.B4
Pickens, Donald K.
"Uncle Tom Becomes Nat
Turner," 1969.B4
Pickrel, P.
"Goodbye to Uncle Tom"
1956.B7,B10
Pierson, Ralph
"A Few Literary Highlights of
1850-1852," 1932.B4
Posin, Jack A.
"A Sportsman's Sketches by
Turgenev versus Uncle Tom's
Cabin by Beecher Stowe,"
1960.B7
"Power of Uncle Tom's Cabin Won
Author World Renown," 1933.B2

Price, Lawrence M.
The Reception of United States
Literature in Germany,
1966.B8
Pringle, Edward J.
Slavery in the Southern States,
1852.A7
Pruette, L.
"Harriet Beecher Stowe and the
Universal Backdrop,"
1926.B3
Purcell, J. M.
"Mrs. Stowe's Vocabulary,"
1938.B4

The Queen's Dream. A Sequel to
Uncle Tom's Cabin, 1852.A6
Quincy, Edmund, 1932.B2
Quinn, Arthur H.
American Fiction, 1936.B4
The Literature of the American
People, 1951.B3
"Saints, Sinners, and
Beechers," 1935.B5

Rammelkamp, C. H. (editor)
"Harriet Beecher Stowe's
Reply," 1932.B5
Randall, D. A. and John Winterich
One Hundred Good Novels,
1940.B9
Randall, James
Civil War and Reconstruction,
1937.B8
Reade, Charles, 1946.B3
"Recent Novels of Harriet Beecher
Stowe," 1863.B3
Redding, Cyrus
"Lord Byron," 1869.B41
"Mrs. Stowe's Second 'True
Story,'" 1870.B12
Reed, Kenneth T.
"Thoreauvian Echo in Uncle
Tom's Cabin?" 1971.B13
Repplier, Agnes
Points of View, 1891.B2
"The Reverend Henry Ward Beecher
and Mrs. Beecher Stowe (by an
American), 1869.B1
Rexroth, Kenneth
"Uncle Tom's Cabin," 1969.B5

Reynolds, R.
    "The Business of Being a
        Beecher," 1943.B6
Rhodes, J. F.
    History of the United States
        from the Compromise of
        1850, I, 1893.B3
Rhodes, M. J.
    "The Minister's Wooing,"
        1860.B5
Rice, C. Duncan
    "Introduction," to "Uncle
        Tom's Story of His Life,"
        1877.B1
Richardson, Charles
    American Literature, 1886.B1
Ridgely, J. V.
    "Woodcraft--Simms' First
        Answer to Uncle Tom's
        Cabin," 1960.B8
Rogers, J. M.
    "Uncle Tom's Cabin in Ken-
        tucky," 1902.B1
Roppolo, J. P.
    "Harriet Beecher Stowe and
        New Orleans: A Study in
        Hate," 1957.B2
    "Uncle Tom in New Orleans:
        Three Lost Plays," 1954.B6
Rossi, Joseph
    "Uncle Tom's Cabin and Pro-
        testantism in Italy,"
        1959.B6
Rourke, Constance
    Trumpets of Jubilee, 1926.B4;
        1927.B5
Russell, Robert L.
    "The Background of the New
        England Local Color Move-
        ment" (dissertation),
        1968.B6
Ryerson, F. and Colin Clements
    Harriet, Appendix II
    reviewed: 1943.B2,B4,B5,B7,
        B8

Sabin, Joseph W. E. and R. W. G.
    Vail
    Bibliotheca Americana,
        1933.B5; 1971.B12

Sanborn, F. B.
    "Mrs. Stowe and Her Uncle
        Tom," 1911.B13
Sand, George [Mme. Dudevant],
        1968.B4
    "Uncle Tom's Cabin," 1852.B52
Santayana, George
    The Last Puritan, 1959.B2
Schrifftgiesser, Karl
    Families, 1940.B10
Scott, Walter, 1853.B22; 1855.B10;
        1856.B10; 1897.B6; 1969.A1
Scudder, H. H.
    "Mrs. Trollope and Slavery in
        America," 1944.B3
See, Fred G.
    "Metaphoric and Metonymic
        Imagery in 19th Century
        American Fiction" (disser-
        tation), 1967.B6
Seiler, Grace
    "Harriet Beecher Stowe,"
        1949.B2
Senior, Nassau W.
    American Slavery, 1855.B3;
        1856.A1; 1857.B1
    Essays on Fiction, 1864.B1
    "Uncle Tom's Cabin," 1855.B3;
        1856.A1
Shepperson, George
    "Harriet Beecher Stowe and
        Scotland, 1852-1853,"
        1953.B7
Sherman, David E. and Rosemarie
    Redlich
    Literary America, 1952.B4
Sherman, James
    "Introduction" to Uncle Tom's
        Cabin, 1852.B54
"A Short Biography of the Author
    of Uncle Tom's Cabin," 1896.B9
Shoup, F. A.
    "Uncle Tom's Cabin Forty Years
        After," 1893.B4
Sillen,
    Women Against Slavery, 1955.B7
Simms, W. G., 1958.B1; 1960.B8
    "A Key to Uncle Tom's Cabin,"
        1853.B29
"The Sixth Beecher," 1937.B1

Sklar, Kathryn Kish
  Catharine Beecher: A Study in
    American Domesticity,
    1973.B11
"Slavery," 1856.B11
Slavery Past and Present, 1852.A1
Smith, Henry N.
  "Feminism and the Household
    Novel," 1957.B3
Smylie, James H.
  "Uncle Tom's Cabin Revisited,"
    1973.B12
Smyth, Albert H.
  American Literature, 1889.B7
"Some Thoughts in Connection with
    Byron's Name," 1869.B26
"Southern Slavery and its Assail-
    ants," 1854.B2
Stanton, Elizabeth Cady
  "The Moral of the Byron Case,"
    1869.B42
Starke, Catherine J.
  Black Portraiture in American
    Fiction, 1971.B14
Stearns, E. J.
  Notes on Uncle Tom's Cabin,
    1853.A8
  reviewed: 1854.B1
Steele, George M.
  Living Celebrities of New
    England, 1864.B2
Steele, Rev. Thomas J., S.J.
  "Tom and Eva: Mrs. Stowe's
    Two Dying Christs,"
    1972.B7
Stephen, Sir George
  Antislavery Recollections,
    1854.A2
  "Uncle Tom's Cabin and The
    White Slave," 1853.B30
Stern, Philip Van Doren
  The Annotated Uncle Tom's
    Cabin, 1964.B6
Stone, Albert, E.J.
  The Innocent Eye, 1961.B8
Stone, Harry
  "Charles Dickens and Harriet
    Beecher Stowe," 1957.B4
Stovall, Floyd
  "The Decline of Romantic
    Idealism, 1855-1871,"
    1953.B8

Stowe, Calvin, 1942.B1; 1962.B5
Stowe, Charles E.
  "Harriet Beecher Stowe, Friend
    of the South," 1911.B14
  "How My Mother Wrote Uncle
    Tom's Cabin," 1911.B15
  The Life of Harriet Beecher
    Stowe, 1889.A2
  reviewed: 1889.B2,B3,B5;
    1890.B2,B3,B4,B5,B6,B7,B8,
    B10,B11
Stowe, Charles and Lyman B. Stowe
  "The Girlhood of Harriet
    Beecher Stowe," 1911.B16
  "How Mrs. Stowe Wrote Uncle
    Tom's Cabin," 1911.B17
  Harriet Beecher Stowe: The
    Story of Her Life, 1911.A1
  reviewed: 1911.B1,B2,B3,B7
Stowe, Frederick, 1953.B2; 1973.B6
Stowe, Harriet [Elizabeth]Beecher
(1811-1896)
  Bibliography:
  works (descriptive): 1933.B9;
    1946.B10; 1958.B9; 1959.B3;
    1960.B9; 1961.B2,B10;
    1965.B1; 1972.B1,B8
  works (listed): 1897.B4;
    1932.B3,B4; 1933.B5;
    1938.B3; 1944.B1; 1948.B8;
    1965.B1,B6
  works about (listed): 1878.B9;
    1921.B1; 1936.B4,B5;
    1938.B2; 1948.B8; 1954.B3;
    1961.B2; 1963.A1; 1965.A1;
    1969.A1; 1970.B6,B12;
    1971.B5
    See Uncle Tom's Cabin
    (bibliography)
  Biography:
  full length: 1889.A1,A2;
    1896.A1; 1897.A1; 1911.A1;
    1913.A1; 1922.A1; 1926.B4;
    1927.B5; 1937.A1; 1941.A1;
    1948.A1; 1949.A1; 1954.B1;
    1963.A1,A2; 1965.A1,A2;
    1969.A1;
  short: 1852.B1,B33,B45;
    1853.B1,B20; 1856.B12;
    1864.B2; 1869.B1,B14,B15,
    B37; 1870.B5; 1871.B1;

"Stowe versus Byron," 1869.B27
Strout, Cushing
  "Uncle Tom's Cabin and the
    Portent of Millenium,"
    1968.B7
Styron, William, 1969.B4
  "Nat Turner and Dred,"
    1970.B13
Suckow, Ruth
  "An Almost Lost American
    Classic," 1953.B9
"Supposing it to be True,"
  1869.B29
Symington, A. MacLeod, "Harriet
  Beecher Stowe," 1890.B14

Talbot, William
  "Uncle Tom's Cabin: First
    English Editions," 1933.B6
Tandy, Jeanette R.
  "Pro-Slavery Propaganda in
    American Fiction of the
    Fifties," 1922.B1
Taylor, Gordon O.
  The Passages of Thought,
    1969.B6
Taylor, Hugh Alfred, 1963.B13
Taylor, W. R.
  Cavalier and Yankee, 1961.B9
Taylor, Walter F.
  History of American Letters,
    1936.B5
Teetor, H. D.
  "The Origin of Uncle Tom's
    Cabin," 1890.B15
Terrell, Mary Church
  Harriet Beecher Stowe: An
    Appreciation, 1911.A2
Thackeray, William M.
  The Virginians, 1859.B2
Thayer, William
  Success and its Achievers
    Illustrated, 1891.B3
Thompson, George
  American Slavery, 1853.A9
Thompson, John R., 1940.B3;
  1961.B7
  "Uncle Tom's Cabin," 1852.B54
Thompson, Maurice
  "Harriet Beecher Stowe,"
    1891.B4
Thoreau, H. D., 1952.A1
  Civil Disobedience, 1871.B13

Thorpe, T. B.
  The Master's House, 1968.B3
"Those Dear Blacks," 1853.B10
Timpe, Eugene
  American Literature in Germany,
    1861-1872, 1964.B7
Tinker, Edward L.
  "Uncle Tom's Cabin," 1938.B5
Tolstoy, Leo
  What is Art? 1913.B5
Trautmann, Frederick
  "Harriet Beecher Stowe: Public
    Readings in the Central
    States," 1973.B13
  "Harriet Beecher Stowe: Public
    Readings in New England,"
    1974.B3
Trent, William P.
  Great American Writers,
    1912.B2
  A History of American Litera-
    ture, 1807-1865, 1912.B6
Trollope, Frances
  Jonathan Jefferson Whitlaw,
    1944.B3
Troughton, Marion
  "Americans in Britain,"
    1957.B5
  "Eminent Victorians,"
    1953.B10
The True Story of Lord and Lady
  Byron, 1869.A3
"The True Story of Mrs. Shake-
  speare's Life," 1869.B29
Tuckerman, C. K.
  "Sir John Bowring and American
    Slavery," 1890.B16
Turgenev, Ivan, 1896.B15; 1911.B4;
  1960.B7; 1965.B3
  "Uncle Akim's Inn," 1960.B7,
    1965.B3
Turner, Lorenzo D.
  Anti-Slavery Sentiment in
    American Literature Prior
    to 1865, 1926.B5; 1929.B3
Turner, Nat
  "Confessions," 1964.B4;
    1970.B10,B13
Twain, Mark [Samuel Clemens],
  1959.B1; 1960.B5; 1961.B3,B8;
  1964.B3; 1965.A1; 1967.B2;
  1970.B3

Ward, Julius H.
"Harriet Beecher Stowe,"
1896.B24
Ware, L. G.
"The Minister's Wooing,"
1860.B6
Warner, Charles D.
"The Story of Uncle Tom's
Cabin," 1896.B25
"Introduction" to The
Writings of Harriet Beecher
Stowe, 1896.B26
Warren, R. P., 1967.B2
Warren, Samuel
"Uncle Tom's Cabin and A Key
to Uncle Tom's Cabin,"
1853.B31
"Was It a Mystification?" 1869.B52
Warterloo, Stanley
Famous American Men and Women,
1896.B27
Wayne, J. L.
"The History of Uncle Tom's
Cabin," 1945.B1
Weaver, Raymond
"Introduction" to Uncle Tom's
Cabin, 1938.B6
Weeks, Stephen B.
Anti-Slavery Sentiment in the
South, 1898.B6
Weisert, J. J.
"Louis Dembitz and Onkel Toms
Hütte," 1953.B11
"Mrs. Stowe First Writes of
Kentucky for Kentuckians,"
1957.B6
Wendell, Barrett
A Literary History of America,
1900.B1; 1925.B5
Westbrook, Percy D.
Acres of Flint, 1951.B4
Wetherill, Martha and Rebecca,
1961.B9
Whicher, George
"Harriet Beecher Stowe,"
1948.B9
Whitcomb, Ida P.
Young People's Story of Ameri-
can Literature, 1934.B4

Whitcomb, Selden
Chronological Outline of
American Literature,
1914.B3
Whittier, John G., 1936.B5
Widdemer, Mabel C.
Harriet Beecher Stowe--Con-
necticut Girl, 1949.A1
Wilbour, Charlotte
"Harriet Beecher Stowe,"
1869.B43
Willard, Frances E.
"Harriet Beecher Stowe at
Home," 1888.B4
Williams, Ben Ames (editor)
A Diary from Dixie by Mary B.
Chesnut, 1949.B3
Williams, Tennessee, 1969.B5
Wilson, Edmund
"Harriet Beecher Stowe,"
1955.B8
"No! No! No! My Soul Ain't
Yours, Mas'r," 1948.B10
Patriotic Gore, 1962.B5
Wilson, R. Forrest
"The Book That Brewed A War:
Uncle Tom's Cabin,"
1941.B13
Crusader in Crinoline, 1941.A1
reviewed: 1941.B1,B2,B3,B6,
B7,B10,B11,B12; 1942.B21
letter, 1941.B14
use of sources, 1963.B3
Winter, A. A.
"Little Woman Who Made a Great
War," 1927.B6
Winterich, John T.
"Bookmarks," 1953.B12
Books and the Man, 1929.B4
Wise, Winifred
Harriet Beecher Stowe: Woman
With A Cause, 1965.A2
Wolfe, Theodore F.
Literary Haunts and Homes,
1898.B7
Wood, Ann Douglas
"The Literature of Impoverish-
ment," 1972.B9
"The Scribbling Women and
Fanny Fern: Why Women
Wrote," 1971.B15

Wood, George
  "The True Story of Eliza,"
    1903.B3
Woodress, James
  "Uncle Tom's Cabin in Italy,"
    1967.B7
Woods, John A.
  "Introduction" to Uncle Tom's
    Cabin, 1965.B5
Woodward, A.
  A Review of Uncle Tom's
    Cabin, 1853.A10
Woodward, William E.
  Years of Madness, 1951.B5
"Words that Shook the World:
  Uncle Tom's Cabin," 1946.B1
Wright, Henrietta
  Children's Stories in American
    Literature, 1896.B28
Wright, Henry C., 1852.B44,B55
Wright, Lyle
  American Fiction, 1965.B6
Wright, Nathalie
  American Novelists in Italy,
    1965.B7

Wyatt, E. V. R., 1943.B7
Wyman, Margaret
  "Harriet Beecher Stowe's
    Topical Novel on Woman
    Suffrage," 1952.B6

"X.Y.Z.," 1852.B35

Yellin, Jean Fagan
  The Intricate Knot: Black
    Figures in American Litera-
    ture, 1972.B10
Young, Stark
  "Gentle Mrs. Stowe," 1942.B8
  "Uncle Tom's Measure,"
    1943.B8
Youmans,_____
  "Mrs. Stowe's Mistake,"
    1869.B43

Zanger, Jules
  "The 'Tragic Octoroon' in
    Pre-Civil War Fiction,"
    1966.B9